Roger Wilkes is a retired journalist. Born in North Wales in 1948, he was educated in Shropshire and joined the BBC in 1972. He worked in television and radio and is the author of several true-crime books.

Also by Roger Wilkes

Blood Relations: The Definitive Account of
Jeremy Bamber and the White House Farm Murders
The Mammoth Book of CSI
The Mammoth Book of Hard Men
The Mammoth Book of Famous Trials
The Mammoth Book of Unsolved Crime
The Mammoth Book of Murder and Science

The Wallace Case

Britain's Most Baffling Unsolved Murder

ROGER WILKES

ROBINSON

ROBINSON

First published in hardback in Great Britain in 1984 by The Bodley Head Ltd

First published in paperback in Great Britain in 1985 by Triad Paperbacks Ltd, an imprint of Chatto, Bodley Head & Jonathan Cape Ltd and Granada Publishing Ltd

This updated edition published in Great Britain in 2021 by Robinson

Copyright © Roger Wilkes, 1984, 2021

1 3 5 7 9 10 8 6 4 2

The moral right of the author has been asserted.

A CIP catalogue record for this book is available from the British Library

ISBN: 978-1-47214-522-2

Typeset in Adobe Garamond Pro by Hewer Text UK Ltd, Edinburgh
Printed and bound in Great Britain by Clays Ltd, Elcograf S.p.A.

Papers used by Robinson are from well-managed forests and other responsible sources

MIX
Paper from
responsible sources
FSC® C104740

Robinson
An imprint of
Little, Brown Book Group
Carmelite House
50 Victoria Embankment
London EC4Y 0DZ

An Hachette UK Company
www.hachette.co.uk

www.littlebrown.co.uk

For Robert

If once a man indulges himself in murder, very soon he comes to think little of robbing; and from robbing he comes next to drinking and sabbath-breaking and from that to incivility and procrastination.

Thomas de Quincey, *Supplementary Papers*

Contents

29 Wolverton Street [1931]

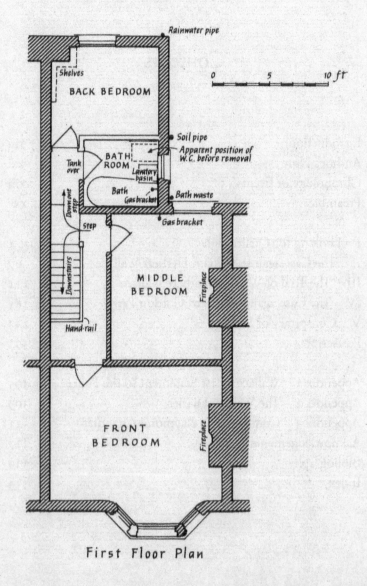

Rainwater pipe

Shelves

BACK BEDROOM

0   5   10 ft

Soil pipe

Apparent position of
W.C. before removal

BATH
ROOM

Tank
over

Lavatory
basin

Down one
step

Bath
Gas bracket

Bath waste

Step

Gas bracket

Downstairs

MIDDLE
BEDROOM

Fireplace

Hand-rail

FRONT
BEDROOM

Fireplace

First Floor Plan

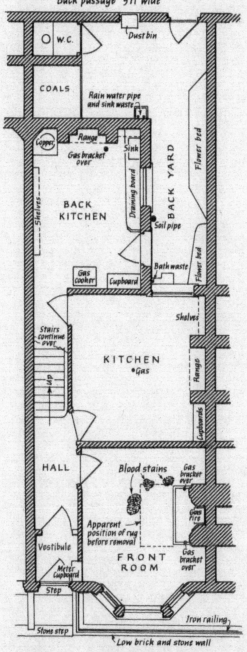

Ground Floor Plan

Introduction

T HE WALLACE CASE of 1931, one of the best-known real-life whodunnits, ranks among the most baffling murder mysteries in history. Did William Herbert Wallace, the mild-mannered Liverpool insurance agent, really bludgeon his wife Julia to death at their home in Wolverton Street, Anfield? Almost a century later, the question still divides opinion. Convicted and sentenced to hang, Wallace was sensationally freed on appeal and died from cancer less than two years later. Since then, many have argued, cogently and convincingly, that Wallace was, indeed, innocent and that the real murderer got away with it. In October 1980, when I first suggested a radio programme about the case, I believed the killer not only cheated the hangman but was still living with his terrible secret intact. I intended to identify the killer and confront him. In the event, I was too late – but only just. Richard Gordon Parry had died six months earlier, perhaps taking with him the truth about what many claimed to have been the perfect murder. The radio programme went ahead anyway, and was broadcast on the fifti-eth anniversary of the murder, on 20 January 1981. This book tells the story of the case as well as the extraordinary sequel to our programme, in which an elderly man called John Parkes, interviewed in hospital, told us how he encountered Parry in the immediate aftermath of the murder and how Parry threatened him if he talked.

Wallace's story was a strange one. At about 7.20 on the night of Monday 19 January, 1931, a man had telephoned the City Café where the Liverpool Central Chess Club was holding its regular meeting. The caller said his name was R. M. Qualtrough and that he wished to speak to Wallace, a club member. Told that Wallace had not yet arrived, Qualtrough explained that he wanted to see him on insurance business (Wallace was an agent for the Prudential) and that he would be at 25 Menlove Gardens East the following night if Wallace would call. These particulars were recorded and the message passed on. The next night, shortly before 7 p.m., Wallace (apparently eager to sell a new policy) left his home at 29 Wolverton Street to keep the appointment. After a fruitless search during which he approached several residents and passers-by, Wallace concluded that neither Qualtrough nor Menlove Gardens East existed. Returning home, he found Julia battered to death in the front parlour. Beneath the body, soaked in blood, was Wallace's own mackintosh.

Wallace was the first and only suspect produced by the police. Det. Supt Hubert Moore of Liverpool CID was in charge of the case. With no other suspect to hand, he arrested Wallace.

But the police had two big problems: Wallace's near-perfect alibi, and his absence of motive. The alibi, the police claimed, was too perfect; it could only have been the invention of a brilliant and cold-blooded murderer. As for motive, Wallace's diaries showed that he and his wife had quarrelled one day three years before. Besides, there were examples of murders committed for no reason at all. Even before his arrest, everyone in Liverpool was convinced of Wallace's guilt. An extraordinary prejudice accompanied the trial, infected the jury and brought Wallace, calmly protesting his innocence, to the brink of the gallows. In the public mind, rumour and the prosecution case transformed the meek Man from the Pru into an arch fiend.

Gordon Parry was first identified as an alternative suspect in 1967 when Jonathan Goodman published *The Killing of Julia Wallace*, in which, for legal reasons, he called Parry Mr X. Parry also claimed an alibi, but it was manifestly fabricated, concocted on the night of the murder or very shortly afterwards, and certainly before the police came knocking. Furthermore, Parry was a member of an amateur dramatic society that met at the City Café. Two points arise from this: first, his histrionic ability would have stood him in good stead during the masquerade telephone call; second, by simply glancing at the noticeboard in the café, he would have known when Wallace was due to play a chess match.

He had an abundance of motives, both for committing murder and implicating Wallace: revenge was the principal one (Wallace had played a big part in getting him sacked from the Prudential and – indirectly – in revealing his embezzlements to his father, whom he idolised); then there was financial gain, and the possibility of a sexual motive. When Goodman and his fellow crime historian Richard Whittington-Egan called at his home in south London in the mid-1960s, Parry let slip that he often visited Julia when Wallace was out at work, ostensibly for

musical afternoons, with Parry singing while Julia accompanied him at the piano. Wallace knew nothing of this, and one
wonders why Julia kept these sessions a secret from her husband.
Another important point (and not forgetting that Parry knew
exactly where Wallace kept his money), Parry was one of the
very few people the timid Julia would have admitted to the
house at night when her husband was absent. And while not
legal tender, it is surely revealing that, a few years later when he
was charged with indecent assault, the girl in the case claimed
that Parry had threatened to murder her if she resisted him.

After Goodman had canvassed these points in our fiftieth-
anniversary programme, an anonymous man called the radio
station offering to identify – for money – a mystery witness,
still living, who would clinch the case against Parry. Producer
Michael Green was particularly struck by Goodman's conversation with Parry more than a decade earlier. Parry had clearly
been ruffled when he told Goodman about his alibi for the
murder night, saying that his car had broken down in Breck
Road, not far from Wolverton Street. Green was convinced
that, although Parry had lied, he had let a half-truth slip out,
and had revealed that he owned, or had the use of, a car, and
that he was using it on the night of the killing.

Irked by the caller's demand for money, Michael Green took
up the challenge of finding the mystery witness himself, and
drew up a list of garages operating in the Anfield vicinity in
1931. Something that the caller had said stuck in his mind –
'You might stumble across it yourselves' – suggesting that the
garage was still in business fifty years on. Knowing where Parry
had been living in 1931, Green thought it likely that the garage
would have been near his home. One seemed to fit the

description exactly: it had a workshop and was only five streets away from Parry's house. But having spoken to the staff and the owner, Green drew a blank. After more head-scratching, Green lighted on Atkinson's Taxis and Motor Engineers, listed in the 1931 street directory in Moscow Drive, just two streets from Parry. 'It was too much to hope that it was still listed in the 1981 phone book,' Green recalled. But then: 'Good God – it was there! The same name and the same address!'

Next morning, Green walked into Atkinson's office, introduced himself, explained he was investigating a famous local murder, and asked if they knew anything about a bloodstained car supposed to have been brought into a local garage on the murder night. 'It was here,' a voice behind him announced. This was Gordon Atkinson, one of the brothers still running the family business, who recalled the story told him by his father. 'You want to go and see Pukka, he worked here then,' he said. 'He lives round the corner.' In fact John 'Pukka' Parkes was in hospital for a minor operation. That evening, Green talked his way in, found the ward, and spoke to the nurse on duty. She showed him an old man asleep in his bed and gave him his son's telephone number. Green rang him and got his permission to see his father the following day.

The whole case turned on time. To catch the tram that took him to Menlove Gardens, Wallace would have had to have left home no later than 6.49. But a milk boy swore seeing Julia alive on her front doorstep at 6.45. In the time available, could wheezy Wallace, at fifty-two, a heavy smoker, out of condition with a chronic kidney complaint, really have stripped naked (wearing the mackintosh to shield himself from splashing blood), beaten his wife to death, cleaned and disposed of the murder weapon (never found), faked a burglary, attended to various gas jets, fires, locks and bolts, and dressed himself for a journey across Liverpool, calm and composed, on a winter's night?

A dozy Liverpool jury thought he could. Wallace was convicted of murder and sentenced to death. He got off on appeal, left Wolverton Street and his suspicious neighbours and moved across the Mersey to a bungalow in the Wirral. He died a broken man less than two years later, having first identified Parry, a local Jack the Lad ('rather foppish, wears spats, very plausible'), as his own prime suspect.

Parry's alleged involvement in this notorious case came as a shock to his daughter, living in the south of England in 1981. She told me she had never heard of the Wallace case and declined to talk to us about it, but her husband described his father-in-law as 'a bit of a recluse' and 'secretive', and to some extent the black sheep of the family. His wife, he added, had very little to do with her father, and there was nothing in his few papers after his death that even hinted at the case. Neither could Parry's younger sister and brother add anything, and they declined to speak to us also, preferring to 'let sleeping dogs lie'.

Since my radio programmes and the original publication of this book in 1984, there has been no shortage of conflicting theories. James Murphy, in The *Murder of Julia Wallace* (2001), insisted that Parry did have an alibi for the time of the murder, one that had nothing whatsoever to do with his girlfriend Lily Lloyd. 'That alibi,' Murphy declared, 'was thoroughly checked and verified by the police and when the tests on Parry's clothes and his car proved negative, he was rightly eliminated from their enquiries.' While Murphy named Wallace as the murderer, John

Gannon, in *The Killing of Julia Wallace* (2012), identified him as the mastermind behind his wife's murder but, having implicated Parry as an accomplice, named the actual killer as another ex-Prudential employee, Joseph Marsden, nephew of a high-ranking officer in the corrupt Liverpool police force of 1931.

For myself, as I make clear in these pages, I was convinced beyond reasonable doubt that the *prima facie* case against Parry half a century after the event was every bit as strong as the case against Wallace, and in several important respects much more damaging. Forty years on, I am still of that view. I regret not getting to Parry in time to confront him with Parkes's evidence, and that of his former girlfriend, who in 1981 demolished his alibi for the time of the killing. The fact that I was refused access to the case file by the then chief constable of Merseyside in 1980 strongly suggested an official whitewash. I was subsequently able to establish that the file had been 'weeded' and statements and notes about Parry removed.

The crime historian Edgar Lustgarten considered the Wallace murder to rank in a class by itself. 'It has all the maddening, frustrating fascination of a chess problem ... Any set of circumstances that is extracted from it will readily support two incompatible hypotheses; they will be equally consistent with innocence and guilt. It is pre-eminently the case where everything is cancelled out by something else.'

And so the case endures, both intriguing and frustrating in equal measure. With police files ransacked and every participant now dead, it seems likely that the Wallace conundrum is destined to remain in perpetual check.

ROGER WILKES, 20 JANUARY 2021

Author's Note

SOME READERS WILL be unfamiliar with the legal procedures obtaining in England at the time of the Wallace case. As a prisoner charged with murder – an indictable offence – Wallace was required to be tried by a judge and jury, but only after the case against him had been heard by an examining magistrate in committal proceedings at a police court. It was the magistrate's function to decide whether a *prima facie* case had been made out against Wallace. Satisfied that it had, the magistrate sent – or committed – Wallace for trial at the assize court. This two-tier judicial system still applies today, but police courts are now known as magistrates' courts, and assizes have been replaced by Crown courts.

Because English solicitors are not allowed to argue a case before a judge, both the prosecution and the defence lawyers are obliged to brief barristers. Wallace's solicitor, Hector Munro, had already briefed a young local barrister, Sydney Scholefield Allen, to represent his client at the committal. But at the trial, an eminent KC (King's Counsel), Roland Oliver, was briefed to lead for the defence, with Scholefield Allen assuming a junior, supportive role. Munro himself, as a solicitor, remained in the defence team, but his role was confined to giving advice to the barristers and dealing with Wallace's routine welfare and legal problems.

Ranged against the defence at the trial were another KC, Edward Hemmerde, and his junior, Leslie Walsh. They were briefed on behalf of the police by J. R. Bishop, a prosecuting solicitor employed by Liverpool Corporation. The circumstances surrounding the decision to brief Hemmerde are fully described in the text.

While marked parallels exist between modern legal procedures and those obtaining in 1931, there is an important difference. Whereas at the time of the Wallace case newspapers were free to report fully on the proceedings of the lower court, the Criminal Justice Act of 1967 has since been introduced to restrict pre-trial publicity. Today, unless the defendant elects otherwise, none of the evidence produced at committal hearings can be reported. The news media are restricted to reporting matters of fact, such as the name of the accused, the charge he faces, and the decision of the court. Had modern practice been followed in 1931, none of the police court evidence, so damaging to Wallace, would have got into the newspapers, except in the unlikely event of his lawyers asking for reporting restrictions to be lifted.

The Court of Criminal Appeal, which subsequently freed Wallace, was abolished in 1966 with the passing of the Criminal Appeal Act. Since then the functions of that court have been assigned to the Court of Appeal, which has both a criminal and a civil division.

The death penalty in England was abolished in 1965, and the penalty for murder is now life imprisonment. In practice, a convicted murderer is usually released, on the orders of the Home Secretary, after he has served some years of his sentence.

Chronology of Events

xxiii

Preamble

LIVERPOOL, FEBRUARY 1981. He came shuffling out of another time, the old man with a story to tell. They led him gently by the arm. He blinked at us and wheezily returned our greeting. When they had made him comfortable on the bed the nurses smiled and left. 'Try not to tire him out,' they said.

We were in a hospital ward in the middle of the afternoon.

The toothless old man on the bed was trembling.

'Do you know who we are?'

He looked at us both and nodded.

'And why we've come?'

'Aye.'

We had come to listen.

He had come to tell us his story.

After the telling, we knew we had the truth. The truth about a so-called perfect murder.

It had happened in our city.

Half a century ago.

I

Looking for Qualtrough

I

LIVERPOOL, JANUARY 1931. Fog, the worst for a generation,[*] had set the city brooding in the first raw week of the year. For three days and nights shipping on the river was at a standstill. Men from the docks, the sheds and wharves huddled in dockside pubs and wondered when the fog would lift, and whether there would be money at the end of the week. At last, on the Wednesday, the weather cleared, and one by one the ships that had fretted impatiently on each sluggish tide were eased from their berths and put to sea. Ten days passed and the evening mists that had lingered over Liverpool were swept away by fierce gales. But these were short-lived, and a wintry weekend gave way to a Monday morning that shivered in persistent sleet. By afternoon, the sleet had turned to drizzle.

Dusk.

And finally nightfall.

Monday 19 January. Seven fifteen p.m. In the Anfield district of the city a man pulled open the door of a telephone kiosk and stepped inside. Lifting the receiver he asked the operator to

[*] *Liverpool Red Book* (1931).

connect him with Bank 3581, the telephone number of a café in central Liverpool, some four miles distant, the meeting place of the Central Chess Club. At the exchange operator Louisa Alfreds connected the call and heard a voice answer at the distant number.

A moment or two later the girl sitting alongside her, Lilian Kelly, took a second call from the man in the kiosk, Anfield 1627. Again he asked for Bank 3581. 'Operator,' he explained, 'I have pressed button A but have not had my correspondent yet.'

It scarcely seemed important at the time, but later, in evidence. Miss Kelly was asked to describe the voice she heard:

Q: 'What kind of voice was it?'

A: 'Quite an ordinary voice.' [TT v. 1 p. 13]*

Lilian Kelly muttered something to her friend, Louisa Alfreds. She could see from a light on the switchboard in front of her that the man at Anfield 1627 had pressed not button A, which would have completed the connection, but button B, which would have aborted the call and returned the man's money.

Miss Kelly turned and spoke to the exchange supervisor, Annie Robertson. She scribbled the two numbers on a slip of paper, noted the time (it was now twenty past seven) and in the margin marked NR (no reply). Then Annie Robertson dialled the number herself. It rang for a moment, then a woman's voice came on the line: 'Hello, City Café.'

'Are you Bank 3581?'

'Yes.'

---

* Trial Transcript, with volume and page reference.

'Anfield calling you. Hold the line.'

Annie Robertson passed the headset to Lilian Kelly.

At the City Café in central Liverpool waitress Gladys Harley listened as the line crackled. Eventually, she spoke again: 'Do you require this number?'

Slightly vexed, Lilian Kelly now told the man in the kiosk: 'Insert two pennies, caller.'

Two clicks. Then, the man spoke once more.

'Is that the Central Chess Club?'

'Yes.'

'Is Mr Wallace there?'

Gladys Harley, standing in the telephone booth at the foot of the stairs leading from the basement café to North John Street, turned and glanced through the glass door. 'I don't know,' she said, 'I'll just see.'

Still holding the receiver she pushed open the door and looked across the room. The café was almost empty, but Samuel Beattie, captain of the chess club which met there twice a week, was sitting at one of the tables, playing a game with a man called Deyes.

'Mr Beattie, someone's on the phone for Mr Wallace.'

Beattie looked up. 'Well, he's not here yet. But he's down to play a game, so he should be along later.'

'Will you speak to this man?'

Beattie frowned. He was enjoying his game. 'I suppose I better had.' He strode across and took the receiver. 'Samuel Beattie, club captain here. May I help you?'

Several weeks later, in court, Beattie would recall the voice he heard:

Q: 'What sort of a voice?'

5

A: 'A strong voice, a rather gruff voice.' [TT v.1 p. 18]

'Is Mr Wallace there?'

'No, I'm afraid not.'

'But he will be there?'

'I can't say,' said Beattie. 'He may or may not. If he is coming he'll be here shortly. I suggest you ring up later.'

'Oh no, I can't.' The voice at the end of the line was insistent. 'I'm too busy. I have my girl's twenty-first birthday on, and I want to do something for her in the way of his business. I want to see him particularly.'

A momentary pause, then the man continued: 'Will you ask him to call round to my place tomorrow evening at seven thirty?'

'I will if I see him,' said Beattie, 'but he may not be here tonight. You'd better give me your name and address so that I can pass it on.'

'The name is Qualtrough,' said the caller. 'R. M. Qualtrough.'

Beattie took an envelope from his pocket and scribbled the name down at the man's dictation. 'And the address?'

'Twenty-five, Menlove Gardens East.'

Beattie closed the phone booth door behind him and noticed that several members of the chess club were drifting in. On the wall to his right hung a large old-fashioned noticeboard on which fixtures and other notes were pinned for the benefit of members. Some had been posted for several weeks, including one that had been gathering dust since the previous October, advertising the fixtures for the club's second-class championship.

It was getting on for twenty-five past seven now and it was a rule of the club that games should start no later than a quarter to eight. Players who broke the rule were penalised. Beattie scanned the faces of the men who had arrived with time to spare, and who were sitting in pairs at various tables. No sign of Wallace.

It occurred to Beattie that with chess-club fixtures suspended over Christmas and the New Year he hadn't seen Wallace for about a month. He made a mental note to pass on Qualtrough's message. Wallace was an insurance agent with the Prudential. 'Something in the nature of his business' and mention of a twenty-first birthday could mean that Qualtrough was contemplating an endowment policy for his daughter. Wallace could stand to earn quite a substantial sum by way of commission.

Four miles away in Anfield, Qualtrough pushed open the door of the phone box that stood at the corner of Breck Road and Lower Breck Road. It was a thin night with a few specks of sleet still in the wind.

Perhaps as he strode into the darkness he pulled up his coat collar to keep out the cold.

Maybe a tram car clanked out of the gloom, bound for the middle of town.

One thing was for certain. The following night, 20 January 1931, Qualtrough would murder Julia Wallace.

James Caird arrived at the City Café at about twenty-five to eight. He knew that tonight was another round in the club's second-class championship, and that he was not paired to play. But he'd come along anyway, on the off chance of a casual game with anyone who would join him. He strolled around the various tables for several minutes watching the games progress.

Caird was a grocer, living not far from Wallace in the same part of Anfield. The two men had known each other for years. So when, at about a quarter to eight, Caird saw Wallace arrive and hang up his hat and coat, he ambled over.

'Evening, Wallace. Care for a game?'

But Wallace explained that he was down to play a tournament match against a man called Chandler. He wanted to get the game wiped off because he was already in arrears.

Wallace moved away, threading his way between the tables in search of his partner. It seemed that Chandler hadn't turned up, so Wallace sat down to play a game with an opponent called McCartney. Caird – who was in a class above Wallace at chess, and therefore ineligible to play him in tournaments – stood and watched the opening moves.

After some minutes Caird mooched over to where Beattie was engrossed in his match with Deyes. Several moments passed before Beattie looked up.

'Hello, Mr Caird.'

Caird nodded a greeting.

'You know Wallace's address, don't you?'

'Yes,' replied Caird, 'but he's here. Look, playing McCartney.'

Beattie looked round and saw where Wallace was sitting. Excusing himself once again to Deyes, he pushed back his chair and got up. 'I've got an important message for Wallace,' he explained, and moved over to where Wallace was seated.

'Good evening, Mr Wallace.'

Wallace scarcely looked up. 'Hello, Mr Beattie.'

'I've got a message for you.'

'Oh,' Wallace replied, apparently only half listening.

'From a Mr Qualtrough. He rang here earlier.'

It was a second or two before Wallace seemed to take notice. Then he looked up and said, 'Qualtrough. Qualtrough? Who is Qualtrough?'

'Well,' said Beattie, 'if you don't know who he is, I certainly don't.'

'Is he a member of the club?'

'No, we've no one called Qualtrough.'

'I've never heard of the chap,' Wallace declared. 'What did he want?'

Beattie fished in his pocket and pulled out the envelope on which he had written the message. 'Mr R. M. Qualtrough said he wanted to see you tomorrow evening at half past seven. Here's the address: twenty-five, Menlove Gardens East. He says it's something in the nature of your business.'

Again Wallace said, 'I don't know the chap.'

Then he asked, 'Where is Menlove Gardens East? Is it Menlove Avenue?

'No,' said Beattie, 'Menlove Gardens East.'

Wallace sat staring blankly back at Beattie.

'Wait a moment,' Beattie said, remembering something. 'I'll see if Mr Deyes knows where Menlove Gardens East is. He lives down that way somewhere. I know one Menlove Gardens comes into Menlove Avenue and the other one, I think, goes into Queens Drive.'

'It's an awkward place to be knocking about in the dark.'

Beattie returned to the table where Deyes sat waiting. Wallace and Caird saw Deyes shake his head.

'No, he's not much help, I'm afraid,' said Beattie, walking back.

'Well,' Wallace announced, 'I belong to Liverpool. I've got a Scotch tongue in my head. I'll find it.'

Wallace pulled out a pocket notebook and started to copy the address from Beattie's envelope. Beattie suggested that a tram to Penny Lane would be the best way of getting at least to Menlove Avenue.

Wallace finished writing out the address, emphasising the word 'East' in block letters. Beattie walked back to his game with Deyes, Caird continued to amble among the tables, while Wallace pocketed his notebook and resumed his game with McCartney.

About 11 p.m. the same night Wallace and Caird were walking side by side through the gloomy streets of Anfield on their way home. On the tram from town Wallace had talked of nothing but his victory over McCartney at chess. But now, as they trudged from Belmont Road, the conversation had turned to the telephone call.

'Qualtrough? It's a funny name,' Wallace was saying. 'Have you heard it before?'

Caird thought for a moment. 'I've only heard of one person of the name of Qualtrough.'

'What about Menlove Gardens East?' Wallace asked. 'Do you know how to get there?'

'If I were you, I'd get the bus from Queens Drive.'

Wallace considered it. 'No. I think the most direct route would be to go into town and out to Menlove Avenue from there.'

'You're definitely going then?' asked Caird as they turned into Letchworth Street.

'No, I'm not sure about going yet,' Wallace replied, 'but if I do go, that's the way I'll do it.'

And the conversation turned from Menlove Gardens to Wallace's health. Caird asked Wallace about his kidney complaint, and if he was still taking some German medicine he'd bought. 'No,' said Wallace, 'if my kidney doesn't trouble me, I won't trouble *it*.'

Outside Caird's front door the two men parted. Wallace, his shoulders hunched against the cold, disappeared into the darkness towards Wolverton Street and home.

2

T HEY WERE QUAINT times, but life in lower-middle-class Liverpool between the wars was mean and grey. The depression brought on by the Wall Street Crash was deepening across all Europe, and by 1931 Britain had three million unemployed. Children ran barefoot in the cobbled and gaslit streets, gathering at corners for games of cherrywags and ollies (marbles) before scuttering home for a skimpy meal: perhaps rattle-in-the-pan or connyonny butties. In Liverpool hardship and despair went hand in hand; traditional industries were spiralling into decline. The city itself, meanwhile, was expand-ing, great housing estates fanned out from Dingle in the south to Norris Green, and new middle-class suburbs were ribboning into the surrounding countryside. Beneath the River Mersey men were digging like moles to scoop out the miraculous £7½-million tunnel linking Liverpool and Birkenhead, to be opened by the King and Queen in 1934. The city skyline too was changing, with the appearance of the colossal central tower of the Anglican Cathedral, while the famous twin towers of the Liver Building at the Pier Head had already acquired a grey naevus of soot, less than twenty years after completion.

This was Wallace's Liverpool: a city of crowded streets, criss-crossed by trams painted crimson and ivory, with an overhead railway hoisted aloft alongside the dock road and running nois-ily between Dingle and Seaforth.* A city where night made the river run inky black, black churned grey at dawn by the wakes of the restless ferry boats.

Winter had been cruel with snow and gales. An outbreak of influenza at the turn of the year kept hundreds of people indoors, to seek relief with bottles of patent cures like Sloan's Liniment, Irwin's Chest and Lung Mixture ('the best protec-tion against weather treacheries') or even Bent's Strong Ale ('cures flu for 5d per nip bott.'). Wallace, himself a flu victim in the third week of January, contented himself with a mustard bath and a little whisky.

Outside, the careworn streets of Anfield seemed to sway in the gales. Winter seemed to pinch them even tighter together. But behind the grimy net curtains of 29 Wolverton Street, behind his blank, rimmed glasses, William Herbert Wallace, the eternal Stoic, passed an uncomplaining week-end, reading, writing up his diary, and listening to the wireless.

Sunday afternoon brought relief from the flu.

Monday brought sleet in the wind.

It was a solid little house, slightly squat, terraced of course, but a cut above the ordinary two-up and two-downs that stretched apparently into dreary infinity through the meaner

---

* Liverpool's trams and overhead railway ('the dockers' umbrella') disappeared in the fifties.

parts of inner Liverpool. This was the area of Anfield known as Richmond Park, a quiet, respectable but essentially drab neighbourhood; not quite the kind where everyone was forever in and out of other people's houses minding other people's business, but where people at least knew the name of the folk next door and took a polite interest in their comings and goings.

Richmond Park itself, in spite of its name, was a rather glum street shaped like a dog-leg, one section running from Breck Road, the other at right angles into Lower Breck Road, hugging the perimeter wall of what was then Belmont Road Hospital, now Newsham General. Wolverton Street runs off the shorter section of the dog-leg, and although blind to traffic connects with neighbouring streets by a small network of back entries, some cobbled or flagged, others simply earthed over. The thirty-four houses in the street, built of red glazed brick, were completed in 1912. Each had six rooms, including an inside bathroom and back scullery with hot and cold running water. Not undesirable, but hardly fashionable.

The Wallaces had moved into 29 Wolverton Street in the summer of 1915, two years after their marriage and four months after their arrival in Liverpool from Yorkshire. Their first home in the city had been at 26 Pennsylvania Road in the neighbouring district of Clubmoor. It was in Clubmoor that William Herbert Wallace conducted his humdrum business collecting insurance premiums for the Prudential, the company to which, for fifteen years, he had rendered entirely satisfactory service.

Julia Wallace was in the kitchen preparing a late supper when her husband arrived home from the chess club.

Although the couple were quite comfortably off – Wallace had more than £150 in the bank – Julia dressed shabbily, often in homemade clothes. Tonight, as on any other, she was grubbing about in her kitchen amid the usual clutter of newspapers and needlework and a hundred and one other bits and pieces.

The kitchen was the room in which the Wallaces spent their evenings. They had no children, and kept little company apart from each other's. When friends and relations came to call they would be entertained in the front sitting room, or parlour, away from the shambles in the kitchen. And it was in the parlour that the Wallaces made their music, he struggling to coax a tune from his violin, she – with far greater accomplishment – accompanying on the upright piano. The parlour, then, was for best, for guests, for occasions, for music. Meals were always taken in the kitchen, and it was there that Wallace greeted his wife on his return.

It may have been over supper, or over breakfast or lunch the next day, that Wallace mentioned to his wife that he had an appointment to keep with a stranger called Qualtrough. On Wallace's own evidence: 'She knew all about it. As a matter of fact we had discussed it during the day and it was really because we discussed it together that I finally decided to go . . .'

Q: 'Had you told her the man's name and where you were going?'

A: 'Yes, everything about it.' [TT v. 2 p. 245]

Tuesday 20 January. Rain. As usual, Wallace left Wolverton Street shortly after ten and took a penny tram ride to

Clubmoor. Even on a grey winter's morning this grey man cut a striking figure. His height – he was six feet two – was exaggerated still further by the inevitable bowler hat perched at the top of an elongated, skeletal frame. On his rounds he strode with a curious stamping gait, as though his long, bony legs had been made upside down, the part below the knee longer than the part above. Strange to behold, gaunt, and some would say rather sour-faced. Certainly old-fashioned to look at and somehow musty too, with the raggedy moustache, grimy mackintosh, bad teeth, and long, tapering fingers heavily stained with nicotine from countless cigarettes, the smoke shrouding his head and shoulders in a smelly and perpetual ectoplasm.

Eleven o'clock. Window cleaner Arthur Hoer and his wife Emily knocked at the front door of 29 Wolverton Street. It was opened by Julia Wallace, who padded into the kitchen to fill their bucket from the tap. The Hoers often worked together, especially when Arthur Hoer got behind with the business. This was quite often, because Hoer was a Labour member of the city council and regularly attended to council business during the day. Between them Hoer and his wife took just a few minutes to clean the front windows. Their routine was to clean the front windows at every house in the street before starting on the back, working down the entries and yards behind. They moved on along Wolverton Street with their cart, their buckets and ladders.

By lunchtime, the rain had eased. At two o'clock Wallace had completed his morning round of collections and returned home. Julia was suffering from a slight cold, possibly passed on to her by Wallace himself. Over lunch the table talk may have been of each other's state of health, or it may have been of their black cat, which had gone missing. Or again, it may have been of Wallace's appointment that evening with Mr Qualtrough. At any rate, the afternoon had turned fine. So Wallace hung his mackintosh in the hall and put on his fawn overcoat before setting out again for Clubmoor.

At three thirty Amy Wallace, wife of Wallace's brother Joseph, called for a chat. She enquired politely after Julia's cold and as they sat talking, Julia mentioned the appointment her husband planned to keep that evening with a man 'in the Calderstones district'. Both women agreed that neither knew anyone in that area. The bread boy called, but no one else. Julia asked Amy to stay to tea, but Amy was in a hurry and left shortly after four o'clock.

As Amy Wallace was arriving at Wolverton Street to visit Julia, in Clubmoor PC James Rothwell was cycling to work at Anfield Road bridewell. At about half past three, in Maiden Lane, he saw Wallace some thirty yards away walking towards him. Rothwell was a client of Wallace's and had known him for a couple of years. The two men met in the street occasionally and often passed the time of day. This afternoon, though, Rothwell said nothing as he cycled past. Wallace's face, he said later, was haggard and drawn, and he was very distressed – 'unusually distressed'. He was dabbing his eye with his coat sleeve and seemed to have been crying. He seemed, said Rothwell, to have suffered some bereavement.

Rothwell bicycled on down Maiden Lane, and Wallace turned into Pennsylvania Road to call on Mrs Louisa Harrison at number eleven:

Q: 'At about what time?'

A: 'About half past three.'

Q: 'Did he appear to have been crying and dabbing his eyes with the end of his sleeve?'

A: 'He was joking with me.' [TT v. 2 p. 312]

Wallace's next call was at the home of Mr and Mrs Lawrence at 16 Londonderry Road. Mrs Amy Lawrence asked him in for a cup of tea. He was, said Mrs Lawrence later, the same as usual.

Four thirty. Dusk was coming on.

Charlie Bliss, an unemployed labourer and brother-in-law to Arthur Hoer, had cleaned the top back windows at 29 Wolverton Street and was pulling his ladder over the wall into number 31 when Mrs Wallace appeared at the back door. Bliss propped the ladder against the back wall of number 31 and climbed up to the bedroom window with his bucket and leather. Mrs Wallace called to him, and asked where Mr Hoer was. Bliss explained that his brother-in-law had been called into town on council business.

'I'd better pay you then,' said Mrs Wallace.

Bliss climbed down the ladder and Mrs Wallace reached over the wall to give him a shilling. Bliss gave her threepence change, and Mrs Wallace pattered back into her kitchen.

Five fifteen. It was dark now as Emily Hoer opened the back entry door at 29 Wolverton Street and walked up the yard to clean the downstairs windows. The kitchen door was shut, but Mrs Hoer could see a light in the room behind the drawn blinds. She noticed too a light in the back bedroom. And seeing no sign of Mrs Wallace she wondered whether she was unwell. Left alone, the two women would sometimes speak to one another, but Emily Hoer found Mrs Wallace to be the quiet type, and a disappointing source of gossip.

From inside the house, there was no sound.

Wallace's last call that evening was at 19 Eastman Road, where Mrs Margaret Martin asked him to explain how to surrender a policy. Wallace left a form for her to sign. According to Mrs Martin, Wallace – 'calm and the same in appearance' – left her house shortly before six.

Wallace took a bus back to Anfield, arriving at Wolverton Street (he said) at about five past six. He and his wife had their tea, and Wallace collected together a number of papers and forms which he thought he might need to transact any business with Mr Qualtrough. Everything ready, he went upstairs to the bathroom, washed his hands and face, went into the bedroom, changed his collar, brushed his hair, and went downstairs again.

Six thirty. Walter Holme had arrived back from work, and was, sitting having his tea in the kitchen of 27 Wolverton Street. He and his wife Bertha were chatting quietly over the meal when Mrs Holme heard a noise coming from the front of Wallace's house next door. It sounded to her as though someone had fallen.

'Is that someone at our front door?'

Walter Holme had heard the noise too. 'No,' he said, 'it's at Wallace's.'

Six thirty-five. The front door of 29 Wolverton Street was heard to close.

According to Wallace, it was a quarter to seven when he left the house by the back door and, patting his wife on the shoulder and promising to be as quick as he could, set off for Mossley

Hill. Julia, he said, went with him down the back yard as far as the door leading to the rear entry. He left her standing there (so he said) with an instruction to bolt the door after him. That was their usual practice.

The police, on the other hand, would contend that before leaving Wolverton Street to see Mr Qualtrough, Wallace took an iron bar to his wife and beat out her brains.

3

AT SIX MINUTES past seven – roughly twenty minutes after claiming to have left home – Wallace boarded a number 4 tram at the junction of Lodge Lane and Smithdown Road in Wavertree, more than two miles from Wolverton Street. Wallace, dressed in a grey trilby hat and overcoat, stepped on to the car and asked the conductor if it went to Menlove Gardens East. Conductor Thomas Phillips said it didn't, and explained to Wallace that he could get a number 5, 5a, 5w or a number 7 car. Just as Wallace turned to get off, Phillips changed his mind.

'Stay on the car,' he said, 'and I'll give you a penny ticket for a transfer at Penny Lane.'

Wallace was still on the platform as the tram moved off along Smithdown Road. 'I'm a stranger in the district,' he explained, 'and I've got an important call to make. It's Menlove Gardens East I want.'

Wallace stepped into the tram's saloon and sat down in the right-hand corner seat just inside the door. When Phillips appeared collecting fares, Wallace again asked about Menlove Gardens East. 'You won't forget, mister?' he asked. Phillips punched him a penny ticket and went upstairs. A ticket inspector travelling in the car told him to change at Penny Lane. And when Phillips came clumping down the stairs Wallace leaned round the partition and, for a fourth time, reminded the conductor of his destination. Once again Phillips told him to change at Penny Lane.

The journey from Lodge Lane to Penny Lane took ten minutes. Wallace stepped down from the car and walked across to where a number 7 tram was in the loop, waiting to move off towards Calderstones. The conductor, Arthur Thompson, hopped on to the platform, rang the bell, and the car moved off. As it did so, Wallace – sitting this time on the left-hand side of the tram's saloon – beckoned him over and asked to be put off at Menlove Gardens East.

The tram car had travelled only some six hundred yards, to the top of Menlove Avenue, when Thompson called Wallace to the platform. Pointing to a road running off Menlove Avenue to the left, Thompson said, 'That's Menlove Gardens West. You'll probably find the street you want in that direction.'

'Thank you,' said Wallace, stepping off the tram. 'I'm a complete stranger around here.'

Indeed, Wallace was well off his normal beat, and a good four miles from his own neighbourhood in Anfield. In 1931 the houses in Menlove Gardens were little more than five years old. Some were still being built. It was an affluent district, quiet and secluded, whose pleasant, tree-lined roads were a far cry from the dingy streets of Clubmoor.

Twenty past seven. Twenty-four hours since the telephone call from Mr Qualtrough.

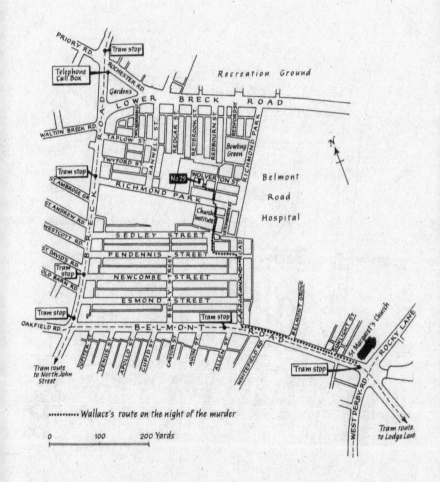

·········· Wallace's route on the night of the murder

0   100   200 Yards

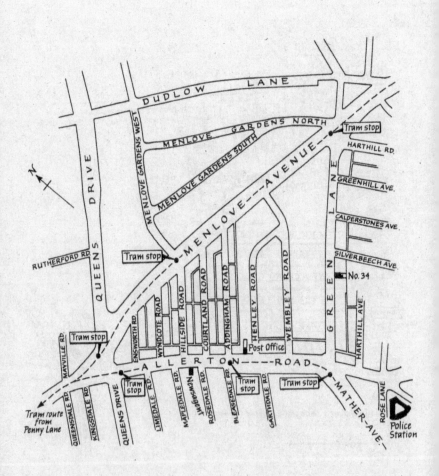

Wallace turned into Menlove Gardens West, walked up the road on the right-hand side past the end of Menlove Gardens South and turned into Menlove Gardens North. Some little way down the road Wallace saw a woman coming out of one of the houses on the other side. He crossed into the middle of the road and asked the way to Menlove Gardens East. The woman seemed uncertain, but suggested it might be along the road that formed a continuation of Menlove Gardens West. Wallace walked back to the corner, turned right and walked to the end of the road. He was now in Dudlow Lane, but apparently didn't realise it until he saw the street sign. At this point Wallace met a young, fair-haired man walking towards him.

Like Wallace, Sydney Green[*] was on his way to keep an appointment. He explained to the tall bespectacled stranger that as far as he knew (and he knew the district well) there was no such place as Menlove Gardens East. Wallace thanked him and said he would ask at 25 Menlove Gardens West.

He retraced his steps and rang the bell at 25 Menlove Gardens West. An elderly white-haired lady came to the door.

'Does Mr Qualtrough live here?'

Mrs Katie Mather looked at the caller standing on her doorstep. 'There's no one of that name here.'

'I'm looking for Menlove Gardens East,' said Wallace, 'but they tell me there isn't any.'

Mrs Mather thought for a moment. 'I don't know the name,' she said.

'Are there any other Gardens around here?'

---

[*] Then twenty-three, Green subsequently became General Manager of the Mersey Docks and Harbour Board. He died in 1981.

Mrs Mather explained that as well as Menlove Gardens West, there were Menlove Gardens North and South. 'Who told you it was East?' she asked.

Wallace explained he'd had a message by telephone. 'It's funny, isn't it, there's no East?' he remarked. Then, bidding the old lady good night, he turned and loped off down the path. Next, he turned into Menlove Gardens South, but saw that all the houses were even-numbered. He walked down the road to its junction with the far end of Menlove Gardens North, but found that in that road too, all the house numbers were even.

Wallace found himself back in Menlove Avenue. He asked directions from a man standing at a tram shelter but he appeared to be a stranger too and said he couldn't help. From this point Wallace crossed over Menlove Avenue into Green Lane. Although claiming to be unfamiliar with the district, Wallace now realised where he was. He'd visited a house in Green Lane on a number of occasions a couple of years before. It was the home of his superintendent at the Prudential, Joseph Crewe, who had given him some tuition on the violin during the winter of 1928. Crewe lived at 34 Green Lane. Wallace claimed later that he rang or knocked at the door, but failed to get an answer. In fact Crewe was out, enjoying an evening at the cinema.

Wallace continued along Green Lane. At the end of the road, where it joins Allerton Road, he spotted a policeman. PC James Sargent had just set out from Allerton Road police station on his duty rounds. Wallace walked over and explained, once more, that he was looking for a Mr Qualtrough at 25 Menlove Gardens East. Sargent, who knew the district well, told him at once that there was no such place. Wallace looked puzzled, and told the constable about the message telephoned to his club the previous evening, explaining that he was an insurance agent and that the appointment was in the nature of his business.

PC Sargent suggested he try 25 Menlove Avenue, and explained how to get there. But as for Mr Qualtrough, he knew of no one of that name in the district.

Wallace thanked him and was just about to walk away when he turned again. 'Is there anywhere that I could see a directory?' he asked. Sargent suggested he try either the nearby post office or the police station.

Wallace looked at his watch. 'Will the post office still be open? Yes, it's not eight o'clock yet, is it? No, it's just a quarter to.'

PC Sargent pulled out his watch and checked the time. 'That's right,' he said, 'it's just a quarter to.'

Wallace thanked him and walked up to Allerton Road to the post office. A man behind the counter, explaining he had no directory, suggested he might see one at the newsagent's over the road. Wallace crossed over. In the paper shop, one of the assistants showed him a directory. Wallace stood at the cigarette counter studying it.

'Do you know what I'm looking for?' Wallace asked the manageress who'd walked over. 'I'm looking,' he said for the umpteenth time that night, 'for Menlove Gardens East.'

Manageress Lily Pinches told him there was no East. Only North, South and West. 'Yes,' said Wallace, 'I've been to a number twenty-five West.'

'Sorry,' said Mrs Pinches.

27

Wallace pored over the directory for several minutes longer. Then, just on eight o'clock, he closed the book. Shutting the shop door behind him, and without another word, he walked to the tram stop near the Plaza cinema and caught a car for home.

His search for Qualtrough was over.

At eight twenty-five Florence Johnston, in her kitchen at 31 Wolverton Street, heard two thumps. Her father lived in the front parlour and she, thinking it was the old man taking off his boots, took no notice.

The Johnstons and the Wallaces had been neighbours for ten years. John ('Jack') Sharpe Johnston was an engineer employed at the huge Cammell Laird shipyard over the water at Birkenhead. Although he and Florence had lived next door to the Wallaces for long enough to form a reasonable acquaintance, the two couples – according to Mrs Johnston – were just chummy, and not on visiting terms. The Johnstons hadn't seen Mrs Wallace for over three weeks. Tonight, they were going out.

At eight forty-five Johnston had just opened the back door leading into the entry behind Wolverton Street when Wallace appeared out of the gloom, walking quickly towards his own back-yard door from the direction of Breck Road.

Mrs Johnston greeted him. 'Good evening, Mr Wallace.'

Wallace looked at her anxiously. 'Have you heard anything unusual tonight?'

'No, why? What's happened?'

Wallace explained that he'd been away from home since a quarter to seven. On his return he had been round to the front door and also to the back. Both had been fastened against him, and he couldn't get in. Johnston suggested that he try the back door again. If it still would not open he would try with his own back-door key.

The Johnstons waited in the entry as Wallace hurried up the back yard to the door of his house. As he did so, he looked back over his shoulder: 'She won't be out. She has such a bad cold.'

There was no sound, and Wallace seemed to turn the door handle without difficulty. 'It opens now,' he muttered.

Johnston glanced at his wife, then at Wallace. 'We'll wait here while you see that everything's all right.'

Wallace disappeared into the house, and the Johnstons watched and waited. The house was in darkness, save for two low lights, one burning in the middle bedroom, the other in the back room upstairs which Wallace used as an amateur laboratory. They heard him call out twice, and at once the light went up in the middle bedroom. Silence again. A match was struck and flickered in the laboratory. For a full minute, perhaps a little longer, nothing happened. Then Wallace hurried out into the yard.

'Come and see!'

His voice was agitated, excited.

'She has been killed!'

The door to the parlour was open and the gas mantle to the right of the fireplace lit, suffusing the room with a yellowish glow. Wallace led the way, the Johnstons following, through the scullery, the back kitchen and into the hall. Wallace stepped into the parlour to the left, leaving his neighbours framed in the doorway, frozen with horror. Lying diagonally across the black rug in front of the gas fire the body of Julia Wallace sprawled like a hideous ruin, feet almost touching the fender, head bathed in a massive pool of blood some eighteen inches from the edge of the open door. Her left arm lay outstretched towards the piano behind the door, her eyes staring at the pedals. She was lying with the left side of her head uppermost. A huge wound above the left ear where the skull had burst revealed bone, brains and blood. Two spent matches lay in the doorway nearby.

Wallace was standing in the middle of the room. He stooped down and felt his wife's left hand. Mrs Johnston edged into the room between the body and a sideboard on the left-hand wall; she, too, bent down and took her hand. 'Oh!' she gasped, 'you poor darling!' She looked up into Wallace's face, and saw it had drained from sallow to deathly pale.

Mr Johnston, who had also leaned over to inspect the body, straightened up. 'I'm going for the police,' he declared. 'Don't disturb anything.'

Wallace spoke. 'Get the police and a doctor. But I don't think it's much use. They've finished her.'

Johnston hurried out, Wallace and Mrs Johnston following as far as the kitchen. Wallace gazed around the cluttered little room. The kitchen table in the middle was covered with a cloth. A copy of that night's *Liverpool Echo* was spread across it, opened at the centre pages. Two armchairs were drawn up at the table, together with a third, upright chair. Julia's handbag was just visible beneath the fold of the tablecloth. On a shelf to the left of the kitchen range stood Wallace's microscope, a box of chessmen, some books, and a homemade cabinet containing some photographic equipment. The door of this cabinet had been wrenched off, and lay in two pieces on the floor.

Mrs Johnson picked up some coins which lay nearby. Wallace reached to the top fireside shelf for the cashbox in which he kept money belonging to the Prudential.

'How much have they taken?'

'About four pounds, I think,' said Wallace, rifling through the contents, 'but I can't be certain until I've checked my books.'

Upstairs, in the middle bedroom, Wallace found a roll of £1 notes, apparently untouched, in an ornamental jar. Returning to the kitchen he sat in silence for several minutes with Mrs Johnston. Then he got up and went back into the parlour, she following in his wake. Again Wallace stooped over the body.

'They've finished her,' he repeated. 'Look at the brains.'

Mrs Johnston tried hard not to.

'Whatever have they used?' Wallace seemed to be talking to himself. Once again he felt his wife's hand. Once again, Mrs Johnston did the same.

Wallace straightened up and moved round the body to the right shoulder. 'Why!' he exclaimed, bending forward. 'Whatever was she doing with . . .' he hesitated a moment '. . . my mackintosh?'

Mrs Johnston hadn't noticed it before, but saw now that something appeared to be tucked under the right shoulder. 'Is that your mackintosh?' she asked.

Wallace stooped down and fingered it. 'Yes, it's mine.'

For a few seconds neither moved nor spoke. The scene was more than Mrs Johnston could bear and she walked back to the kitchen. Wallace followed. The two sat in silence again for two, maybe three, minutes. Then Wallace put his hands to his head and began to sob.

Embarrassed and distressed, Mrs Johnston decided she had to do something. 'Well,' she said, 'we'll have a fire.'

The fire in the range had burned very low, and only a few live embers remained. Mrs Johnston fetched some fresh coal and chips from the scullery and banked it up. Wallace seemed to have recovered some of his composure and as the warmth of the fire began to steal across the room, Mrs Johnston turned to him with a reassuring smile. But he was crying again. She squeezed his hand, and he dried his eyes and swallowed hard. There were no words, just the hiss and crackle from the embers in the fire.

Outside, in Wolverton Street, PC Fred Williams propped his bicycle against the low wall in front of number 29, hurried to the door and knocked. For a few seconds someone inside fumbled. Then the door opened and Wallace stood at the threshold.

'Come inside, officer,' he said. 'Something terrible has happened.'

It was nearly nine fifteen.

'How did this happen?'

PC Williams was kneeling by the body. He took the right wrist, felt no pulse, but noticed that the flesh was slightly warm.

'I don't know,' murmured Wallace. And he began to pour out his story, about the fruitless journey to Menlove Gardens, and his return home to find the doors of his house locked against him. Williams listened attentively. Then he and Wallace began to search the house. In the middle bedroom Wallace explained that it was here that he had changed before setting out for Menlove Gardens. Williams asked about the lighted gas jet, which was still burning, and Wallace said he had probably left it on after changing his collar. On the mantelpiece, Williams saw the ornament containing five or six £1 notes. 'Here's some money which hasn't been touched,' said Wallace, fingering the notes.

The two men crossed the tiny landing to the back room which Wallace had turned into an amateur laboratory. 'Everything seems all right here,' he muttered. In the bathroom Williams flashed his torch and asked about the small light burning there. Wallace explained that he and his wife usually kept that room lit. This seemed to satisfy the constable because he was already out on the landing again, making for the front bedroom.

The room was in darkness, even though the blinds weren't drawn, and it was by the light of Williams's torch that the two men beheld a scene of inexplicable disorder. The bedclothes were half on the bed and half on the floor, exposing part of the mattress. There were a couple of pillows lying on the floor near the fireplace. On the mattress, as though just thrown there, were two women's handbags and three old hats, women's hats of the type Julia Wallace had worn on her expeditions to the local shops.

No words were spoken as Wallace and PC Williams surveyed the room. The officer noticed that the drawers in the dressing table and the doors of the wardrobe were all closed. Downstairs in the kitchen, where Mrs Johnston was still pottering, there was more disarray. Wallace pointed out the little cabinet, its door wrenched off and broken in two. He also pointed out the small cashbox lying on top of the bookcase to the left of the fireplace. Wallace told Williams, as he had told Mrs Johnston, that he thought about £4 had been stolen from it. Wallace also picked up Julia's handbag from the chair, half-hidden by the tablecloth. He rummaged inside and pulled out a £1 note and some silver. Evidently the robber, if such a person existed, had been less than thorough.

Williams decided it was time to revisit the scene of the crime in the parlour. He led the way, Wallace following, stopping just inside the door to survey again the killer's handiwork. The window blinds, he noticed, were drawn. As he stood in the doorway taking in details, Wallace, who'd been standing just behind him, stepped forward round the body of his wife to the fireplace at the far side. He took a match and lit the left-hand gas mantle. Now both mantles were burning, giving the shabby little room the appearance of a ghastly sacrificial altar. Wallace retraced his steps round the body and both men left the room, PC Williams closing the door behind him.

In the kitchen the officer noticed that the windows over-looking the back yard were heavily curtained. Parting the drapes slightly he asked Wallace if he'd noticed any lights in the house as he entered on his return from Menlove Gardens. Wallace explained that with the exception of the lights upstairs, the house had been in darkness. Anyway, he added, if there had been a light in the kitchen, the curtains would have stopped any of it escaping. This did not seem to satisfy PC Williams. 'I'll try them,' he said.

'It's no use now,' Wallace replied. 'You've disturbed them.'

It was nearly ten minutes to ten. Wallace and PC Williams had spent about half an hour touring the house, and the constable seemed little the wiser for his trouble. A second police officer arrived, a sergeant called Breslin, and now all three men stood in the blood-spattered parlour looking balefully at Julia Wallace's broken body. It was Williams who spoke first.

'That looks like a mackintosh.'

Wallace, standing in the open doorway, looked at the rumpled coat stuffed under his wife's right shoulder. 'It's an old one of mine,' he said. Glancing into the hall he added, 'It usually hangs here.'

But further discussion about the mackintosh was cut short by another knock at the door. Professor MacFall had arrived.

John Edward Whitley MacFall, who'd been summoned to conduct the medical examination of the body, was rated as one of the most distinguished practitioners in the field of criminal pathology. As Professor of Forensic Medicine at Liverpool University he had acted for many years as medical adviser to the Liverpool police, and was enormously experienced in murder cases. Silver-haired, pipe-smoking and twinkle-eyed, he looked like everyone's idea of a favourite uncle. MacFall set to work at once, herding Wallace and the two policemen out of the room to join Mrs Johnston in the kitchen.

It was obvious, at first glance, that Julia Wallace had been savagely beaten to death by repeated blows to the head. Bending over her, and pulling the hair aside, MacFall saw several split wounds at the back of the head, as well as the huge, gaping wound some three inches long on the left temple from which bone and brain had burst. How this woman had died was perfectly plain. But when did she die? It was to this crucial question that MacFall now addressed himself.

In 1931 there were two basic methods of working out the time elapsed since death: body temperature, and the progress of rigor mortis, the stiffening of the body after death. Both methods were known to be pretty inaccurate; in particular, the observation of rigor mortis was known to give only the very roughest estimate of time since death. Yet, for some reason, it was this method that MacFall chose to make the all-important calculation. At no time during that first, critical, examination, when Julia Wallace's flesh was not yet cold, did he seek to crosscheck his estimate by measuring the body temperature.*

It was getting on for ten o'clock when MacFall first examined the body. He knew that rigor mortis could set in between two and six hours after death. Crouching over Julia Wallace's corpse in the tiny cluttered parlour, MacFall saw in the gaslight that the rigor was just beginning. The hands were cold but the body still warm, and the tell-tale stiffening was noticeable only in the upper part of the left arm. By one o'clock, rigidity had spread to the right arm and right leg. The following day MacFall was able to assert with confidence in a report to the CID that 'it was most likely death had taken place approximately two hours before my arrival.'

* The procedure would have involved placing a low-reading thermometer in the rectum or vagina, and applying the following formula to arrive at an estimate of the number of hours since death:

$$\frac{\text{normal body temperature } 37^\circ \text{C (99 }^\circ\text{F)} - \text{recorded rectal temperature}}{1.5} = \text{hours since death}$$

In other words, at about eight o'clock on the murder night.

Looking around the room MacFall could find no sign of any disturbance, and surmised that the woman had been taken by surprise and felled by the first blow, almost certainly the blow that caused the terrible gaping wound to the left side of the head. This first great blow, he deduced, was delivered while Julia was sitting down, probably on the chair to the left of the fireplace, with her head turned to the left as though talking to someone.

MacFall himself perched on the arm of the chair to make a rough sketch, showing the position of the body, and of the various blood splashes, some of which had shot as high as seven feet. He was still sitting there, making notes, when, at about five past ten, he heard a minor commotion coming from the hallway. The Criminal Investigation Department had arrived.

First came Hubert Moore, a red-haired Irishman recently promoted to the rank of superintendent in charge of what was then known as the Special Branch. With him was his sergeant, Adolphus ('Dolly') Fothergill. Moore had been alerted by a phone call to his home in Newsham Park, only a mile or so from Wolverton Street. He, Fothergill and MacFall exchanged pleasantries in the parlour. Moore made a quick appraisal of the scene and spoke briefly to PC Williams and Sergeant Breslin, who had been waiting in the kitchen with Wallace and the Johnstons. Moore asked Wallace a few desultory questions. Neither Wallace nor his neighbours, it seemed, had seen anyone loitering around the house that night. Neither had they seen or heard anyone in the house on Wallace's return from Mossley Hill.

There was no telephone at Wallace's house, so Moore drove the short distance to the bridewell in Anfield Road to phone details of the murder to a CID inspector at police headquarters in Dale Street. He in turn alerted each police division in the city, ordering an immediate search of all lodging houses, railway stations, all-night cafés, clubs and brothels. Moore's specific instruction was to find a man whose clothing was heavily bloodstained.

The hunt for Qualtrough was on.

4

I T WAS ABOUT half past ten when Moore returned to Wolverton Street. His first thought was to find the murder weapon, and he ordered other detectives who were arriving at the house to make a thorough search, inside and out. Moore himself took a look at the front-door lock, but finding no marks concluded that no one had broken in. Back in the kitchen he conducted a second interview with Wallace, who again described his meanderings in Menlove Gardens and his return home to find his wife murdered. Then there were the contents of the smashed-up cabinet strewn on the floor, and the cashbox. Moore reached up for it and opened the lid. Inside he found three compartments, the middle one containing an American dollar bill. 'I can't understand,' he said, 'why a thief would go to all this trouble putting the lid on the box and putting it back where he'd found it.'

Upstairs, Wallace showed Moore his home laboratory, and checked that none of his tools were missing. A couple of hammers and other implements were apparently untouched. The two men peered into the bathroom and into the middle bedroom, where Moore noticed that the few photographs and trinkets on the dressing table were undisturbed. He noticed, too, the ornamental pot on the mantelpiece containing a small roll of banknotes. Leaving these untouched, they looked finally at the disordered front bedroom before returning downstairs to the front door.

Here, Moore again looked at the lock, watched this time by Wallace and another detective, Inspector Herbert Gold. Moore asked Wallace for his latchkey, which he wiggled in the lock for a second or two. Moore opened the door, stood on the front step, closed the door, inserted the key and opened the door again at the first attempt. 'I can open it all right,' said the superintendent, 'but the lock is defective.'

'That's strange,' replied Wallace, 'it wasn't like that this morning.' Moore said nothing, but pocketed the key and walked back to the parlour, telling Wallace to wait in the kitchen.

'Julia would have gone mad if she'd seen all this' Wallace muttered to Mrs Johnston.

In the parlour Moore again stooped over the body. He began to ponder the significance of the blue-grey mackintosh, crumpled and blood-soaked, which had been stuffed or tucked against the woman's right shoulder. Moore stared at the mackintosh for several moments. Then he took a torch and, crouching on all fours, flashed it into the various folds and creases. Moore got to his feet again and called Wallace into the room. 'Is this your mackintosh?'

It wasn't the first time that Wallace had been asked that question. He stooped slightly and put his hand to his chin. Moore watched as Wallace gazed unblinking at the pile of bloodstained gaberdine. A good half minute passed.

Silence.

'Did Mrs Wallace have a mackintosh like this?' Moore's voice was a trifle tetchy. Still Wallace stared down, rubbing his chin slightly with his hand. Moore had had enough. He spoke brusquely to Detective Sergeant Harry Bailey, who was standing by the sideboard. 'Take it up,' he snapped, 'and let's have a look at it.'

Bailey picked up the mackintosh and held it out. Moore stepped forward and pulled out the sleeves. 'It's a gent's mackintosh,' he exclaimed, barely suppressing the note of triumph in his voice.

By now Wallace had got hold of the mackintosh himself and was looking at it closely. 'If there are two patches on the inside it's mine,' he said. Moore twirled the mackintosh, matador-style, to reveal two patches in the lining. 'It is mine,' said Wallace. 'I wore it this morning, but the day turned out fine so I wore my fawn coat this afternoon. Of course,' he added, 'it wasn't burnt like that when I wore it.' Wallace was pointing at the part of the garment that had been badly scorched.

'Where did you leave it?' asked Moore.

'Hanging in the hall,' said Wallace, 'at half past one.'

It was now getting on for eleven o'clock. In the past two hours Wallace had spoken to PC Williams and later to Superintendent Moore, both of whom had made written notes of the conversations. But these notes, hastily recorded, contained only the barest outline of Wallace's version of events, and Moore decided it was time that he made a full and detailed statement. Besides, the tiny house was filling up with detectives, medical people, police photographers and others. It was all too hectic; Wallace would have to go to the Anfield Road bridewell to collect his thoughts. Moore packed Wallace into a police car with Inspector Gold and Sergeant Bailey.

Outside, in Wolverton Street, it seemed as though the whole of Anfield had gathered in the chilly night. As the car turned the corner into Richmond Park the sight of Wallace being rushed to the police station was one to relish for the local tattle-tales. Within minutes the buzz in the crowd was that Wallace had been arrested. But Hubert Moore, stroking his moustache behind the grimy blinds of 29 Wolverton Street, was thinking hard. He knew that in cases like this it was usually the husband who was the culprit. A simple domestic crime. And yet, he must have mused to himself, the whole thing seemed far from simple. A real puzzler, in fact.

By now Professor MacFall had completed his examination of the body, and had set off on his own tour of the house in the search for more blood. Bloodstained footprints? None. Smears or drips? None. Neither the broken cabinet nor the cashbox was in the slightest way bloodstained. At last, at about eleven o'clock, in the bathroom, MacFall found something that no one else who'd traipsed in and out that night had found. On the rim of the lavatory pan, at the front and slightly to the right, was a blood clot. It was just a tiny one, measuring only three-sixteenths of an inch in diameter and an eighth of an inch in height. It was shaped like a little pyramid. Very carefully, MacFall removed it and wrapped it in a piece of paper. It had been difficult to find; in fact MacFall had missed it himself at first because the gas mantle by the window cast a shadow over the pan. It wasn't until he took a pocket torch to the bathroom that the tiny clot was noticed. But elsewhere in the grubby little room there was little to gladden the professor's heart. A rather grimy white towel hanging over the side of the bath was completely dry; so was the bath itself. Only a nail-brush, its bristles damp, showed any sign of recent use. MacFall knew that the murderer must have been drenched in blood. Before leaving the house he surely must have cleaned up in some way. But where? And how? Evidently not in this cramped little bathroom. But how to explain the tiny blood clot? It was a mystery, thought MacFall.

Eleven fifteen. A mile or more from Wolverton Street, garage hand John Parkes was leaving home in Stoneycroft to start his night shift. Pulling his muffler close around him, he darted into a back entry, into the gloom, humming a tune to himself and the listening shadows.

At the bridewell in Anfield Road, Inspector Gold and Sergeant Bailey were conducting an exhaustive interview with Wallace. Gold asked whether, on his return home from Menlove Gardens, Wallace had heard anyone moving about in the house. And Wallace explained that although he had heard no noise in the house, he thought someone had been inside, because both front and back doors were locked against him.

Wallace gave the detectives a list of the contents of the cash-box. Everything, it seemed, had been taken except for four penny stamps.

'Does your wife have any money?' asked Gold.

'I think she had some,' said Wallace, 'but I don't know where she keeps it.'

'Do you know anyone called Qualtrough?'

'No. I know no one of that name.'

'Do you know of anyone who might have sent the message to the chess club?'

'No, I can't think of anyone.'

'Would your wife be likely to let anyone into the house if you were out on business?'

'No, she wouldn't admit anyone unless she knew them personally. If anyone did call, she would show them into the parlour.'

Gold was getting nowhere. 'Is there anyone, besides the paper boy – any tradespeople or anybody like that – who'd be likely to call?'

'I can't call to mind anyone likely to call, and I don't know that she had any friends unknown to me.'

Gold changed tack. 'Who gave you the message at the chess club?'

'Captain Beattie.'

'Do you know of anyone who knew you were going to the chess club? Or had you told anyone you were going?'

'No, I'd told no one I was going, and I can't think of anyone who knew I was going.'

The interview lasted about a quarter of an hour. Then Wallace was examined for any bloodstains. His clothes, his hands, his boots, all were inspected, but Gold could find no sign of blood at all. Shortly before midnight. Wallace volunteered his first, full statement. (See Appendix 1.)

At Wolverton Street, Professor MacFall, fresh from his triumphant if enigmatic find in the bathroom, had been joined by the official police surgeon, Dr Hugh Pierce. It was ten minutes to midnight when Pierce first examined Julia Wallace's body. He found rigor mortis in the neck and upper left arm, and, finding the hands and feet cold, estimated the time of death at about six o'clock, two hours earlier than the estimate arrived at by MacFall. Pierce examined the body at intervals of fifteen or twenty minutes, but – like MacFall – failed to supplement these observations with measurements of the body temperature.

Q: 'You know what is called the rectal temperature is generally considered the best test?'

A: 'Yes.'

Q: 'That was not done?'

A: 'No, it was not done. I did not do it.' [TT v. 1 p. 157]

No one did it. In the early hours of Wednesday morning, while Wallace was helping the police inquiries at the Anfield bridewell, and Moore and his men were crawling over the house looking for blood by the light of two lamps borrowed from the fire brigade, the body of Julia Wallace was driven from Wolverton Street to the mortuary at Princes Dock. MacFall packed his murder bag and left the house at about one o'clock, accompanied by Pierce. In the interview room at the bridewell Wallace sat smoking cigarettes, wondering when and whether he would be allowed to leave. And at Atkinson's Taxis and Motor Engineers in Stoneycroft, John Parkes brewed himself a pot of tea to warm himself against the night's long and chilly watch.

I T WAS FOUR o'clock in the morning before Superintendent Moore finally left the murder house in Wolverton Street and drove to the Anfield bridewell. Wallace was anxious for news of developments, but Moore had little to say. He thought it was time that everyone got some sleep. Wallace said he wanted to spend what was left of the night in his own bed, but Moore said that going home was out of the question, and arranged for a police car to take Wallace to the home of his sister-in-law in Sefton Park. Amy Wallace had visited the murder house as soon as news of the killing reached her. She and her son Edwin returned to their flat in Ullet Road to make up a spare bed on the sitting-room sofa, and it was there that Wallace snatched a few hours' sleepless rest before reporting, as requested, to the police headquarters in Dale Street at ten o'clock on the morning of Wednesday 21 January. He remained there all day and well into the evening – twelve hours in all – making statements, giving information and answering endless questions from the police.

News of the murder had spread the length and breadth of Merseyside. Liverpool's morning newspaper, the *Daily Post*, carried a short report quoting various unnamed neighbours who spoke of the Wallaces' manifestly harmonious domestic life. But by the Wednesday evening the story had exploded to become the main item in that night's *Liverpool Echo*. 'The police admit, after their twelve hours' hunt, that they are baffled,' wrote the reporter. 'They are without a clue.'

While Wallace submitted to the barrage of police questions at the Dale Street detective office, Professor MacFall arrived at the Princes Dock mortuary to conduct a post-mortem exam-ination on the body of Julia Wallace.

He shaved off the hair, which was matted with blood and brain tissue, to reveal the massive wound on the left side of the head. On the back of the head, on the left, MacFall found ten wounds, apparently incised. Further examination showed that the whole of the left side of the back of the skull was driven in and broken into pieces. In his report to the coroner, MacFall wrote that it looked as though 'a terrific force with a large surface had driven in the scalp, bursting it in parallel lines'. Death, he concluded, was due to fracture of the skull by some-one striking the woman 'three or four times' with terrific force using a hard, large-headed instrument.

MacFall refined these deductions in a second report, this time for the police, in which he reckoned there were 'two main blows struck with terrific force and several small ones'. As for the weapon, it must have had 'a large heavy head covering a big area', a different thing altogether from the iron bar MacFall had supposed had been used on first seeing the body.

Not for the last time in the course of the Wallace case, MacFall had changed his mind.

* * *

As the morning wore on a group of detectives began house-to-house inquiries in Wolverton Street. The entire Richmond Park area was combed for traces of a weapon or bloodstained clothing. At eleven o'clock Superintendent Moore himself accompanied the Chief Constable, Mr Lionel Everett, to Wallace's house, where he was joined by MacFall and the Liverpool City Analyst, Professor W. H. Roberts, who performed a minute examination of the front parlour to see just where blood had spilled. Pictures on the wall, a photograph, Wallace's violin case, even the brown paper cover of the violin score on the music stand, all were spattered with blood. Yet on Wallace's suit of clothes, the suit he had worn on the night of the murder, there was not a trace.

Detective Sergeant Harry Bailey was given the job of cracking the riddle of the name given by the telephone caller to the chess club, R. M. Qualtrough. He found there were fourteen families of that name living in Liverpool, but none could shed any light on the mysterious message. Other detectives contacted Captain Beattie and Gladys Harley, the two people at the City Café who had actually spoken to Qualtrough on the night before the murder. Wallace's story about wandering around Menlove Gardens was checked out, and witnesses were contacted.

In the absence of any positive leads, reporters joined the detectives in knocking on doors in Wolverton Street. They discovered that Wallace had been 'very ill for some time'. According to the *Liverpool Echo* he had recently been treated in the Royal Southern Hospital for an internal growth. Neighbours said that his wife had not only nursed him back to health, but had also kept his insurance agency going for him.

This sort of humdrum information must have seemed scant reward for the reporters scouring the street in search of lurid background details, but they were able to shed a curious sidelight on the affair. Chatting to Wallace's neighbours on the well-scrubbed doorsteps of Wolverton Street, the inquiring journalists learned that the area had recently been the target of an elusive housebreaker. Using duplicate keys, he had burgled between twenty and thirty houses in the Anfield area while the occupants were out. And there was something else. No fewer than five widows were to be found living in Wolverton Street. Their husbands had all died in tragic circumstances. Three had committed suicide, a fourth had dropped dead at a football match and another had died while away on holiday. It was, one reporter wrote, a street of tragedy.

At police headquarters the phones scarcely stopped ringing. It seemed as though everyone in Liverpool thought they could tell the police something that might help them solve the murder. Most of the calls were useless, but one man did have something of interest to say to the police. Did they know, he wondered, that Wallace employed a maid? 'Maid' was putting it a little strong, because when detectives taxed Wallace on the point it turned out that the caller was talking about Sarah Draper, the Wallaces' weekly charwoman, who called each Wednesday morning to help with the cleaning. At last, some of the detectives might have muttered to themselves. Another woman in the case.

At a quarter to seven that evening a group of children gathered outside the Parochial Hall in Richmond Park. Elsie Wright, a pert thirteen-year-old, was talking excitedly to two newspaper boys, Douglas Metcalf and Harold Jones. Elsie had just come from the dairy in Sedley Street where she worked part-time. There she had spoken to Alan Close, whose parents ran the dairy, about the deliveries he had made the previous evening in Wolverton Street. Hadn't he called at the Wallaces' house on his round?

'Yes,' Alan Close had replied.

'What time would that have been?'

'Oh, about a quarter to seven.'

Elsie Wright had been quick to grasp the point. The time of Close's visit could be crucial. His estimate that he had called to deliver milk to Mrs Wallace at a quarter to seven seemed to fit Elsie's own recollection of seeing Close carrying cans of milk along Letchworth Street on his way to Wolverton Street at turned half past six.

'And you saw her alive and well at a quarter to seven?'

'Well, yes.' Close was thinking back. 'In fact, she said I'd better hurry up home because of my cough. And she said she had a bad cough too.'

Elsie Wright was telling Douglas Metcalf and Harold Jones what Alan Close had told her. Metcalf considered the point for a moment. 'Do the police know that Alan called to give Mrs Wallace her milk last night?' Elsie shook her head.

Just then Kenneth Caird, the son of Wallace's chess-playing friend, sidled up the entry from Letchworth Street on his way to the library. Metcalf shouted over to him and young Caird walked across to join them. Metcalf asked him if he had heard about Alan Close's sighting of Mrs Wallace, but Caird said he had not. As the four stood talking, Alan Close himself appeared, on his way home to the Sedley Street dairy.

'Hey, Alan!' Metcalf's voice echoed up Richmond Park. Close crossed over, still carrying his empty milk cans.

'What time did you see Mrs Wallace last night?'

'Quarter to seven.'

'You ought to go and tell the police. You might get a reward.'

'Oh?'

Metcalf pulled an *Echo* out of the bag he had laid on the pavement. 'Look,' he said.

He turned to the back page, and the report of the murder. 'According to this, Mr Wallace went out at quarter past six. So if you saw her alive at a quarter to seven, people couldn't think that Mr Wallace did it.'

Close pulled a face. 'I don't want to go to the police.'

'I'd go if I were you,' said Metcalf. 'You could help the police a lot if you did.'

'You're a fool for not going,' piped up Caird.

'Well, I've already been to the house once tonight.'

'How do you mean?' asked Metcalf.

Close explained that he had knocked at the door to see if the police inside wanted any milk. But he had not mentioned calling the previous evening and seeing Mrs Wallace alive.

'I know,' said Metcalf. 'If you go back, we'll go with you.' The others nodded agreement. 'But you've got to go, Alan, it's really important.'

Alan Close looked at each of the others in turn. Then, slowly, a smile began to crease his cheeks. Then a grin. Then a laugh.

'Ha ha! I'm the missing link!' The lad had dropped his milk cans and was sauntering in a circle round the others, his thumbs stuck in the armholes of his waistcoat. 'I'm the missing link,' he sang. 'Ha ha! I'm the missing link!'

Elsie Wright and the three boys, Metcalf, Jones and Caird, followed as Close strutted across the road, down the entry leading into Wolverton Street. At Wallace's house, Close marched up the little steps and knocked. A policeman came to the door. 'What, you back again?'

Close looked back to where the others were grouped on the pavement, nodding encouragement. 'My name is Alan Close and I've come to tell you that Mrs Wallace answered the door last night when I called with the milk at a quarter to seven.'

By now a second policeman had come to the door and was peering over the shoulder of the first. Alan Close stood on the step, fidgeting.

The first policeman looked at Close, then at his friends standing wide-eyed on the pavement. 'Right,' he said, fixing Close with a meaningful look. 'You'd better come inside.'

That evening Wallace got permission from the police to leave the headquarters in Dale Street to go to Lime Street railway station with his sister-in-law Amy and nephew Edwin. Julia's sister, Amy Dennis, was arriving by train from Harrogate. There was a tearful reunion, followed by a discussion about where everyone would spend the night. The flat at Ullet Road had only two bedrooms, and it was left to Wallace to decide whether or not to spend a second night there, or to return home to Wolverton Street. Edwin and the two grieving women left in a taxi for Ullet Road; Wallace walked back to Dale Street and, after another interview session with detectives, was driven to Anfield in a police car, accompanied by Inspector Gold and Sergeant Bailey. They left him at Wolverton Street, alone with his thoughts and his ghosts.

6

S HORTLY BEFORE NOON on Thursday 22 January, Wallace
again presented himself at police headquarters. Pressed to
suggest some ideas about the identity of the killer, he made a
second, lengthy statement, drawing attention to a man –
'rather foppish . . . very plausible' – with whom Wallace had
had business dealings a couple of years before. In it, Wallace
claimed that this man was untrustworthy with money, was
well acquainted with the domestic arrangements at Wolverton
Street, and would have been admitted to the house by his wife
'without hesitation' had he called, even if Wallace himself was
out. Wallace gave the police the man's name and address, but
if the detectives regarded the information as a breakthrough,
they did not show it. They seemed much more interested in
another new piece of information that had come to light as a
result of inquiries elsewhere. It seemed they had managed to
trace the origin of the mysterious Qualtrough telephone call.
It had come from a call box in Anfield, not far from Wallace's
house. And, according to information given to the police, it
had been made at about seven o'clock on the night before the
murder.

Without delay, Hubert Moore drove to the telephone exchange in Anfield Road. On his arrival it took less than an hour to piece together the faintly farcical sequence of events surrounding the Qualtrough call. Moore and his detectives took statements from Lilian Kelly, Louisa Alfreds and the supervisor, Annie Robertson, in which they described how the call from Anfield 1627 came to be logged, and how the caller apparently tried to swindle twopence out of the Post Office by claiming to have pressed button A instead of button B.

But Moore evidently thought the most significant aspect of the phone call, other than its function of triggering either an alibi (for Wallace) or a decoy (for someone else), was the location of the call box. It was only some four hundred yards from Wallace's front door. And only a few paces from a tram stop from which the caller Qualtrough could have easily caught a car to take him into central Liverpool. Surely, Moore must have reasoned as he was driven back to his office, Wallace and Qualtrough were the same man.

That afternoon the Liverpool coroner, Dr Cecil Mort, opened and adjourned the inquest on Julia Wallace. The only witness was Wallace's sister-in-law, Mrs Amy Wallace, who gave evidence of identification. Wallace himself did not attend the coroner's court. He was at Wolverton Street with Inspector Gold and Sergeant Bailey. From a drawer in the middle bedroom Wallace retrieved some of his wife's jewellery and a Post Office savings book. After searching the house he told the detectives that he could find nothing missing except possibly a small wood chopper which used to be in the back kitchen 'but which I haven't seen for about twelve months'.

A second search was made and the chopper was found in a basket under the stairs. Gold told Wallace that according to the charwoman, Sarah Draper, a small poker was missing from the fireplace in the kitchen. And an iron bar was missing from the parlour.

'Perhaps she's thrown the poker away with the ashes,' Wallace replied. About the iron bar Wallace said he knew nothing.

Elsewhere in the house they found a Prudential insurance policy in the name of Julia Wallace in the sum of £20. 'That's the only one,' Wallace told the police.

Later, Gold took away the suit Wallace was wearing on the murder night, together with a towel from the bathroom.

Wallace spent the rest of that Thursday at police headquarters, and didn't leave until well after ten o'clock that night. It had been another gruelling day of questions. He walked wearily down Dale Street in the direction of the Pier Head, and turned left into North John Street. It was now twenty past ten. At the corner of Lord Street, Samuel Beattie and James Caird, who had just left the City Café after an evening's chess, were waiting at the tram stop. Their talk was of the killing. It was Caird who first noticed that Wallace was approaching. He looked a changed man, distraught and shaken.

'Mr Beattie,' murmured Caird, 'he is here.'

Caird, Beattie and Wallace exchanged greetings.

'Oh,' said Wallace, 'about that telephone message. Can you remember definitely what time you actually received it?'

Beattie thought back to Monday night. 'About seven o'clock or shortly after.'

Wallace seemed dissatisfied with this answer. 'Can't you get a bit nearer than that?' he asked.

'I'm sorry,' said Beattie, trying his best to be helpful, 'but I can't.'

'Well, it's very important to me,' Wallace went on, a note of urgency trembling his words a little. 'I'd like you to be more exact.'

'I'm sorry, I can't.'

Wallace's lips were quivering. Caird thought he looked ghastly.

There was a pause. Then, Wallace spoke again. 'I've just left the police. They've cleared me,' he said.

'Well,' Beattie replied, 'I'm very pleased to hear it, very pleased. But if you'll take my advice, you won't discuss the case any further, because it's quite possible that a simple thing you say may be misconstrued.'

Sure enough, the following day there was trouble.

'You saw Mr Beattie of the chess club last night?' Superintendent Moore was pacing in his office; Wallace, dressed in mourning, was seated, smoking a cigarette. It was early evening on Friday 23 January.

'Yes.'

'You asked him about the telephone message, and what time he received it?'

'Yes.'

'In what way,' Moore asked, narrowing his eyes, 'did you mean the time was important?'

Wallace drew on his cigarette. 'I had an idea,' he said. 'We all have ideas. It was indiscreet of me.'

Moore had stopped pacing. 'I wish you would tell me what your idea was. It might help me in the inquiry.'

Wallace blew a stream of smoke at the ceiling. 'I can't explain any further. I recognise it was an indiscretion on my part.'

*   *   *

That night both local and evening papers, the *Liverpool Echo* and the *Evening Express*, carried an extraordinary story. It seemed that at seven o'clock on the murder night a man called at a garage not far from Wolverton Street, asking to be driven to Sefton Park. (In the days before mass car-ownership, most garages provided a taxi service.) 'Drive quickly, I'm in a hurry!' exclaimed the man. Taking his seat beside the driver he added, 'You won't kill me, will you?'

Surprised, the driver reassured him, and asked what he meant by such a strange remark.

'I'm in a nervous state,' the man explained.

The story went on to describe the route the taxi took to Kingsley Road, at which point the man paid his fare, got out and hurried off into the darkness towards Princes Road.

There followed a description of the panicky passenger: '. . . well spoken, and about fifty years of age; about 5'11" in height, of a thin build with sharp features; hair is turning grey; he had a moustache and sallow complexion; he was wearing a pair of rimmed glasses, a dark overcoat and carried an umbrella.'

In almost every detail, the description fitted Wallace to a T.

Elsewhere in the story, the *Echo* reported: 'An important move might take place on Monday, when it is possible that a legal representative of the police will journey to London for an interview with the Home Office.' To the initiated, this was supposed to indicate that the police were getting a lot further with the investigation than was actually the case. There would only be one reason for such a trip to the Home Office: to seek the opinion of the Director of Public Prosecutions about the strength of the evidence against the only suspect, Wallace, and the DPP's recommendation on whether or not the Liverpool police should arrest him.

As for the panicky passenger in the taxi, this was surely a piece of outright mischief-making by the CID, who presumably had fed the story to local journalists. (Over the weekend someone must have thought better of it, because by Monday morning the *Echo*'s sister paper, the *Liverpool Daily Post*, was able to report that the passenger had come forward and had been interviewed by the police, who now declared that they were satisfied he had no connection with the crime. The truth of the matter, it seems, was that the whole episode was pure fabrication: the mystery fare was never mentioned again during the investigation or Wallace's trial.)

Seventy-two hours after the murder Superintendent Moore was evidently convinced that Wallace was the killer. Moore sat down and did some hard thinking. He thought, in particular, about the time factor, about the evidence from the milk boy Alan Close that he had seen Mrs Wallace alive at 6.45 p.m. on the murder night, and the statement from Thomas Phillips that his tram had left the junction of Smithdown Road and Lodge Lane at 7.06 p.m. Twenty-one minutes was not very long for Wallace to murder his wife, clean up, dispose of the weapon, fake a burglary, bolt doors, attend to the lights, then make his way on foot to a tram stop a good third of a mile away, await the arrival of the necessary tram, then travel in it for more than a mile and a half with not so much as a hair out of place. It was not very long. But was it long enough?

Moore decided to find out.

He assigned seven detectives to time the journey, in a series of so-called 'tram tests'. Over a period of days, working in pairs and singly, the detectives – who became known as a consequence as the Anfield Harriers, such was their zeal in trying to make the journey in the shortest possible time – walked, strode, jogged and scuttled from Wallace's house to the stop outside St Margaret's Church where he had said he had boarded the first tram to Menlove Gardens. There they caught the first available tram for Lodge Lane.

About two dozen tram tests were carried out in this way. The detectives found that the journey took anything between seventeen and twenty minutes. (One particular test, in which two CID men made the journey in a staggering fifteen minutes, was discounted on the ground that they had sprinted after a distant tram, a feat quite beyond the athletic prowess of Wallace with his kidney condition.)

Moore and his men were far from happy with the outcome of these tram tests, which simply proved that Wallace could not have left the house later than 6.49 P.M. on the night of the crime. Given Wallace's own estimated time of departure, and Close's sighting of Mrs Wallace at the same time – 6.45 p.m. – the police had the task of proving that Wallace accomplished the killing in four minutes flat.

The first weekend of the inquiry did produce some evidence that seemed, on the face of it, to be of value. A young typist, Lily Hall, who lived near the Cairds in Letchworth Street, told detectives that she had seen Wallace on the murder night talking to a man by the passage leading from Richmond Park to Sedley Street. According to Miss Hall, the time was 8.35 p.m.

– about ten minutes before Wallace was seen by the Johnstons trying to get into his house. Moore put the point to Wallace, who immediately denied having spoken to anyone in Richmond Park on his way home from Menlove Gardens. Indeed, he had already said that he spoke to no one as he hurried home from his fruitless search for Qualtrough.

Moore was undeterred. He spent that Saturday evening in conference with the other senior CID men and an official of the police prosecutions department, weighing up the evidence against Wallace and trying to convince themselves and each other – if no one else – that there was enough evidence to constitute a *prima facie* case against him on a charge of murder.

There was another conference early on the following Monday morning. And on Tuesday afternoon, 27 January, a week after the killing, Liverpool's Assistant Prosecuting Solicitor, Mr J. R. Bishop, accompanied by Inspector Herbert Gold of the CID, travelled by train to London.

This was the 'important move' foreshadowed at the weekend, although according to Tuesday's *Liverpool Echo* the two men set off lamentably unprepared. As the paper put it: 'Although the police have garnered a great mass of evidence, no vital clue has yet been discovered . . . Spiritualists and clairvoyants have communicated with the police too, but the officers are satisfied that the lines of investigation that they are now following will provide something definite within the next day or two. Of course the discovery of the weapon with which the frenzied attack was made would be a most valuable clue, as would the discovery of any bloodstained garments.'

Hubert Moore must have read his *Echo* with a growing sense of despair. 'Something definite' was precisely what the po-faced detective sorely needed. He had no weapon, no bloodstained clothes, no real idea of a motive, no unassailable witnesses, no proof. Just a suspect – and a gut feeling.

Bishop and Gold spent Wednesday morning with the Assistant Director of Public Prosecutions at his office in Richmond Terrace, just off Whitehall in London. They laid before him everything they had in the way of evidence, but the official was not impressed. His advice was simple: do not go ahead on the present evidence, and if you cannot get any more, leave the question of charging Wallace to the coroner at the resumed inquest.

Glumly, the two men caught the train home.

In Liverpool, Superintendent Moore's despair was turning to desperation. He had busied himself by preparing a report on the murder for the Chief Constable. 'As a result of the investigations,' he wrote, 'the present position is that the husband of the murdered woman is strongly suspected.'

Moore supported his assertion with a recital of numerous facts, an explanation of the police theory that Wallace himself sent the telephone message, and an assessment of Wallace's behaviour in the days following the murder. Moore was forced to admit that everything Wallace had said about his movements on the murder night and the night before had been checked and found to be perfectly true.

'The motive,' wrote Moore, 'is obscure, but a solution is probably to be found in his affliction – he has only one kidney and that is failing – which is often associated with various forms of insanity.'

The idea that the police were dealing with a madman was obligingly backed up by a neurologist at Liverpool's Royal

Southern Hospital, where Wallace had been treated for a kidney complaint the previous summer. Interviewed by Gold, the surgeon confirmed that Wallace's left kidney had indeed been removed many years before. According to the surgeon, Wallace's physical condition was such that it would 'affect his mentality and it would be quite consistent with his condition for him to premeditate and commit the crime'.

Encouraged by such eminent medical opinion, Bishop, Moore and their colleagues held another series of conferences. On Thursday 29 January, and again on Friday, the newspapers ran police appeals for the man said by Lily Hall to have been talking to Wallace in Richmond Park on the murder night to come forward. Wallace himself, meanwhile, had started work again. He had returned to lodge at his sister-in-law's flat in Ullet Road, and made the journey to Clubmoor and his insurance round by way of the city centre. Each morning he called at police headquarters in Dale Street to inquire about the progress of the investigation.

But on Monday 2 February, it was the turn of the police to go calling on Wallace. At seven o'clock that evening, a car carrying Superintendent Moore, Superintendent Charles Thomas and Inspector Gold drew up outside 83 Ullet Road. The three men walked up to the first-floor flat, the home of Amy Wallace. She was out, and it was her son Edwin who answered the door. From the sitting room where he was writing letters Wallace heard footsteps and voices. The door opened, and Edwin poked his head in. 'Someone from the police station wants to see you, Uncle,' he said.

The door opened wider and the three detectives came into the room. Wallace got to his feet. 'Take a seat, gentlemen.'

They stayed standing, hats on heads. Then, all three moved in closer, giving Wallace the impression of being surrounded. Gold stood directly in front, Moore to one side, Thomas to the other. It was Gold who spoke.

'Mr Wallace, you know who I am?'

Wallace nodded and began to say something, but Gold cut him short.

'It is my duty to arrest you on the charge of having wilfully murdered your wife, Julia Wallace, and I have to caution you that anything you may say in reply to the charge will be taken down in writing and used in evidence against you.'

Wallace, stunned, looked at each of the detectives in turn. He noticed that Gold had pulled a notebook from his pocket and was poised with a pencil.

There was silence. Again, Wallace's eyes flicked across the faces of the officers, set like stone beneath their hats.

'What can I say in answer to this charge, of which I am absolutely innocent?'

Wallace's reply, blurted out, brought no reaction. Gold calmly scribbled it in his book. The two others seemed to unfreeze and set about rifling through the papers on the table where Wallace had been sitting. They collected every piece, including the unfinished letter he had been writing to a friend. Wallace was allowed to get his coat and hat, and to speak briefly to his nephew.

'Edwin,' he said, his face pale and shocked, 'they have come to take me away.'

'I'm awfully sorry, Uncle,' the boy whispered. 'Is there anything I can do?'

'No. Tell your mother not to worry. It'll be all right.'

Wallace was hustled out of the flat, down the stairs and into the waiting car.

Thirteen days after the murder of Julia Wallace, the police hunt for Qualtrough was over.

II

*The Case against William
Herbert Wallace*

I

LIVERPOOL'S MAIN BRIDEWELL, or central lock-up, stands a few yards up Cheapside off Dale Street in the city centre, next to the magistrates' courts. It is an uninviting building, likened by some to a disused public lavatory, screened from the street by a high, forbidding wall.

On the evening of Monday 2 February, 1931, Wallace stood, flanked by the CID men, at the main entrance. One of them pushed a bell and after a moment or two the arrivals were scrutinised through a sliding peephole in the huge brown steel door. Moore, Thomas and Gold ushered Wallace into a big room with a barrel-vaulted ceiling supported by cast-iron columns with fluted tops. An official behind the long charge-office counter filled Wallace's particulars in a ledger, then formally charged him with murder, to which Wallace made no reply. There and then, he was searched. Everything he had, except his clothing, was taken from him. Even his spectacles. Then he was led downstairs to a cell. It was quite empty, with not a stick of furniture. Wallace stood in the middle of the cell and looked despairingly at the four walls surrounding him. The warder who had led him there reappeared with a big tin cup containing about half a gallon of drinking water. Later he returned with an armful of bedding: a fibre mattress with a couple of blankets. Wallace laid them out to form a bed; still fully clothed, he slipped beneath the blankets. But sleep was impossible. Several times a warder opened the cell door to ask if there was anything he wanted. At last, shortly before dawn on Tuesday 3 February, at seven o'clock in the morning, a tin mug of tea and some coarse bread and butter were brought in. Wallace drank the tea and chewed a little of the bread.

It was to be a momentous day.

At ten o'clock, half an hour before the court was due to sit, the public gallery in the Stipendiary's court in Dale Street was crowded with spectators, mostly men. News of Wallace's arrest had raced around the city like a lighted fuse, and police had to break up a crowd of about two hundred people who jostled in the anteroom trying to get a seat in court.

There was a stir when Wallace's name was called. He stepped swiftly but calmly into the dock, wearing a heavy black overcoat over his dark suit and, putting his bowler hat on a seat in the corner, leaned against the rail of the dock to hear the charge read: that he did murder his wife on 20 January at 29 Wolverton Street.

Wallace stood propped against the rail, resting his head on his left hand, apparently perfectly calm, and looked around the court with evident interest. He could see Superintendent Moore sitting with a man he did not recognise. This was the Chief Constable, Lionel Everett. To their right sat the Assistant Prosecuting Solicitor, J. R. Bishop. The court rose as the magistrate, Stuart Deacon, took his seat. A buzz of excitement ran round the room as police, officials and spectators resumed their seats to hear the evidence begin.

Bishop stood to deliver his statement. Wallace listened attentively. After evidence of arrest, Bishop began to outline the case against the prisoner, saying he proposed at the end to ask for a remand.

'His business takes him about Liverpool at various times in the day,' said Bishop, in the first of a series of mis-statements (Wallace's business was confined to Clubmoor, a small area). 'He usually returned about midday for a meal [2 p.m. in fact] and in the evening for his tea. His story is that on this particular evening he arrived home about 6.05 and had tea, and left again about 6.45 and when he returned about 8.40 he discovered that his wife had been murdered.

'After the accused, the last person to see the unfortunate woman alive was a milk boy, at 6.31 [the time was not established], and it is the suggestion of the prosecution that after this boy called at 6.31 [ditto] the accused murdered his wife and left the house at about five minutes to seven [this time would have been impossible, as the police tram tests had proved]. He had an appointment – so he says – which required him to leave the house about seven o'clock and it is a fact that he was seen a short distance away [in fact, over two miles] at about ten past seven [more like 7.06]. To get to that spot he may have left the house at any time from five to four minutes to seven [again, quite impossible, as proved by police tests].'

Bishop related how Wallace had claimed to have had an appointment with a man who, the previous night, had left a message at the chess club. 'It is the suggestion of the prosecution,' he declared, 'that this message was sent to the accused by himself. In fact, it will be proved that the message emanated from a call box two or three hundred yards from the house [in fact, over four hundred yards].

'It would have taken him just as long to get from that call box in time to reach the café where he received the message, as did time elapse between the time the message was received and accused arrived at the café [in fact, this crucial time lag was never tested]. One curious fact is this: but for the fact that that message was sent from a call box, and that the number to which it was sent was engaged [a point that was never proved, the call being logged at the exchange as "no reply"], one could never have traced the call box from which the message was sent.'

Next, Bishop outlined the call itself. 'While the message was given to the telephone official in one voice, a totally different voice was assumed on speaking to the gentleman who received the message [no evidence to support this was ever produced].'

And so to the details of how Wallace, in response to the message, went in search of the non-existent Qualtrough and the non-existent Menlove Gardens East, a quest which Wallace finally abandoned. 'He says he hurried home,' said Bishop, 'but as a matter of fact he was seen in conversation with some man within a very few yards of his home, apparently standing and talking [this was not a matter of fact at all, just a matter of opinion, that of Lily Hall, whose evidence was completely uncorroborated].'

Next, Bishop described how Mrs Wallace's body was discovered by her husband. 'It is a curious thing that the accused, having gone into the house, asked his neighbours to wait in case there was anything wrong [in fact, it was Mr Johnston who offered to wait; Wallace made no such request]. He goes into every room in the house before he goes into the front sitting room, where his wife was battered to death. When he comes out he calls his neighbours in, and Mrs Johnston goes in [both Mr and Mrs Johnston went in].

'There they find the woman. She is dead, and lying beside her on the carpet is a mackintosh which belonged to the accused, and which he had been wearing earlier in the day. For some reason, when he went out afterwards he did not wear the mackintosh but wore his coat. Perhaps because it was colder [no, because it was drier]. This mackintosh, which was lying by the side of the woman, had been hanging on the rack. Accused immediately remarks to the neighbour: "What is my mackintosh doing here?" [Wrong: Wallace did not mention the mackintosh until the second visit to the parlour.]

'When the police came and saw the mackintosh they had it up and examined it. It was covered with blood and was burnt to some extent at the bottom towards the right side. There was blood all over it and blood up to the sleeves and over the shoulders. When this was held up by the police and shown to accused it was not until he saw two patches on it that he identified it as his [in fact, as Bishop had just said, Wallace immediately claimed ownership of the mackintosh].

'I suggest,' Bishop continued, 'that that mackintosh was used to protect the murderer from the blood of his victim. That an attempt was made to destroy it by fire afterwards.

'Accused discovered that his house had been robbed. He found that four one-pound notes—' Here, Wallace – who had been keenly following the evidence, fingering his moustache and occasionally scratching his head – interrupted.

'No, sir, that is inaccurate!'

'S-sh,' warned a police officer. Wallace said no more. 'Well, some notes had been stolen from a cashbox, quite a small thing, which had been kept on a high shelf where one would not expect to look for a cashbox [in fact, Wallace had provided the police with the list of the cashbox contents, which presumably was accurate]. He found, strangely enough, that the money had been stolen, and the tray replaced, cashbox closed, and replaced on the shelf. I suggest it is a most unlikely thing for any thief who broke into the house to do.

'Later it was found that four one-pound notes were in a vase, in a bedroom upstairs, and on one of these notes there was some human blood. I need say no more about that. [This bloodstained note was spotted by a detective who had taken them to police headquarters late on the murder night for safe-keeping. The inference that the note had been stained by a guilty Wallace was one of no fewer than five possibilities: that the blood had come from the hand of Wallace after killing his wife; from the hand of an innocent Wallace after holding his dead wife's hand and handling the blood-soaked mackintosh; from the hand of an unknown murderer; from the hand of an investigating police officer; or from the hand of anyone at all at any time before the murder: in other words, the smear of blood may have had no connection with the crime.]

'In the bathroom of the house, on the first floor, there is a water closet, and on the top rim of that there was found a bloodstain which, there is no doubt at all, was of the same period of time as the murdered woman's death [in reality, all that had been established about this blood was that it was human blood, and not of menstrual origin]. The suggestion of the prosecution is that whoever murdered the woman went upstairs into the bathroom and washed away all stains of blood from his person. It is suggested that no person or stranger who broke into the house with robbery as his motive would have gone upstairs into the bathroom when there was plenty of hot water in the kitchen below. No weapon could be found. I suggest that that is a most significant fact. The suggestion is put forward that if a stranger broke in and robbed and murdered the woman he would not take his weapon away.'

His statement complete, Bishop remained on his feet. His only task before applying for a remand was to call evidence of arrest. Inspector Herbert Gold took the stand. He told the court how he visited the house in Wolverton Street on the murder night, and had found the body of Mrs Wallace lying on the rug. Gold then described how Wallace had been arrested, cautioned and charged with his wife's murder.

Still standing, Bishop then applied for Wallace to be remanded for eight days. The Stipendiary looked at Wallace and asked if he had anything to say. Wallace gripped the rail of the dock tightly. Drawing himself up to his full height, he said dramatically: 'Nothing, sir, except that I am absolutely innocent of the charge.'

Wallace was duly remanded in police custody for eight days, and led down to the cells. But before being transferred to Walton Gaol, he was led into a small yard to the side of the bridewell. Lined up with nine other men 'of similar age and appearance', Wallace faced his first, and only, identity parade. From a side door, a police officer appeared with the young woman called Lily Hall. Miss Hall walked along the line of men, touching Wallace on the shoulder as she passed. The girl was led out of the yard, to be replaced by a man, tram-car conductor Thomas Phillips. He too walked the length of the line, identifying Wallace as the man who had boarded his tram car on the murder night at Lodge Lane and asked the way to Menlove Gardens.

It was nearly time to leave for Walton, but before that Wallace was allowed to telephone a solicitor. He chose a young lawyer named Hector Munro. Munro shared two things with Wallace, although the two men had never spoken. Munro was a member of the Central Chess Club (Munro was a much better player than Wallace and the two were never paired in tournaments) and Munro's office was in the same building as the Prudential, at 36 Dale Street, about two hundred yards from the court building. As Munro recalled shortly before his death in 1981: 'I didn't actually know Wallace, but he knew me by sight. And I suppose when he was charged with murder, he felt that I'd be the person who could deal with the case for him.'

Quite why Wallace chose to put his faith in Munro is hard to judge. Munro was no seasoned courtroom campaigner; he was a comparative stripling, aged thirty-one, recently returned from his honeymoon, and without any experience in a murder case. But Munro knew the drill. He arranged to acquaint himself with the facts of Wallace's case, while his client was driven from Cheapside to Walton Gaol in a Black Maria, along with a sundry collection of sentenced felons. At Walton, Wallace was taken to the reception room. With the other prisoners newly arrived from court he stood in line, answered to his name, gave his occupation, his religion and other personal details, and answered to the charge against him. The men were then put in open cells, a temporary measure while they awaited the arrival of a prison doctor who would carry out an exhaustive medical check. When the doctor arrived Wallace and his fellow inmates were stripped naked and told to take a hot bath. After his medical Wallace was given a suit of prison clothes – a blue set, the colour ordained for a remanded prisoner – and told to put them on. The clothes had been tailored for a man of average height, and Wallace, standing over six feet tall in his stockinged feet, looked like a gangly schoolboy on his first day in class.

By afternoon Hector Munro had arrived. He had read a copy of Bishop's speech to the police court – it had been reported in full in that day's *Liverpool Echo* – and formally accepted Wallace's case, on the basis that 'the absence of proof was conclusive in his favour. There was not enough evidence to convict.' Munro scribbled a draft contract, which Wallace shakily signed. Then Munro, accompanied by his managing clerk Norman Wheeler, drove to Anfield and the scene of the crime.

Later, in gaol, Wallace was handed a greasy pan containing a pint of equally greasy cocoa, a half-pound hunk of bread spread thinly with margarine, and told gruffly that this was supper, that he would get nothing more until the following morning. Because he had been remanded on a capital charge, Wallace was entitled to accommodation not in an ordinary cell but in the prison hospital, under the observation of the prison medical officers. Passing through several iron-barred gateways, Wallace was met by the chief hospital warder and led to the ward where he was to spend the next few weeks.

There were twelve beds in the room. Wallace took the only one left vacant. The other prisoners were mainly mental defectives, most of whom had been in prison at least once before. Like Wallace they were on remand awaiting trial. Wallace surveyed them balefully. The man in the bed next to his was charged with housebreaking, a second crime committed while bound over for a first offence. Another was accused of bigamy.

A third, an old soldier clearly insane, also charged with house-breaking, was eventually transferred to an asylum. Another man was charged with manslaughter, having stabbed a woman in the throat (he was later sentenced to seven years' penal servitude). There were two cretinous tramps and an epileptic, who frightened everyone else in the cell by rolling out of his bed in the middle of the night in a fit.

Wallace sat on his bed eating his bread and doing his best to swallow the cocoa. He felt relieved when at eight o'clock a warder arrived, announced it was bedtime, and turned out the light.

The next morning, as the people of Merseyside and south-west Lancashire were devouring every detail of the police case against Wallace, reported verbatim in the *Liverpool Daily Post*, Munro again visited Wallace in the prison hospital. The news was encouraging. Munro was able to report that he had traced the children to whom Alan Close, the Wallaces' milk boy, had spoken the day after the murder. The three boys, Douglas Metcalf, Harold Jones and Kenneth Caird, were all certain that Close had claimed to have seen Mrs Wallace alive at a quarter to seven on the murder night. Elsie Wright was certain too. But Munro was able to produce an ace from up his sleeve. He had managed to find a moon-faced newspaper delivery boy named Allison Wildman, who swore he had seen Close standing on the Wallaces' doorstep delivering milk as late as 6:38 p.m. Wildman had explained that he was a sixteen-year-old dock worker, who had a spare-time job delivering newspapers for a shop in Lower Breck Road. His evening round began in Hanwell Street at about half past six. It took him along Taplow

Street, through two entries into Richmond Park, down a third entry by Campbell's dance hall into Wolverton Street, where he delivered papers at five houses, including number 27 – next door to the Wallaces.

According to young Wildman, on the murder night (as on every other night) he had glanced up at the clock of Holy Trinity Church, at the corner of Breck Road and Richmond Park. It was then twenty-five to seven. By the time he had walked down Richmond Park and through the entry into Wolverton Street, it would have been two or three minutes later, making it 6.37 or 6.38. Pushing an *Echo* through the letterbox at number 27, Wildman had noticed a milk boy on the steps of number 29. Because he had his back towards him, Wildman did not recognise the boy, but noticed he was wearing a Shaw Street School cap. It was dark, but the door of the house was open, and the boy was evidently waiting for his milk can to be returned.

Munro was satisfied that there was evidence to show that Mrs Wallace was alive and well as late as twenty-two minutes to seven. If Wallace was the killer (and Munro never thought he was), then even on the police evidence he would have had just eleven minutes to murder his wife, remove every spot of blood from his person and clothing, change his clothes, fake the burglary, dash upstairs with four £1 notes, stuff them in a jar in the bedroom, turn down the lights, bolt the front door, and – leaving not a scintilla of blood in the place other than in the murder room itself and a spot of blood on the lavatory pan – let himself out of the house by the back way in order to stroll with total nonchalance to the tram stop some distance away in Belmont Road to begin a journey on which he would meet at least ten people, not one of whom would suspect him of anything other than being lost in a strange neighbourhood.

Munro updated Wallace on his inquiries in Richmond Park, and drove back to his office in town. Munro and Norman Wheeler began writing out, in longhand, statements from the youngsters to whom they had spoken, genuinely buoyed at what they had found. The Wallace defence file was beginning to take shape.

At police headquarters, at the further end of Dale Street, the police file on the Wallace case was also filling up. Statements were taken from just about everyone whom Wallace had encountered on the murder night and the evening before. And CID men were assigned to assemble a picture of the Wallace ménage. This presented them with a difficulty, because there was little to learn, and even less to support the idea of domestic disharmony. Most of what the police did find out was supplied by the chess-playing grocer Caird. Caird and his wife were on friendly terms with the Wallaces: friendly but hardly intimate. Mrs Caird and Mrs Wallace knew each other well and used to meet in the street from time to time, but neither visited the other at home. The two men, though, were rather matier, and Caird was a fairly frequent visitor at Wolverton Street for games of chess. 'I think the last time I was there was in October 1930,' said Caird. 'He [Wallace] had been in the Southern Hospital having an operation, and I visited him about three or four times shortly after he came out.'

Caird found Wallace to be quite sprightly, despite his stay in hospital, and remembered Mrs Wallace making quite a fuss of the convalescent. 'I should say that he was her sole thought,' he told the police. 'Mrs Wallace was always very careful in the way she looked after her husband's health. They were a very happy couple and I never saw anything approaching a quarrel between them.'

Caird thought back to the previous summer, shortly after Wallace's discharge from hospital. Wallace, newly tutored on the violin, was anxious to accompany his wife, who was an accomplished pianist. But Mrs Wallace was worried: 'No, Herbert,' she had told her husband, 'you're not strong: you'll only upset yourself if you play.' But Wallace insisted, and the couple played over a couple of pieces in the front parlour.

All this, of course, took Superintendent Moore and his team nowhere at all. So he set Inspector Gold to work on compiling a detailed dossier on Wallace's background and antecedents. It is an illuminating comment on the quality of police work in Liverpool in 1931, shot through with spite and inaccuracy in almost equal measure.

'I beg to report that the accused, William Herbert Wallace, was born at Millom, Cumberland, in 1979 [*sic*]. [Fact: Wallace was born on 29 August 1878, at 44 Newton Street, Millom.]

'He attended the board school at Dalton-in-Furness, and on leaving he commenced to work for a firm of drapers in that town or in Barrow-in-Furness. [Fact: It was Barrow, at Tenants in Cavendish Street.]

'He remained there for some years and then obtained a position with a firm of cotton manufacturers and went to India and China as their representative. I have been unable to ascertain the names of the firms by whom he was employed. [Fact: It was Whiteway, Laidlaw and Co.]

'In 1906 he was admitted to hospital at Shanghai, where he underwent an operation for kidney trouble.

'He afterwards returned to England and on 3 April 1907 he was admitted to Guy's Hospital, London, where his left kidney was removed.

'On his discharge from hospital he obtained a post with a political association in the Harrogate district* and there he met his wife, the deceased woman, who at that time was keeping a boarding house at 157 Belmont Avenue, Harrogate. [Fact: The actual address was 11 St Mary's Avenue.] She had previously held a situation as a lady's maid. They were married at St Mary's Church, Harrogate, in 1913. [Fact: The date was 24 March 1914.]

'In 1914 the accused obtained employment as an agent with the Prudential Insurance Co., and he and his wife went to reside at 29 Wolverton Street, Liverpool. [Fact: The couple lived first at 26 Pennsylvania Road, Clubmoor, before moving to Wolverton Street, in 1915.] He remained in this employment up to the date of his arrest. His average earnings were about £6 a week.

'Since his operation at Guy's Hospital, in 1907, the accused appears to have suffered considerably from his complaint and for the past five or six years he has been attended by Dr Curwin, 59 Anfield Road. There are frequent references in his diaries since 1928 regarding his state of health. From 9 June until 10 July 1930 he was in the Royal Southern Hospital, Liverpool, where he was treated for kidney trouble. A copy of a report on his case is attached.

---

* Wallace was Liberal agent for the Ripon division in the West Riding of Yorkshire from 1910 until 1915, by which time, according to Wallace, the job 'ceased to be worth keeping up' because of the outbreak of the Great War.

'There are no children of the marriage and the accused and his wife appear to have led a very secluded life. They had resided in Wolverton Street for sixteen years but the other residents in the street knew very little about them. He is a very reserved type of man and outside his business acquaintances and a few members of a chess club, he does not appear to have formed many friendships. His hobbies were science and music. He did not drink to excess. His wife also appears to have been a reserved kind of woman and old-fashioned. She was also fond of music and they occasionally entertained two or three of their friends to a musical evening. These friends all say that the accused and his wife appeared to have been happy together.

'Mr J. E. Wallace, 31 Bentley Road, Liverpool, is the accused's brother. He holds a position as a printer in the Malay States, and returned to England about a month ago after a prolonged absence abroad. His wife, Amy Margaret Wallace, and her son, Herbert Wallace [Edwin], 20 years, have resided in Liverpool for the past two years and one or the other saw the accused or his wife practically every week.

'Mrs Wilson, matron of the police remand home, Derwent Road, nursed the accused at his home about eight years ago through an attack of pneumonia. She describes the accused and his wife as being a very peculiar couple and says their attitude towards each other appeared to be strained and that that feeling of sympathy and confidence which one usually found existing between man and wife appeared to be entirely absent.

'She describes the accused as a man who appeared to have suffered a keen disappointment in life. Mrs Wallace was peculiar in her manner and dirty. During her husband's illness she slept on the sofa in the kitchen although the front bedroom was vacant, and was much more convenient to the room occupied by her husband. The house itself was dirty and Mrs Wallace did not seem to have any desire to keep it clean. She did not appear to have any enthusiasm for anything.

'Mrs Wilson says that she formed the opinion that the relations between them were not those of a normal couple, and they were certainly not the "happy and devoted couple" as described by other people. She was at the house for about three weeks.

'Alfred Mather, retired Prudential agent, 8 Hornsey Road, informed me that he had known the accused for about twelve years. He describes him as the most cool, calculating, despondent and soured man he had ever met. He was not liked by his clients and some spoke of him as "a bad-tempered devil". He says that Wallace detested his work and thought it was beneath him to have become an insurance agent. He would not associate with his fellow agents and his pride is described as "nauseating" and his manner very morose. During an illness in 1930 Mather visited him and was admitted by Mrs Wallace. She treated him in a very offhand manner. When he inquired about her husband, she showed him into the parlour and left him without speaking. Mather says he was the only agent with whom Wallace would converse, and he was fairly intimate with him. Mather also told me that a Mr Jones, now deceased, who was a Prudential agent, knew Mr Wallace and his wife very well. He described Mrs Wallace to Mather as a proud and peculiar woman who thought she had lowered herself by marrying an insurance agent. She hated the business and would give no assistance to her husband. She would keep clients standing at the door when they called to see him on business, and she would not take in premiums which clients brought during her husband's absence.

'Dr Louis Curwin, 59 Anfield Road, informed me that he has attended both the accused and his wife at their home fairly often during the past five years. Since the death of Mrs Wallace he had considered their attitude towards each other and had come to the conclusion, from his observations, that they did not lead the happy and harmonious life that outsiders supposed they did.

'On one occasion when the accused was ill in bed he visited him but Mrs Wallace did not go upstairs. When Dr Curwin came downstairs, Mrs Wallace asked him how her husband was and on being told she said, "He wants to stay at home" and from her tone and manner the doctor was in no doubt that she meant that her husband was malingering.

'On other occasions when Mrs Wallace was ill in bed he had noticed when visiting her that the accused appeared to be indifferent about the state of her health.

'Dr Curwin also told me that after the accused was discharged from hospital in 1930 he told him that his condition was serious and warned him to be careful. The accused treated the matter with indifference and said he would have to carry on.

'Annie Elizabeth Spencer, 235 Lisburn Lane, a client of Wallace's, says that a week after the murder Wallace called to collect her premiums. During a conversation he told her that some friend of his wife's had killed her because she never allowed a stranger over the doorstep. Spencer thought he meant it was a friend of both of them, and asked if that was so. "No," replied Wallace, very excitedly. "A friend of my wife."

'The general feeling amongst Wallace's clients regarding him is that he was a surly type of man who would hardly return a greeting but would simply collect his premiums and then leave abruptly.

'The accused's superintendent, Mr Crewe, says that he was a competent agent and did his work well. His accounts were in perfect order.'

This pen picture of Wallace and his wife had now run for five pages of typescript. But at the end, Gold could not resist adding his own ha'porth. 'The accused was my agent for about nine or ten years,' he wrote. 'I saw him occasionally and the impression I had of him was that he was a man who attended to his own business. He was very reserved and did not encourage conversation.'

Herbert Gold was a prolific contributor to the police file on the Wallace case. At an early stage of the investigation he had drawn up a report, intended apparently for the perusal of the Director of Public Prosecutions. It comprises a rough guide to the case, and begins with a three-page summary of the bare facts of the killing, and Wallace's journey to Menlove Gardens. There follows a three-page list of reasons why Wallace was suspected of the murder, but against each reason Gold wrote, where possible, the argument in Wallace's favour.

The list starts with the telephone call to the chess club. Gold points out that membership was very limited, and the number was not listed in the telephone directory. Moreover, Wallace was only a casual attender, he had not been there for at least a fortnight before the killing, and an unknown murderer would have scarcely relied on Wallace receiving a message telephoned to the club. It was plain that the message had been sent from a call box about three hundred yards from Wallace's own front door within, on his own admission, a few minutes of his leaving home for the City Café. The call box was by a tram stop where Wallace could have boarded a car to get him to the chess club in twenty minutes or so. On the other hand, assuming the murderer to be not Wallace but 'Qualtrough', such a shadowy figure could have watched Wallace leave home on the night of the murder, entering the house and attacking Mrs Wallace without any resistance. Either Wallace sent the message himself to establish an alibi, or the message was a deliberate ploy to get Wallace away from the house. This was possible, the police argued, if Qualtrough had good grounds for believing Wallace would go to play chess that night, and would run the risk of the message being delivered.

Gold pointed out that whoever sent the telephone message used one tone of voice in speaking to the telephone operator and another when speaking with Captain Beattie at the chess club. (In fact, as already noted, there was not a scrap of evidence to support that assertion.) Beattie, of course, would have recognised Wallace's voice. There was also the business of Wallace's conversation with Beattie and Caird two days after the killing, when Wallace pressed Beattie about the time of the telephone call. Moreover, Wallace had aroused further suspicion by telling Beattie that the police had cleared him, when in fact Wallace had never been accused. And another point against him was that if the message had been sent by the mysterious murderer Qualtrough to lure him out of the house the next night, how could Qualtrough be certain that Wallace had received the message? Beattie had told the caller that he was not sure whether Wallace would definitely get the message.

Gold's document moved on to the crucial question of timing. Accepting the story of the milk boy Close, and assuming that Mrs Wallace was indeed alive and well at 6.35 p.m., where did that leave Wallace? He claimed to have left home roughly ten minutes later, at 6.45 p.m., and there is no definite sighting until he is seen waiting for his tram at Lodge Lane at a little before 7.10 p.m. So, the police reasoned, he could have committed the murder any time after 6.35 p.m. and had at least until 6.50 p.m. before leaving Wolverton Street to reappear at Lodge Lane at 7.10 p.m. Qualtrough, of course, would have had plenty of time to accomplish his mission. The unknown murderer would have had from about 6.45 p.m. until 8.40 p.m. to commit the crime. But – assuming again that Wallace was the killer – how did he murder his wife and clean up to everyone's evident satisfaction in the space of just twenty minutes?

This was a mystery in itself.

So was the fact that there was no evidence of a forced entry into the house, or of a struggle having taken place in the parlour before or during the murder itself. But what about the cash-box? For one thing, it had been kept well out of the way both of prying eyes and itchy fingers, on a shelf in the kitchen more than seven feet from the ground. A thief looking for money would have surely been more interested in the cash in Julia's handbag on the kitchen chair and the roll of notes in the jar in the bedroom; both more conspicuous and accessible than the contents of a partly hidden cashbox. As for the broken wooden cabinet, why bother to smash it open – as the murderer had done – and create a totally unnecessary commotion: the cabinet would have opened quietly and without fuss simply by unlatching a small metal hook on the door. It all smacked of a careful set-up by Wallace, Gold argued. On the other hand, an unknown thief, having got into the house through the unbolted back door, might have rifled the cashbox in the kitchen, only to be disturbed by the sound of Julia Wallace moving about in the front parlour. After the murder, the thief would have made off without ever having noticed or sought the other cash.

Suppose the murderer had actually been admitted to the house by Mrs Wallace herself, under some pretext? That would solve the mystery of the unforced entry, but surely such a person would have murdered first and thieved second, leaving bloodstains on the cashbox, the wooden cabinet and anything else he happened to touch on the killer's frantic rampage through the house.

As for bloodstains, there was plenty of blood in the murder room – a couple of pints was one expert estimate – but apart from that, and the tiny clot in the bathroom, the entire house was unblemished. Gold reasoned that a mystery intruder would inevitably have left bloodstains, but thought it improbable that such a thief would have used the upstairs bathroom to perform the necessary washing. After all, there was a sink with hot and cold running water in the scullery – a few steps from the scene of the murder, and conveniently situated for someone planning to leave the house by the back door. That the murderer left by the back door was accepted by Gold without hesitation. The front door, he stated unequivocally in his report (despite the recollection of PC Williams on his arrival at Wolverton Street), was found bolted.

All this weighed against Wallace, in the police view, and may even have proved conclusive had it not been for the inescapable fact that Wallace and his clothing had been minutely examined for bloodstains without the tiniest spot being found.

The mackintosh belonged to Wallace, and had been tucked under Julia's right shoulder. It had been soaked with blood – there were bloodstains inside both sleeve cuffs – and was badly burnt. It was a fair assumption by Gold that the mackintosh was worn by the murderer to shield himself from most of the spilled blood, but in the burning (presumably on the gas fire) there would have been a smell of scorched rubber. Yet, Gold pointed out, there was no such smell at a quarter to nine when Wallace and the Johnstons beheld the body in the parlour. Gold reasoned that the absence of such a smell pointed to the murder having been committed considerably earlier. So did the fact that the kitchen fire had all but burned out (assuming that the killer had tried to destroy the mackintosh there rather than in the murder room). However, it was plain that anyone could have snatched the mackintosh from the hook in the hall where Wallace claimed to have left it hanging, to protect himself from splashing blood.

How then to explain Wallace's hesitation in identifying the garment to Superintendent Moore? It was only after he had examined it closely and discovered a recent repair that Wallace had confirmed it was his. On the other hand, Mrs Johnston was saying that Wallace claimed ownership of the mackintosh almost as soon as he had first noticed it. Another quandary. But Gold's assumption, weighing it all up, was that Wallace, realis-ing that the mackintosh might be identified by the tell-tale patches which were still intact despite the burning, had been *forced* to admit it was his.

There were half-a-dozen other crucial points that occurred to Inspector Gold. They are listed here, exactly as they appeared in his report to Superintendent Moore.

AGAINST WALLACE

Wallace, when questioned, denies any knowledge of a bar of iron being missing from the fireplace, and denies knowledge of its existence. This is proved to be missing by the charwoman, Mrs Draper. No other murderer would bother to dispose of such a weapon seeing it belonged to the house.

Wallace, having struck one blow, would strike sufficient subsequent blows to ensure death, since his wife would denounce him. A thief would probably only strike one blow to ensure his escape.

Wallace appears to have taken elaborate pains to establish the fact that he was in the Menlove Gardens district, even going so far as to tell a constable his business and that he was an insurance agent.

Why did Wallace go all over the house (including his workshop) before visiting the parlour where his wife lay murdered?

Dr Unsworth* states that Wallace's medical condition is one frequently associated with mental changes, delusions, mania and temporary fits of insanity.

Deceased was insured for £20 and had £90 in the Post Office Savings Bank.

FOR WALLACE

Any murderer may have used a weapon and taken it away with him afterwards.

A homicidal maniac would strike several blows.

He may have been very anxious not to miss the chance of getting new business.

Wallace may have thought she had gone to bed. He knew she had a cold.

He is not known to have been in financial difficulties.

---

* The physician who treated Wallace at the Royal Southern Hospital in 1930.

The *Liverpool Evening Express* of Wednesday 11 February, 1931, carried a story which read:

> For more than an hour before the case was due to be heard, crowds waited outside Liverpool police court today when William Herbert Wallace, aged 52, the Liverpool insurance agent who is accused of the murder of his wife, Julia Wallace, aged 53, at their home, Wolverton Street, Richmond Park, Anfield, again appeared before the magistrate.
>
> . . . Wallace, a grey-haired, sparsely built man, wearing gold-rimmed spectacles, listened closely to the application of Mr J. R. Bishop, prosecuting for the police, for a remand.
>
> Occasionally he glanced around the court. He was wearing a black overcoat and a black tie.
>
> Mr Bishop applied for a further remand for eight days. He said that Wallace was now represented by Mr H. Munro.
>
> Mr Munro said this would suit him, and the Stipendiary remanded Wallace for eight days.
>
> Wallace bowed slightly to the magistrate when he was remanded.

2

BY TEN O'CLOCK on Thursday 19 February, 1931, half an hour before time, hundreds of people had gathered in the courtyard outside the Liverpool police court in Dale Street. Twelve constables formed them into an orderly queue to the lobby leading to the court on the first floor. There was confusion about which court would hear the Wallace case. When the door of the Stipendiary's court opened, about half the crowd swarmed in, filling the public seats and anywhere else not actually allocated to the police, lawyers, press, officials and the magistrate himself. It was standing room only. Those who could not actually squeeze past the double doors were herded back into the street. But when the Stipendiary took his seat at ten thirty, and the defendant in the first case turned out not to be Wallace, there was a rush for the door and the neighbouring number two court. Hardly had the breathless onlookers taken their seats and stashed their coats, sandwiches and vacuum flasks safely away when Wallace bobbed up into the dock, flanked by two officers. Wearing a black overcoat and black tie, he answered briskly 'Yes' when his name was called. His lawyer, Sydney Scholefield Allen, said it would be convenient if Wallace could sit immediately behind him, and the magistrate, Mr R. J. Ward, agreed. As Wallace took his seat, J. R. Bishop rose to outline the case for the prosecution. It was a familiar story: Wallace, it was claimed, had sent the Qualtrough message to himself, the first step in establishing an alibi for the murder night. Bishop described how the call came to be logged at the telephone exchange, and how Wallace arrived at the City Café 'in just such time as it would take him to get from the call box to the café comfortably by tram car' – a curious assertion in that no one had actually bothered to time the journey on behalf of the police.

The message, Bishop explained, was duly delivered to Wallace on his arrival at the café. It was to the effect that Wallace should call on a Mr Qualtrough next evening, on business, at Menlove Gardens East. It was very strange, said Bishop, that Wallace did not know the name, or even the district of Menlove Gardens or Menlove Avenue at all, and that he entered into a discussion as to where the place was.

'It is curious for this reason,' Bishop went on, 'that his chief . . . lives at a house, 34 Green Lane, which runs out of Menlove Avenue. Menlove Gardens North, South and West all run out of Menlove Avenue on the opposite side. The accused has been in the habit of visiting his chief for some time past at this house [WRONG] and must know the district well [WRONG] apart from the fact that he has lived in Liverpool for many years, and that, when his chief had been laid up as he was some two years ago [WRONG] he went there regularly two or three times a week [WRONG AGAIN].'

Wallace's 'chief' was his superintendent, Joseph Crewe. He had not visited Crewe at home for over two years, and when he did, it was only once a week during the winter of 1928 for his violin tuition. It was patently absurd to suggest, as Bishop did, that such journeys would have acquainted Wallace with the layout of the surrounding streets and roads. In any case, Crewe's house is nearer the Allerton Road end of Green Lane than the Menlove Avenue end; Wallace, on his musical visits, would have almost certainly taken a tram down Allerton Road to minimise the walking time between the tram stop and Crewe's house. As for Crewe being laid up, he himself would shortly testify that he had never had a day's sickness in his life, rendering pointless frequent visits from Wallace or, indeed, any visits at all.

Bishop ploughed on, describing the sighting by PC Rothwell of Wallace, distraught, in Maiden Lane on the afternoon before the murder, Wallace's departure from Anfield to Menlove Gardens, his return to discover the body of his wife, and the mystery of the burnt mackintosh. Wallace had worn the garment on the morning of the murder, but had changed into his overcoat because the afternoon had turned fine. That, at least, was Wallace's explanation. 'I suggest,' said Bishop, 'that the reason he hadn't worn it was that it had played some part.'

That was too much for Scholefield Allen, who had been listening with growing amazement to the catalogue of misinformation being laid before the court on behalf of the prosecution. He jumped to his feet.

'Time after time,' he exclaimed, 'Mr Bishop is suggesting things. It is his duty to present this case fairly, without bias and on the facts. Wallace is on trial for his life and my friend seems to forget that. He is not addressing a jury, but presenting a case for committal proceedings, and he is not entitled to make suggestions against the prisoner in this manner.' Scholefield Allen fixed Bishop with an icy glare. 'My friend's duty is coldly and dispassionately to present the case for the Crown as the minister of justice. Cold, hard logical facts are needed, and not things to prejudice Wallace.' And, turning to the magistrate, he added, 'I protest strongly about this, and this is not the first time it's been done.'

The magistrate blinked sagely. 'You can take it from me,' he said, 'it is having no effect on me.'

Scholefield Allen pressed the point. 'What Mr Bishop says will be taken down by the press representatives here and there will be full reports of his speech in the press tonight. They will be read by people wise and people ignorant. They will also be read by people who have a logical faculty and people who have not. It is from among those people that the twelve men and women will be selected to try this man at a later stage for his life. Mr Bishop has already told us that this man has committed a crime. Surely Wallace is presumed to be innocent until he is proved guilty, and Mr Bishop is not entitled to give his opinion.

'What we must have are the cold, hard facts,' barked Scholefield Allen. 'If any.'

It was Bishop's move. 'It would be difficult to produce a mackintosh,' he said, 'without giving reasons, and the evidence must be explained. That, I hope, is the limit to which I will go.'

Scholefield Allen countered, 'It is the cumulative effect of suggestions made that I object to. For example, there is some suggestion that the accused himself sent the telephone message. There is no proof of that.

'It is your duty to present logically facts which tell against the prisoner and not attempt to flare up the imagination of the public.'

Bishop smiled at this. 'I'm trying simply to put the facts before the magistrate, and before him only.' Anyway, Bishop was nearly finished. At the end of this opening statement he turned to Scholefield Allen. 'I hope my learned friend was not serious when he suggested that I was opening any facts which I should not open,' he said blithely. 'I hope I have not been unfair, but it would be useless for me to present my case to you without first of all explaining what it is you have to listen to.'

And with that Bishop sat down.

The second day was no less entertaining. Nearly two hundred people piled into the public gallery in number two court. They were instantly rewarded for taking the trouble to come. First into the box was a new witness, PC James Rothwell, who claimed to have seen Wallace, head down and crying, on the afternoon of the murder. 'I saw he was dabbing his eye with the end of his sleeve, and he appeared to me to be very distressed. His face was very pale, haggard and drawn.'

Here, one of the spectators in the well of the court burst out laughing. The magistrate peered over the bench. 'Do not let us have so much humour, please. Take this thing seriously,' he snapped.

Everyone had the weekend off, but on Monday morning, 23 February, the lawyers were at it again. In the witness box this time was Wallace's superintendent, Joseph Crewe, who was explaining to Bishop that he had lived at his present address, 34 Green Lane, for three and a half years.

'Has Mr Wallace ever visited you there?' asked Bishop.

'Yes.'

'How many times?'

'Four, five or six.'

Bishop blinked. 'Four, five or six?'

Up jumped Scholefield Allen to object. 'He said four or five, Mr Bishop.' Bishop tried to straighten the point out with Crewe. 'Don't put words into his mouth that he didn't use,' cried Scholefield Allen.

Bishop turned, empurpled with rage. 'Will you please sit down, Mr Scholefield Allen?' he roared.

The Assistant Magistrates' Clerk, Henry Harris, sought to defuse the crisis. 'What were your original words, Mr Crewe?'

'Four, five or perhaps six, but I now want to give it as four or five,' said Crewe.

Another 'breeze', said that night's *Liverpool Echo*.

Jack Johnston, Wallace's neighbour, was giving evidence. Bishop was asking the questions; Scholefield Allen was objecting again. 'The suggestion is made against the prisoner that he was waiting there [in the entry behind his house] for someone, and when he got someone he asked them to wait while he made the discovery,' spluttered Scholefield Allen.

'I haven't got that idea,' murmured the magistrate.

'No, but that idea has got out to the public, and it has been proved to be entirely inaccurate.'

'The public', said Ward, 'are not judging this case.'

'No,' said Scholefield Allen, thoroughly exasperated. 'But some members of the public will have to deal with it.'

*   *   *

On day four a long queue snaked under the archway of the central police buildings in Dale Street. The public gallery filled to capacity with spectators, again mostly men. Plenty of lurid detail was provided by Professor MacFall, whose evidence, the *Echo* agreed, was 'eagerly awaited'. MacFall described the terrible wounds on Mrs Wallace's head 'as if a terrific force had driven in the scalp, bursting it in parallel lines'. Death, he estimated, was caused by one of eleven blows, and would have taken place in less than a minute.

Later, the court heard, 'We did not take careful notes.' The speaker was not MacFall, but Dr Pierce, police medical officer. Scholefield Allen pounced.

'You go there as scientific witnesses forming expert opinions and you do not take notes?'

Bishop came to the rescue. 'If you would ask questions and not make so many speeches to the witnesses, we would get on better.'

Scholefield Allen ignored this, and turned again to Pierce. 'Do you realise this man's life may depend on what you say?'

Pierce nodded.

'Then you will appreciate why I am so anxious to get at the facts.'

Only later did Pierce manage to explain that he had meant to say that he and MacFall had not made *detailed* notes, not that they had not made *careful* ones.

The case was adjourned until Thursday, at first. But when on Thursday morning another big crowd gathered outside the court, the doors remained closed. After it had milled around for some time a policeman came down and told everyone that the hearing had been adjourned again, until Monday. The crowd broke up, cheated. As he left the court Wallace raised his hand to someone in the gallery.

On Monday, for the fifth day, crowds besieged the court, and many people were turned away, having failed to get a seat. On Tuesday, the sixth day, the same thing happened again. Wednesday, 4 March was the seventh, the last and most rewarding day of the committal, so far as the spectators were concerned.

First of all there was an opportunity for more hilarity in court when Inspector Gold was questioned about the exhibit of hair which had been produced. He agreed that 'it was hair that had been worn by a lady'.

'The suggestion,' Scholefield Allen was saying, 'is that it is false hair.'

The public gallery fell about laughing.

'I wish,' said Ward wearily from the bench, 'that we could treat this inquiry quite seriously. It is a serious matter. I want people at the back of the court to realise that too.'

Secondly, there was the delicious spectacle of Wallace, for the first time, publicly betraying his feelings. At the invitation of Scholefield Allen, Inspector Gold was reading an extract from Wallace's diary, dated 7 January 1931: 'A night of keen frost. The heavy fog gives a wonderful appearance to all plants and trees. Every twig and leaf was most beautifully bordered and outlined with a white rim of frost. Holly leaves, owing to their wavy edges, presented a most charming appearance, and I cannot recollect an occasion on which the hoar has produced such wonderfully beautiful effects. After dinner I persuaded Julia to go into Stanley Park. She was equally charmed. A gradual thaw seems to be setting in now.'

'That,' said Scholefield Allen, 'is a beautiful and tender incident.' But his comment was lost to most of those in the public seats, who were craning forward to watch Wallace, overcome with emotion, weeping freely and holding a handkerchief to his face. The magistrate adjourned the court for lunch. Wallace sat for a few moments to recover his self-possession, then disappeared down the steps to the cells.

When the hearing resumed, with Gold still in the witness box, Scholefield Allen referred to another diary entry, dated 25 March 1929: 'Julia reminds me today it was fifteen years ago yesterday since we were married. Well, I don't think either of us regret the step. We seem to have pulled well together and I think we both get as much pleasure and contentment out of life as most people. Our only trouble is that of millions more, shortage of £ s d.'

That afternoon the prosecution completed its case. The clerk read out the formal charge. Wallace rose, and in a firm voice replied, 'I plead not guilty to the charge made against me, and I am advised to reserve my defence.

'I would like to say that my wife and I lived together on the very best of terms during a period of some eighteen years of our married life. Our relations were those of complete confidence in and affection for each other.

'The suggestion that I murdered my wife is monstrous. That I should attack and kill her is to all who knew us unthinkable and unbelievable, all the more so when it must be realised that

I could not gain one possible advantage by committing such a deed. Nor do the police suggest I gained any advantage.

'On the contrary,' Wallace continued, his voice wavering now with emotion. 'In actual fact, I have lost a devoted and loving comrade. My home life is completely broken up and everything that I hold dear has been ruthlessly uprooted and torn from me. I am now left to face the torture of this nerve-racking ordeal.

'I protest once more that I am entirely innocent of this terrible crime.'

Wallace sat down. There was total silence in court.

He was duly committed for trial at the next Liverpool Assizes. 'I have followed the evidence very clearly,' said Magistrate Ward, 'and taken notes, mental and otherwise, from the beginning to the finish.'

Henry Harris, the Assistant Magistrates' Clerk, laid down his pen. In the course of the seven-day hearing he had recorded some fifty thousand words of evidence. After a short talk with Scholefield Allen and Munro, Wallace was taken down. The crowds milled out into the street, to wait on corners for the evening newspapers to check that there was nothing they had missed. WALLACE IN TEARS, read the *Echo* headline. No, they had missed nothing.

The headline in the *Liverpool Evening Express* on Wednesday 4 March, 1931, read INQUEST AGAIN ADJOURNED, and the story was as follows:

'The inquest on Mrs Julia Wallace was today formally adjourned by the Liverpool coroner [Mr C. G. Mort] for another week.

' "I have received a declaration from the clerk to the justices that the case is now being heard, and I adjourn the inquest in order to hear the result of that case," said the coroner.'

Wallace was driven back to Walton Gaol. The dormitory in the prison hospital was occupied chiefly by mental defectives whose manners at the long table in the centre of the room disgusted Wallace. 'One extraordinary character,' he wrote later in his 'life story', 'had the habit of breaking up his bread very small and minutely examining every tiny particle before putting it into his mouth . . . This was a form of imbecility . . . Others would burst from vacancy into uncontrollable laughter, harsh and uncanny, sinking back as suddenly into dullness and apathy. Some would be forever discussing their cases and the wrongs under which they were labouring. Others would stalk moodily about, sombre and silent, wrapped in their own miseries. On the other hand, quite a number were cheerful, even merry, and didn't seem to care a rap what might happen to them. Prison life had evidently no terrors for them.'

Wallace spent most of his time reading from the extensive prison library. Another pastime was draughts or dominoes, played with other prisoners 'out of sympathy for the poor, brainless fellows who could not amuse themselves and who were, I suspect, entirely illiterate'. Wallace was allowed visitors for twenty minutes a day, but his lawyers, Sydney Scholefield Allen and Hector Munro, were permitted to see him at almost any time, and their visits were not curtailed. For exercise Wallace was allowed an hour's walk during the morning around circular concrete pathways that crisscrossed the prison grounds, and a half-hour stint in the afternoons.

The days dragged by, but at the end of March Wallace's spirits were sent soaring by news from Hector Munro, who hurried back to Liverpool from London, where he had secured an undertaking from the Prudential Staff Union that they would guarantee the entire defence costs. But there was even better news: members of the union's executive council had held a secret mock trial, and found Wallace not guilty of murder by a unanimous verdict.

The council had met in secret session in an upstairs room at Holborn Hall. The trial had lasted all day. Wallace's plight had been put before the union by Norman Allsop, who had started Wallace in the Prudential in 1915, and August Evans. It had taken some weeks to organise, but finally, on Thursday 26 March, executive members of the PSU from all over Britain gathered in London to test the evidence for themselves. Wallace, of course, was a union member – the PSU had seven thousand members in all – and was a past chairman of the Liverpool branch. Hector Munro placed before the council all the available evidence and, in an atmosphere crackling with tension, declared that 'no court in the land would convict Wallace'.

Allsop and Evans reported that Wallace, an educated and cultured man, had lived in complete happiness with his wife. They produced statements to show that none of his acquaintances in Liverpool believed that he had committed murder. Finally, in an impassioned plea for his client, Munro rose to his feet and said: 'When he is acquitted he will be a ruined man all the same. All his savings will have gone. He has put all he has

– roughly four hundred pounds – into his defence, and it will cost at least twice this amount on a modest estimate. It is computed it will cost at least one thousand two hundred pounds.'

For several hours members of the executive closely questioned Munro and Liverpool members of the union. By the end there was not a single person in the room who was not convinced of Wallace's innocence. There and then, the men from the Pru decided to set up the Wallace Defence Fund, and one of the most remarkable trade union manifestos of modem times was immediately drafted.

'We are, as we write,' it began, 'sitting in session of executive council in Holborn Hall, and have under our urgent consideration a matter of life and death. One of our members, an agent, Mr William Herbert Wallace, of Liverpool, is in Walton Gaol, charged with the murder of his wife . . .'

The document outlined details of the case, and concluded: 'Those who know him think it inconceivable that he should be capable of such an atrocious murder. No motive has been assigned or suggested, except robbery, which would clear Mr Wallace. The executive council recognises that our duty to Mr Wallace does not arise out of the fact that we are a trade union, and he is our member, although that makes us stand related as brothers, but on the broader, stronger ground of human brotherhood and Christian charity.

'The executive council has agreed to guarantee the whole cost of the defence and to raise what money will be required. We have placed a duty on the conscience of each member, and trust wholeheartedly that there will be a response, immediate and ample, to the needs of this supremely serious occasion.

y person is held innocent until guilt is proved in British
aw and equity.'

The manifesto, signed by the union's top officials, was circulated to members all over Britain and quickly produced £500.
The Prudential Company itself contributed £150, and agreed
to keep Wallace's position open for him, putting a temporary
agent on his rounds to keep the agency in order.

Of course not a word of this appeared in the newspapers at
the time. Public curiosity about the case between the committal and the trial was fed only with scraps of somewhat routine
information. The trial judge, for example, was to be Mr Justice
Wright, a man of sixty-two with a background not in criminal
work but in heavy civil and commercial cases. His reputation
was as a judge of clarity and thoroughness – both great judicial
virtues – but he had a lugubrious, boring voice, which juries
were apt to find tiresome during Wright's rather lengthy
summings-up.

The barrister briefed by Hector Munro to defend Wallace
was the florid and softly spoken Roland Oliver KC, the
Recorder of Folkestone. Oliver was best known as a prosecutor
rather than as a defence lawyer; for some years he had been a
Junior Crown Counsel at the Old Bailey, and had appeared in
most of the notable criminal trials of the day, including the
Thompson–Bywaters murder case.

Just a fortnight before the opening day of the Liverpool
Spring Assizes it was announced that Edward Hemmerde KC,
the Recorder of Liverpool, would lead for the Crown. The news
caused almost as big a sensation in the city as the Wallace case
itself. For Hemmerde was arguably the most notorious and
certainly the most controversial figure on the northern legal

scene. Both in and out of court, Hemmerde's activities and pronouncements had been making news for years.

His career had begun in meteoric fashion: he was a brilliant young silk, and at the age of thirty-five had been elected an MP, the Liberal member for East Denbigh. Hemmerde prospered, was nominated as Recorder of Liverpool by the Liberal government of 1909, and amid a welter of professional, parliamentary and social engagements managed to find time to write a number of plays, one of which, *A Butterfly on the Wheel*, opened in London's West End in 1911 and ran for several months.

At the end of the Great War, Hemmerde was sitting pretty, but then things began to go wrong. He started losing heavily at the gambling tables, and had further bad luck playing the stock market. A creditor dragged him through the civil courts to recover a debt. Hemmerde eventually lost the action, which cost him dearly not just in terms of money he now owed but also in terms of his reputation, having found himself branded as the villain of the piece in the coverage of the case in the popular press. To add insult to injury, other creditors began to press for their money, and before he knew where he was Hemmerde was up to his neck in debt. When, a few months later, his wife successfully sued for divorce, Hemmerde must have felt he had touched bottom.

But he was wrong. Misfortune followed misfortune: after switching his political allegiance, becoming Labour MP for Crewe in 1920, he was passed over for official legal office; not long after this, he heard from East Africa that his twenty-three-year-old son had been killed in an accident. The news appears to have unhinged something in Hemmerde's head, because it was at this point that he decided to lift the lid on a most unpleasant and quite unprecedented episode involving himself and his municipal masters within Liverpool Corporation.

It began in March 1921, when Hemmerde raised the question of his precedence in the city on ceremonial occasions, and his claim to read addresses on important occasions such as royal visits. Hemmerde felt sure he was being made the victim of what he called a ceremonial boycott. Even more galling and certainly a lot more expensive was the fact that despite his office as Recorder, the City of Liverpool kept briefing other people when the Corporation went to law. Hemmerde claimed that it should be he who was briefed on behalf of the Corporation in litigation. Hemmerde called this a professional boycott that had cost him many thousands of pounds. It was a fact that in the twenty-odd years since being appointed Recorder of Liverpool he had not been briefed by the Corporation in one major action. The council's view was that the Recorder had no right to expect to be briefed on their behalf, and therefore Hemmerde had no business complaining on that score.

But the fact was that Hemmerde had upset his political masters during the trial in Liverpool in 1921 of a group of Sinn Feiners. Hemmerde had been briefed not by the Crown but by the defence, and in the course of the case launched a scathing attack on the local police, a tactic which incurred the gross displeasure of the city's watch-committee.

The ceremonial boycott began when Hemmerde switched from the Liberals to the Labour Party in 1920. Hemmerde felt snubbed at civic occasions. Once, after an official dinner for a visiting judge, he felt obliged to write to the Lord Mayor complaining that he had been placed wrongly on the seating plan. 'If either you or any other Lord Mayor do not desire my presence on such an occasion,' raged Hemmerde, 'the remedy is not to invite me.'

It was in this sort of strained atmosphere that Hemmerde was offered the leading prosecution brief in the Wallace case in March 1931. He was jubilant, feeling no doubt that this was a peace offering from the Corporation to settle all the old arguments once and for all. But jubilation was mingled with apprehension: what if Hemmerde were to lose the case? If he did, and Wallace was acquitted, his career would effectively crash in ruins. On the other hand, if Hemmerde were to triumph, and secure a conviction against Wallace, then he would be made for life, able to look forward to many untroubled years of prosperity.

Like Wallace, Hemmerde knew that the trial at St George's Hall in April 1931 amounted to an all-or-nothing gamble. It was a gamble that Edward George Hemmerde was not prepared to lose – at any price.

III

The Trial of William Herbert Wallace

I

It was spring, but spring in Liverpool, and rain lashed across Lime Street with regard neither for the season nor the crowds milling in the dawn of Wednesday 22 April outside St George's Hall, hoping for a seat in the number one court. They huddled beneath umbrellas, mackintoshes and newspapers waiting for the doors to open. At last those at the head of the line were allowed inside, to scuttle into court and take their places in the magnificent circular gallery, where they took off their soaking coats, stuffed them beneath the seats and settled down to await the drama that was to follow. Outside, hundreds more remained in the rain, hoping for a seat later in the day.

'Put up Wallace!'

The words of the Clerk of Assize were the cue to the two prison officers flanking Wallace to usher him up the steps into the dock, a kind of wooden pen surrounded by an iron rail. He clasped his hands behind his back as he gave a friendly nod to his junior counsel, Scholefield Allen. The clerk asked Wallace if he objected to any of the jurors. He leaned over the dock rail, and, after a momentary consultation with Hector Munro, shook his head.

'Silence!'

A door behind the great wooden bench opened, and everyone in the packed court rose. From the door emerged a small procession: first, a man carrying a white wand, then the sheriff and his chaplain, followed by the judge, Mr Justice Wright, in scarlet trappings and a goat-hair wig. As they took their places Wallace glanced around. On his left, boxed into two pews, sat the jury. Above them, the press box, packed with reporters. Behind the dock, Wallace must have been aware of a packed public gallery. In front, in the well of the court, the lawyers and officials. Amid the black gowns and wigs Wallace no doubt picked out the familiar figure of his brother Joseph, sitting alongside Munro. But there was no time even to make a signal. With a rustle of his gown, the clerk rose again.

'William Herbert Wallace,' he intoned. 'You are indicted and the charge against you is murder in that on the twentieth day of January nineteen-thirty-one at Liverpool, you murdered Julia Wallace. How say you, William Herbert Wallace, are you guilty or not guilty?'

In a firm voice, Wallace replied, 'Not guilty.'

Edward Hemmerde KC, Recorder of Liverpool, opened the case for the Crown in a long, shrill speech in which he sought to 'show a very serious case against the prisoner'. And yet, in the course of two hours, there were really only a couple of new points of any interest. The first was the prosecution's amended explanation of the crumpled mackintosh.

At the police court it had been claimed that Wallace had worn the mackintosh to protect himself from the splashing blood. But now the Crown took the theory on to encompass not merely due care and attention on the part of the murderer but also a perverted streak: Wallace wore the mackintosh, Hemmerde suggested, while murdering his wife in the nude.

'The history of our own criminal courts shows what elaborate precautions people can sometimes take. One of the most famous criminal trials was of a man who committed a crime when he was naked. A man might perfectly well commit a crime wearing a raincoat, as one might wear a dressing gown, and come down, when he is just going to do this, with nothing on which blood could fasten, and, with anything like care, he might get away, leaving the raincoat there, and go and perform the necessary washing if he was very careful.'

Hemmerde's reference was apparently to the trial of François Courvoisier for the murder of Lord William Russell in 1840. Courvoisier, a Swiss valet, slit his master's throat, presumably, though not with absolute certainty, while naked. It was a colourful touch, but it conveniently ignored the fact that police tests on the bath and washbasin, and the pipes and drains, had failed to reveal any evidence whatsoever of the necessary washing in the house. Nevertheless, it provided the listening reporters with a fair angle for the evening papers. COUNSEL AND NAKED MAN CASE was that night's headline in the *Liverpool Echo*.

'I tell you quite frankly,' Hemmerde told the jury towards the end of his speech, 'the Crown can suggest no motive. But supposing, to take an extreme case, you saw a murder committed, you'd be unimpressed if someone said to you afterwards: "But there was no motive for his doing it." You would say: "I can't help that – I saw it."

'So if, although there is no motive apparent to the Crown or apparent to you, the facts seem to you to point irresistibly to the conclusion that he DID it, motive has nothing to do with the question!'

Hemmerde was well aware of the need to end an opening speech for the Crown on a high note of rhetoric. 'This is not a case where you will be in any way concerned with other possible verdicts such as manslaughter,' he told the jury. 'If this man did what he is charged with doing, it is murder, foul and unpardonable. Few more brutal murders can ever have been committed; this elderly, lonely woman literally hacked to death for apparently no reason at all.

'Without any apparent enemy in the world, she goes to her account, and if you think that the case is fairly proved against this man, that he brutally and wantonly sent this unfortunate woman to her account, it will be your duty to call him to HIS account.'

Early witnesses for the prosecution were taken through their evidence by Hemmerde's junior, a young Northern Circuit barrister called Leslie Walsh. At twenty-seven, this was his first major murder trial.

Telephone operator Louisa Alfreds, the first of two switchboard girls to speak to Qualtrough – 'just an ordinary voice' – was followed by Lilian Kelly – 'quite an ordinary voice' – and then by the switchboard supervisor Annie Robertson. It was Miss Robertson who explained how the call came to be logged. It had been connected at 7.20 p.m. and the time had been noted 'as is the custom when an operator refers to me a number for which she'd been unable to get a reply'. Qualtrough had, in fact, placed the call twice, claiming on the second occasion that although he'd pressed the button, 'I have not had my correspondent yet.'

Waitress Gladys Harley from the City Café testified to hearing 'just an ordinary voice' but it was Samuel Beattie, the chess club captain, who sent a stir through the court under cross-examination from Roland Oliver.

Q: 'Do you know Mr Wallace's voice well?'

A: 'Yes.'

Q: 'Did it occur to you it was anything like his voice?'

A: 'Certainly not.'

Q: 'Does it occur to you now it was anything like his voice?'

A: 'It would be a great stretch of the imagination for me to say it was anything like that.'

Wallace's chess-playing grocer friend James Caird, who spoke of Wallace as an intellectual, said there'd been nothing unusual about his manner on the night before the killing. Then, the first police witness was called, PC Rothwell, who claimed to have seen Wallace 'unusually distressed' several hours before his wife's murder. He was cross-examined by Oliver.

Q: 'Have you ever made a mistake in your life?'

A: 'I dare say I have.'

Q: 'If I were to call about twenty-five people who saw him that afternoon . . . and they said he was just as usual, would you say you had made a mistake?'

A: 'No, I should stick to my opinion.'

Q: 'You would?'

A: 'Yes.'

Q: 'Then I shall have to call them.'

Exit PC Rothwell. Enter Alan Close, the fourteen-year-old milk boy who had delivered to the Wallaces as usual on the night of the killing.

Q: 'What time?'

A: 'Half past six.'

Q: 'How do you know the time?'

A: 'When I passed Holy Trinity Church, it was twenty-five past six and it takes me five minutes to get to Mrs Wallace.'

Q: 'Can you say why you noticed the time, twenty-five past six?'

A: 'I generally glance at the clock when I pass.'

Q: 'When you delivered the milk, who took it in?'

A: 'Mrs Wallace.'

Q: 'You're sure about that?'

A: 'Yes.'

Close told Oliver in cross-examination that he normally made his deliveries by bicycle, walking only in bad weather or when his bike was broken. On the murder night the machine wasn't working, so Close walked. Warned now by Oliver that his evidence about the timing was 'absolutely vital', Close explained that having passed the church clock at 6.25 p.m. he walked down Breck Road, turned into Sedley Street and went into his father's dairy shop for some fresh cans of milk. These he carried up Sedley Street and along Letchworth Street, turning left at the top into Richmond Park.

One customer in each street. Two customers in all.

Time taken: not very long.

Distance from clock to shop: five hundred yards.

Time taken by Close to walk from church to Wolverton Street via dairy: five minutes. And that included a brief 'hello' to Elsie Wright in Letchworth Street.

Q: 'If Elsie Wright says that the time then was something like twenty to seven, you would not agree with her. Is that right?'

A: 'No, sir.'

Oliver moved to the day after the murder, and the encounter between Close and the other children in the street, Elsie Wright, Kenneth Caird and Douglas Metcalf. 'Did he [Metcalf] ask you this: "What time were you there?"' asked Oliver.

'Don't remember.'

'Just try to remember, will you?' Oliver rattled back. 'Perhaps this next thing will bring it back to your mind. Did you say: "At a quarter to seven"?'

'No, sir.'

'Think!' Oliver snapped. 'I suggest to you that in the presence of Kenneth Caird, Elsie Wright and this boy Metcalf, you said that you were there at a quarter to seven.'

'No,' replied Close, 'between half past six and a quarter to seven.'

'I must put this to you quite seriously: that you, in the presence of those other children, said that it was a quarter to seven when you were at Mrs Wallace's. Now. You think hard. Isn't that right?'

No reply.

The judge leaned forward. 'What do you say about it?'

Again, no reply. Close shook his head.

'Do not shake your head,' rapped the judge.

Still no reply.

'Perhaps he's tired,' mused the judge.

'Are you feeling all right?' asked Oliver.

Close looked sulky for a moment, then said he was.

'Will you just apply your mind to what I put to you?' said Oliver, patiently. 'Did you not say that you took the milk to Mrs Wallace at a quarter to seven?'

Another silence. The longest yet.

At last Close replied, 'No, between half past six and a quarter to seven.'

'It's taken you a long time to answer. You weren't feeling ill, were you?'

'No.'

The judge commented again: 'He shook his head several times and couldn't bring himself to speak.'

Alan Close's ordeal wasn't over yet.

'Did you make a joke about it that evening,' Oliver was saying, 'when they wanted you to go to the police? Do you remember you put your thumbs in your waistcoat like that' – Oliver illustrated the gesture – 'and said: "Well, I'm the missing link"?'

Silence.

'Well, did you?'

'No.'

'Nothing like that?'

'No, sir.'

'If they were to say you used that expression, that is quite wrong, is it?'

'Yes, sir.'

'It's a funny thing to invent, don't you think?'

'Yes,' said Close, smirking.

'Do not answer carelessly!' shouted Oliver. 'Just think if during that evening you didn't use that expression.'

Close was sulking again. 'No, sir.'

'Nobody is saying it's very wicked if you did,' said Oliver soothingly. 'I'm only trying to find out what you did say.'

'Well,' said Close, stubborn to the last, 'I didn't say it.'

'You swear you didn't?'

'Yes, sir.'

After Alan Close came a string of people who'd encountered Wallace on his journey to Menlove Gardens: the tram conductors, Mrs Mather, Sydney Green, PC Sargent and Mrs Pinches from the newsagent's where Wallace had used a directory. They were followed by five members of the Anfield Harriers with evidence concerning the tram tests, and Joseph Crewe, the superintendent from the Prudential. He told the jury of Wallace's visits to his home in Green Lane. Anyone who knew Wallace, or knew his habits and employment, said Crewe, might expect him to have the bulk of the money he had collected on his rounds by Tuesday night. And that money could be anything from £50 to sometimes over £100. 'The reason it varies is this,' he told Hemmerde during re-examination. 'On the fifth of January he paid £35 2s 11d in. The following week, the twelfth of January, is what we call a monthly week. He also collects weekly premiums and monthly premiums. That accounts for £89 being paid that week.'

The final witness on the first day of the trial was typist Lily Hall, who claimed to have seen Wallace talking to an unidentified man at about 8.35 p.m. on the murder night, shortly before the body of Mrs Wallace was found. Hemmerde was hoping to end the day on a telling note, but as his questioning of the girl progressed, things lurched from the troublesome to the shambolic:

Q: 'When did you last see Mr Wallace before the tragedy?'

A: 'On the nineteenth.'

Q: 'You saw him on the nineteenth?'

A: 'Yes.'

Q: 'That was the Monday?'

A: 'No, the Tuesday.'

Q: 'You mean Tuesday the twentieth?'

A: 'Yes.'

Q: 'What time was that?'

A: 'About twenty past nine [*sic*].'

What Miss Hall had actually told the police was that she'd seen Wallace talking to another man in Richmond Park at about 8.35 p.m.

Q: 'What made you notice the time?'

A: 'I was going to the pictures.'

A curiosity, since she'd said earlier that she was walking down Richmond Park towards her home in Letchworth Street.

Q: 'What time do the pictures begin?'

A: 'About ten to nine.'

Q: 'And you noticed from the clock it was eight thirty-five?'

A: 'Yes.'

Miss Hall had now squared her timings, but pressed on with her demolition job on this part of the prosecution case.

Oliver cross-examined.

Q: 'I suppose you saw a good many other people about the streets?'

A: 'Yes.'

Q: 'You never gave those a thought at the time, did you?'

A: 'No.'

Q: 'No. Why should you? Then there was a murder. How long after the murder did you give your statement to the police? About a week?'

A: 'I think it was about a week, but I'm not sure.'

Q: 'What made you wait all that long time before going to the police?'

A: 'I was ill in bed for one thing.'

Hemmerde, in a last desperate bid to salvage something, re-examined.

Q: 'How many of you are there at home?'

A: 'Two.'

Q: 'Your sister and father and mother?'

A: 'Yes, and me.'

Q: 'Was your statement actually taken by the police when you were in bed?'

A: 'Yes.'

Q: 'Did you know how they heard about it?'

To which there was no reply.

'Well!' exclaimed Roland Oliver.

The judge adjourned the court for the night.

On Thursday 23 April at ten o'clock Wallace took his place in the dock, to follow the evidence with close interest. Once again he sat, arms folded, between two warders. Again the court was crowded. Hundreds had queued for a seat; many had been turned away. Into the witness box stepped Wallace's former neighbour Jack Johnston, who had since moved to another part of the city. He said little that was new, except to query one of the photographs of the scene of the crime, claiming that the mackintosh pictured under the body was not there when he and his wife beheld the murder room with Wallace. (In this, Johnston was quite obviously mistaken.)

Like her husband, Florence Johnston yielded nothing startling in the course of her evidence, but at the end of Oliver's cross-examination seemed to support Wallace's contention that the front door was bolted when he opened it from the inside to admit the police.

Q: 'Do you know whether or not the door was bolted?'

A: 'I do not.'

Q: 'If he says he undid the bolt you would not contradict him, would you?'

A: 'I don't know whether he did, but I can't remember that.'

Next came the police officer who was admitted by Wallace 'after a few seconds' fumbling', PC Fred Williams. Without any ado, Hemmerde sought to clear up the point.

Q: 'While the fumbling was going on, did you or did you not hear any bolt drawn?'

A: 'I did not.'

Williams was the first police officer to speak to Wallace after the discovery of his wife's body, and the first to record Wallace's own version of events. This was in a statement written down from memory some time after Wallace had poured out his story in the murder room. Oliver, in cross-examination, had some trouble in pinpointing exactly when Williams committed this recollection of Wallace's story to paper. But eventually Williams said, 'I should say it would be about half past ten when I made my rough notes of what I had ascertained.'

'So,' said Oliver with evident relief, 'at half past ten you sat down to record, quite properly, what had happened during the last hour and a quarter.'

'I did not sit down to it.'

'Then stood up!' barked Oliver.

Only one thing in Wallace's statement to Williams worried Oliver. 'Are you sure he said she walked down the entry with him and not down the back yard?'

'I'm emphatic that he said she walked down the entry.'

'It's a funny thing to do,' mused Oliver. 'I'm going to suggest that he said she walked down the back yard and let him out. You're confident you are right?'

'I am confident,' said Williams, 'absolutely.'

'Have you ever made a mistake?' asked Oliver, not for the first time in the trial.

'I dare say I have,' replied Williams, 'but I'm confident I never made a mistake because I thought of the probability at the time of somebody having sneaked into the house while the accused and his wife were a few yards down the entry. That's how I remember it.'

Perhaps something in Hemmerde's stomach tightened.

Oliver feigned surprise. 'With them in the entry?'

'It's a peculiar neighbourhood,' observed Williams, not choosing his words with care.

'Is it a peculiar neighbourhood?' asked Oliver, seizing the advantage. 'What is peculiar?'

Williams began to busk. 'As regards the laying out of it, the planning of it.'

'There have been troubles there occasionally, have there not?'

'I do not know,' said the officer with breathtaking temerity.

'Perhaps someone else does,' Oliver observed scornfully. 'At any rate, I'm suggesting that you're mistaken about that. Are you quite clear that he told you she bolted the back-yard door?'

'Absolutely,' said PC Williams.

The next two witnesses in turn raised, then considerably lowered, the temperature of the morning's proceedings. First there was the Wallaces' charwoman, Mrs Draper. From an alarming selection of iron bars of various lengths and thicknesses produced from a box by Hemmerde she chose one about fifteen inches long and half an inch in diameter. This, she said, as the bar was passed to the judge, to the jury and back to Hemmerde, most closely resembled the iron bar missing from the Wallaces' parlour since the early weeks of January.

After Mrs Draper came James Sarginson, a locksmith, and not one of the Crown's most scintillating expert witnesses. He told the court about the condition of Wallace's front-door lock – which had some springs missing – and the back-door lock, which was apparently rusty and stiff. Sarginson and Oliver got into a terrible tangle over the technicalities of rusty locks, and at last the judge brought the episode to a close with a question of his own. 'All that is suggested to you,' said the judge with infinite indulgence, 'is that there might be some difficulty with extra stiffness because of the adjustment of the strike?'

'Yes,' said Sarginson, to everyone's huge relief.

Those spectators (and those participants as well) who'd grown restless in the course of all this now settled down with keen anticipation to watch the undisputed star of the second day: Professor MacFall. Unlike the hapless locksmith, MacFall was a highly accomplished performer in the witness box. He knew the form.

'Are you Professor of Forensic Medicine in the University of Liverpool, and Examiner in Medical Jurisprudence in the Universities of Glasgow, Edinburgh, Manchester and Birmingham?' asked Hemmerde.

'I am,' replied MacFall, with evident relish.

MacFall described to the jury his observations about the body of Julia Wallace, based chiefly on the progression of rigor mortis. He said that by 1 a.m. his opinion was that death had occurred 'quite four hours before ten o'clock'. That was to say 6 p.m.

Hemmerde needed that revising, and sharpish.

Q: 'What would you regard as the possible margin of error in that calculation?'

A: 'It could not possibly be in this case more than an hour; it isn't possible because post mortem rigidity isn't merely beginning, it has begun, and has progressed to a certain extent in the neck and arm.'

Hemmerde smiled. He still had his expert witness, his top man, keeping Wallace firmly on the spot with his timings. Six o'clock was no good – it was obvious that Wallace hadn't arrived home by six – and five o'clock was worse still. But a possible time of death of seven o'clock! Just the job.

Evidence was given next about the blood clot on the lavatory pan ('not freshly spilt . . .' said MacFall, '. . . beyond that I cannot go') and a suggestion as to where Mrs Wallace was when the first blow was struck ('sitting . . . with the head a little forward, slightly turned to the left as if talking to somebody').

MacFall's examination-in-chief continued after lunch.

Q: 'What was the demeanour of the accused when he was there?'

A: 'I was very much struck with it. It was abnormal.'

Q: 'In what way?'

A: 'He was too quiet, too collected, for a person whose wife had been killed in the way that he described. He was not nearly so affected as I was myself.'

Q: 'Do you happen to remember anything in particular that led you to that conclusion?'

A: 'I think he was smoking cigarettes most of the time. Whilst I was in the room examining the body and the blood, he came in smoking a cigarette, and he leant over in front of the sideboard. It struck me at the time as being unnatural.'

Oliver rose to cross-examine. 'I want to begin with the last part of your evidence.'

'May I put in this before that,' said MacFall hurriedly, and without a question mark. 'You haven't had the position of these blows . . . which is very important.' He produced a piece of paper.

'I don't want to stop anything,' said Oliver, bemusedly, because MacFall was now waving the slip of paper at the judge, 'but how can this indicate who did it?'

'No, of course not,' said the judge hastily.

Hemmerde bobbed out of his seat. 'The Professor thinks it important,' he explained. 'I hesitated to ask him.'

'I have a great reason for this myself,' said MacFall to nobody in particular.

The judge decided it was time to get a grip on things again. 'Counsel must conduct the prosecution,' he said, gruffly, 'and he will ask you or not ask you as to anything that occurred.'

Hemmerde was still on his feet. 'Can you give me quite shortly what your reason is?'

'I can,' boomed MacFall. 'I formed an idea of the mental condition of the person who committed this crime.'

The court suddenly fell completely silent.

'I've seen crimes, many of them of this kind, and know what the mental condition is,' MacFall continued. 'I know this wasn't an ordinary case of assault or serious injury. It was a case of frenzy!'

Gasps and mutterings filled the court, and even the judge shifted slightly in his chair. 'Well, the jury may already have thought of that. If you have a blow which in itself is fatal, and then a series of violent—'

'Meaningless,' snapped MacFall.

'—blows struck,' the judge ploughed on, 'it does suggest frenzy. But,' he added, eyeing MacFall darkly, 'that is a matter for the jury to consider.'

Oliver had to act quickly to repair the damage.

Q: 'If this is the work of a maniac and he [Wallace] is a sane man, he didn't do it. Is that right?'

A: 'He may be sane now.'

Q: 'If he's been sane all his life and he's sane now, it would be some momentary frenzy?'

A: 'The mind is very peculiar.'

Q: 'It's a rash suggestion, isn't it?'

A: 'Not in the slightest. I've seen this sort of thing before, exactly the same thing.'

Q: 'The fact that a man has been sane for fifty-two years and has been sane while in custody for the last three months would rather tend to prove he's always been sane, wouldn't it?'

A: 'No, not necessarily.'

Q: 'Not necessarily?'

A: 'No. We know very little about the private lives of people or their thoughts.'

Q: 'I want you to deal with evidence and not speculation.'

A: 'You asked me, I think.'

Q: 'Let us go back. You have told the jury that you were very much struck with his callous demeanour?'

A: 'I was.'

Q: 'Why did you not say so at the police court?'

A: 'Because I wasn't asked.'

Q: 'Oh, but you don't mind volunteering things. You've been volunteering things for the last five minutes.'

A: 'I could say many things, but my lord would pull me up.'

Q: '. . . I will get this fact from you: not one word about his demeanour was said by you at the police court?'

A: 'No.'

Q: 'Even though you gave evidence for a long time, and in detail?'

A: 'Yes.'

Oliver was building a theory about the mackintosh, and how it came to be burned. 'Suppose,' he asked MacFall, 'it was round her shoulders and she collapsed, do you not see the possibility of the bottom of the mackintosh falling into the fire and getting burnt too?'

'There is the possibility,' MacFall admitted.

'Do you not see the possibility of someone having grasped her by the hair to pull her from the fire?'

'Yes.'

'Where her clothes were burning?'

'I don't know about the burning.'

Oliver ventured to test the truth of that.

'It is said that my client tried to destroy the mackintosh by burning it, because it was his. That would take time, would it not?'

'I am not an authority on the burning of mackintoshes,' was MacFall's pompous reply.

'Then we'll leave that to our general knowledge,' observed Oliver, urbanely. 'Now, to come to another matter. Whether clothed or naked, it would be necessary, would it not, in all common sense, that many splashes of blood would fall upon the assailant?'

'Yes,' said MacFall, 'I should expect to find them.'

'Would you agree that nothing in this life is certain, but it is almost certain the assailant would have blood on his face and clothes?'

'On his left hand, I think he would.'

'What about his right?'

'No, I don't think so. You don't find the blood so much on the hand that holds the weapon.'

'The last blows being probably struck with the head on the ground, there'd be blood on his feet and lower part of his legs for certain, wouldn't there?'

'I should expect that.'

The judge asked, 'There would be some on his face?'

'There would be some on his legs.'

'And his face?' Oliver persisted.

'Yes.'

'And his hair?'

'Yes, but more likely upon the face.'

Oliver snapped back, 'You agree it would be most likely on the face?'

'Yes,' said MacFall ruefully, 'I agree.'

'How many notes did you make with regard to rigor mortis?' Oliver demanded.

'Practically none, I think.'

'Can you show me one?'

'I don't think I can.'

'You would agree that the progress of rigor mortis from the point of view of crime is important?'

'Very.'

'And not one note made?'

'No, but I know definitely.'

MacFall did not know. And Oliver would later prove it.

MacFall was telling Oliver that the progress of rigor depends, among other things, on whether the dead person is big or small, hefty or slight. MacFall agreed that a powerful, muscular body would be affected by rigor much more slowly.

Q: 'Was this a feeble and frail body?'

A: 'Yes. She wasn't exactly frail; she was a feeble woman.'

Q: 'You have used the word "frail".'

A: 'Yes, she was a weak woman.'

Q: 'Frail?'

A: 'Yes, frail.'

Q: 'Then . . . it comes to this: that she was a woman who was likely to be quickly affected by rigor?'

A: 'No. She would be rather delayed if anything.'

This was a remark so surprising that the judge rocked forward in his chair to clarify matters for himself. 'I thought you said it would be quicker in a frail person and slower in a person of muscularity?' he rasped.

'She would be delayed,' mumbled MacFall.

Oliver spoke again. 'Do you wish to say that a feeble and frail person would have delayed rigor?'

'No.'

'Why do you say it then?'

'She was in a condition of good health although a frail woman.'

'Then,' Oliver sighed, 'I will start all over again. A muscular body would take longer to be affected by rigor than a feeble and frail body?'

'Yes.'

'Was this woman a feeble and frail woman?'

'Yes.'

'Then she would be likely, would she not, to be more quickly affected by rigor?'

'A little.'

'Then why did you say "rather longer" just now?'

'Not rather longer than a muscular person.'

'You are not arguing the case, are you?' snapped Oliver.

'No,' MacFall replied, 'I wish to state what I found.'

'You know what's at stake here?'

'I do.'

'Bearing in mind that this feeble and frail woman would be more likely to be affected by rigor, are you going to swear she was killed more than three hours before you saw her?'

'No, I'm not going to swear,' MacFall said testily. 'I am going to give an opinion, and I swear that the opinion that I give shall be an honest one.'

'Then what,' boomed the judge, 'IS your opinion?'

'My opinion was formed at the time that the woman had been dead about four hours.'

'Now that I have reminded you that, she being feeble and

frail, rigor would come on quicker, does that move your opinion?'

'No.'

'It doesn't?'

'No.'

'You don't think she was killed four hours before you saw her?'

'I do.'

'You DO?'

'Yes.'

'That is your honest opinion?'

'Yes.'

'You saw her at ten past ten?'

'Yes.'

'So if she was alive at half past six, your opinion is wrong, is it not?'

'Yes.'

'Doesn't that convince you what a very fallible test rigor mortis is?'

'No,' said MacFall, obdurate to the last, 'it does not. I am still of the opinion.'

'Do you think the milk boy IMAGINED seeing her alive?' trumpeted Oliver.

'I don't want to think about the milk boy and what he saw at all,' replied MacFall with uncharacteristic candour.

Oliver looked closer at MacFall's assertion that although no notes were taken, the medical man could 'know definitely' about the progress of rigor mortis.

Q: '. . . what was the condition at ten to eleven?'

A: 'I did not make any notes as we went along of progression.'

Q: 'Not making notes! You have a good memory, I suppose?'

A: 'I have.'

Q: 'What was the position [at ten to eleven]?'

Q: 'It had got the right shoulder.'

Q: '. . . is that all?'

A: 'I was not looking at the times as I went on. I did not take the time on any other occasion except when I went to the house.'

So how could he know the progress of rigor at ten to eleven?

The last, bedraggled episode in MacFall's evidence concerned the mysterious blood clot on the rim of the lavatory pan. Oliver spent some time trying to get the unhappy doctor to admit the possibility that the drop of blood was shed not by the killer but by one of the investigators. At last he allowed, 'Yes, I thought the police might have dropped it there.'

Oliver sat down, his cross-examination complete.

Hemmerde rose to re-examine. 'That occurred to you, Professor, because it was the only mark of blood upstairs?'

'The only mark,' MacFall agreed, 'and it is so striking.'

'And you now think,' the judge interposed as if to tidy up the point, 'it may have been carried there by the police?'

'No, my lord.'

'I thought you said so,' said Mr Justice Wright, nonplussed.

'I was asked: did I recognise the possibility? And I said I did recognise the possibility and made inquiries about it.'

'It IS a possibility?' The judge wanted this absolutely clear.

'Yes, certainly,' said MacFall, fumbling now for his trump card, 'but I took care to find out that the police had not been up.'

This was palpably not so: at least four policemen, Williams, Moore, Gold and Bailey, had tramped in and out of the bathroom before MacFall found the blood spot.

Oliver got up. 'I meant the witness to understand that it was he who might have done it.'

'I myself?' squawked MacFall.

'Yes.'

'I am glad you have said that,' wheezed MacFall, beaming disingenuously. 'No, I did not.'

'So far as you are concerned,' said Hemmerde, 'have you any doubt about it?'

'Not the slightest doubt about it.'

Next into the box stepped medical man number two, Dr Hugh Pierce. 'I thought death had taken place about six o'clock,' he told the court. 'Or, it may be, after,' he added, rendering the estimate valueless.

Having allowed himself two hours' leeway either side of a perfectly notional time of death – between four and eight o'clock – Pierce proceeded to get himself into a terrible tangle. Questioned by Hemmerde, he differed from MacFall about the dead woman being frail: she was, said Pierce, perfectly healthy. But he was at one with his hapless mentor on the question of recording the progress of rigor.

Oliver: 'Will you show me any notes you made?'

'I was simply there by order of the Chief Constable. Professor MacFall was doing the examination.'

'At any rate,' continued Oliver, 'you did not take any notes?'

'No, I did not take any notes.'

And the question of the cooling body:

Q: 'You did not take any temperatures, did you?'

A: 'I was not doing the examination.'

Q: 'But you did not, in fact.'

A: 'I did not.'

Q: 'No temperatures were taken?'

A: 'No.'

Q: 'You know what is called the rectal temperature is generally the best test?'

A: 'Yes.'

Q: 'That was not done?'

A: 'No, it was not done. I did not do it.'

Things lurched from bad to worse. At last Mr Justice Wright butted in: 'You have said so many things, it is difficult to follow what it is you have made or have not. So far you have put it [the time of death] at six or perhaps later; with a margin of error two hours either way, which I thought referred to this particular case. Otherwise,' barked the judge, 'what is the use of saying it?'

'Yes,' gulped Pierce, 'that is so.'

Finally Oliver delivered the *coup de grâce*.

'When you got there [at ten to twelve] you said that rigor was present in the neck and what else?'

'The upper part of the left arm.'

'Do you know that is precisely the condition recorded by Professor MacFall hours earlier?'

'I do.'

'It seems rather funny?' mused Oliver.

'If I may explain in this way,' cried Pierce. 'When you move a muscle and rigor mortis is just starting you make it limp and flaccid for a time, but if the muscle has not completely gone so that really it might start again the rigor will come on definitely.'

Oliver considered this piece of incoherent nonsense, tried without success to punctuate it in his mind, and blinked, first at Pierce and then the judge. 'I will leave it there, my lord,' he said. And sat down.

Last on the prosecution's list of 'expert' witnesses was William Roberts, the city analyst who'd examined several articles taken from the murder room, including the mackintosh and the dead woman's skirt. Roberts propounded the theory that the killer wiped his bloody feet on the hearthrug before leaving the murder. But, as Oliver pointed out in cross-examination, 'It would be difficult to wipe the calves and shins on the hearth-rug, would it not?'

'Yes.'

Hemmerde re-examined: 'Would you expect there to be much blood on his calves and shins?'

'No, not much.'

'Surely,' cried Oliver, jumping up, 'that is a medical question?'

Mr Justice Wright agreed: 'He is not a medical man at all; he is an analyst.'

Hemmerde replied, 'I have known him so long, I think he is both.'

'I am an analyst, my lord,' said Roberts.

*   *   *

Into the witness box stepped Detective Superintendent Hubert Moore, the last witness of the day. Under cross-examination by Oliver, Moore ducked and dived, stonewalled and lied.

Q: 'You talked about his [Wallace's] demeanour being quite calm, smoking cigarettes. Is that true?'

A: 'Quite.'

Q: 'You have never mentioned it before today in public?'

A: [Ducking] 'I was never asked it.'

Q: 'It only seems to have occurred to someone quite lately to ask that question. You attach importance to it, do you not?'

A: [Diving] 'No, not that I know of.'

Q: 'If you do not think it is important, I will not trouble with it. Have you ever heard of people smoking cigarettes to try and keep a hold on their nerves, to try and calm themselves?'

A: [Stonewalling] 'I am not a cigarette smoker. I smoke a pipe.'

Q: 'That is a very good reason why you should not.'

And later.

Q: 'You make the point that it is quite wrong to strike a match at the door [of the darkened murder room] to light the gas?'

A: 'I do; there's no necessity for it. A man living sixteen years in a little room like that . . . it was not the natural thing.'

And later still:

Q: 'Do you know a boy named Allison Wildman?'

A: [Lying] 'No, I do not.'

Q: 'The name was given of a youth who said that Mrs Wallace was alive many minutes after six thirty that night. I want to know why shouldn't that boy have been called by the prosecution?'

A: [Still lying] 'I do not know the boy Wildman.'

3

ALFWAY THROUGH THE trial, and nearing the end of the prosecution case, Detective Sergeant Harry Bailey was the first witness on day three, Friday 24 April.

'Do you know a boy named Wildman?' asked Oliver in cross-examination.

'I can't say I know him. I know the family,' said Bailey.

'Do you know why the police haven't called Wildman, or a newspaper boy called Jones?'

'We arrived, as far as I know, at the conclusion that Close was the last person who saw the deceased?'

True, but not the answer to the question.

Oliver: 'I wonder if you know it has been laid down in the Court of Criminal Appeal that it is the duty of the police to call all witnesses who are relevant to assist the jury – not to pick and choose the ones who help to prove the guilt? Do you know anything against Wildman or Jones?'

'No, I don't,' said Bailey.

Detective Inspector Herbert Gold was called next and questioned by Walsh about Wallace's demeanour in the hours following the killing. 'He was cool and calm,' said Gold. 'I didn't see any sign of emotion in him at all at the death of his wife. When I first went into the house on the night of the murder, he was sitting in the kitchen. In fact, he had the cat on his knee and was stroking the cat . . .'

Then he made a remark, a very telling remark, but set down or reported several different ways:

'He did not look to me like a man who had just battered his wife to death.' [Official trial transcript]

Or: 'He didn't look to me like a man who'd just DISCOVERED his wife had been battered to death.' [*Liverpool Echo*]

Or, again: 'He didn't look like a man who'd lost his wife.' [*Liverpool Evening Express*]

At eleven forty-five, the prosecution concluded its case.

'That, my lord, with the accused's statement, is the evidence for the Crown.' Hemmerde's shrill announcement prompted an immediate hubbub in court, but this was cut short by the Clerk of Assize, who stood up, to recite the statement made by Wallace on the last day of the committal. Wallace himself, meanwhile, seemed quite oblivious to what was going on. 'His outward attitude,' the *Echo* journalist reported that night, 'was that of a man resigned to whatever fate might have in store for him . . . arms folded, head resting slightly on one side as though with weariness.'

Oliver's opening speech for the defence lasted less than thirty minutes. To a packed and silent court he declared that apart from police suspicion, there was 'no rag of evidence' to convict Wallace of murder. The Crown case, he stressed, was built 'on the flimsiest circumstantial evidence'. Wallace's behaviour throughout the case had been that of an innocent man. Criticising the methods of the police, Oliver accused them of 'throwing ropes in front of this man to prevent the facts coming out'.

In conclusion Oliver argued: 'Up to the very last moment before his arrest, the police were taking statements from Wallace . . . If he is an innocent man, consider what his condition of mind must have been. He was quiet, stunned by shock. He sobbed – as Mrs Johnston says – when he was alone.

'If he has made a slip or two,' said Oliver finally, 'remember the circumstances.'

At two-thirty Wallace was led from the dock to the witness box by two warders. He looked deathly pale, and swayed a little as he took the oath. The words were barely audible, and Wallace apologised. 'My throat is a little husky,' he explained, feebly. 'It will go in a moment.'

The judge said Wallace could sit if he wished. But Wallace remained standing, and his answers were clear and unhesitating. The examination-in-chief lasted an hour.

'I suppose I must put this question to you,' said Oliver at one point. 'Did you lay a finger on her? Did you lay a hand upon your wife at all that night?'

For a moment, Wallace mulled the question over. Then he replied, 'I think, in going out of the back door, I did what I often enough did. I just patted her on the shoulder and said: "I won't be longer than I can help."'

'I don't mean that,' said Oliver, slightly vexed at not getting the unequivocal No he had wanted. 'Did you do anything to injure her?'

'Oh no,' said Wallace, 'certainly not.'

Later Wallace was asked, 'When you went out, was your wife alive?'

He replied, unhesitatingly, 'Certainly.'

Wallace was giving his evidence with his arms clasped behind him. His voice seemed to become clearer as Oliver's questioning progressed.

Q: 'What was your relationship with your wife?'

A: 'What I should describe as perfect.'

Still later Oliver asked, 'When you got the light on, what did you do?'

'I turned round and examined my wife,' said Wallace. 'I got hold of her left hand . . . and felt the pulse. I couldn't find any sign at all. Then I looked into her face and saw she was obviously quite dead. Well, I can hardly remember what I did then . . .'

'Do you know,' asked Oliver, 'what your demeanour was for the rest of the evening? It is said you were cool and collected.'

'Well,' replied Wallace, 'I remember I was extremely agitated, and also that I was trying to keep as calm and cool as possible. Probably I was smoking cigarettes for something to do. I mean, the inaction was more than I could stand. I had to do something to avoid breaking down . . .'

'Is there anyone in the world who could take the place of your wife in this life?'

'No, there is not.'

'Have you got anyone to live with now?'

'No.'

'Or to live for?'

'No.'

A stir rippled through the court as Hemmerde rose to cross-examine. His initial tactic was to catch Wallace off balance with a bombardment of questions, often disconnected.

'Where was your wife on Monday evening, January nineteenth?'

'In the house . . .'

'Where was Mr Crewe on Tuesday, January twentieth?'

'I understood he had gone to the cinema . . .'

'On that night, the twentieth?'

'On the Monday night.'

'I'm not talking of the Monday; I'm talking of the Tuesday.'

'On the Tuesday I do not know where he was.'

'I thought you did know. On the Monday night you say you knew he'd been to the cinema?'

'No, I am wrong. On the Monday night I do not know where he was . . .'

'This must have been quite a slight cold of your wife's, was it not?'

'We did not regard it as a serious matter . . .'

'Her cold had not been too bad for her to walk out into the yard and see you out?'

'That is so.'

'Her cold was evidently not at all bad?'

'We did not consider it serious.'

'And she was not a singer?'

'She had been at one time.'

And so on. After a time it seemed that Wallace was feeling rattled. 'You do not realise,' he told Hemmerde, who was trying to confuse him with figures, 'that in addition to what is known as an industrial branch collection I might pick up varying sums in the ordinary branch.'

'Allow me to take it in my own order,' snarled Hemmerde.

Wallace had been in the witness box for nearly two hours, and by now his replies to Hemmerde's torrent of questions were becoming distinctly abbreviated.

Q: 'Does not the whole thing strike you as very remarkable that a man who does not know you should ring you up for business in another district and expect you to go there, and yet without knowing whether you had gone there or not come and wait outside your house for the chance of murdering your wife?'

A: 'Yes.'

Q: 'It is a curious thing, is it not?'

A: 'Yes.'

Q: 'It would have been easier for him, would it not, to have given a right address a little further off?'

A: 'I suppose it would.'

Q: 'If you had been given a right address, of course, you need not make a number of inquiries. One would have been sufficient. You follow what I mean?'

A: 'Yes.'

Q: 'If you had been told Menlove Gardens West, the first inquiry would have landed you there?'

A: 'Yes.'

Q: 'If you are told of an address which does not exist, you can ask seven or eight people, every one of whom would be a witness where you were?'

A: 'Yes.'

Q: 'So, to a man who is planning to do this, a wrong address would be essential to his alibi?'

A: 'Yes.'

After a short break for a cup of tea, Hemmerde increased the pressure still further, trying to dislodge Wallace over his recollection of exactly what he said and did on the murder night; about the locks, the iron bar, the theory that an intruder may have still been in the house on Wallace's return, and about Mrs Johnston and the mackintosh. 'You see what I am putting to you,' said Hemmerde at length. 'If you were describing things that really happened, you would be accurate, like when you said your wife went down the entry and things of that sort. Here, you may be wrong about what you said that night about having noticed it [the mackintosh] when you first came in; but what I am putting to you is, you said it that night, apparently giving her the impression as though you had made a discovery: "Whatever was she doing with my mackintosh?"'

The judge leaned forward: 'No, I don't remember that. She was not asked what her impression was: she simply described what she saw . . . I heard no evidence of any impression.'

'My lord, I could not ask her what her impression was.'

'No,' said the judge, 'I know.'

The Hemmerde–Wallace battle ended nearly three hours after it began.

'You could not open that door?'

'Which door?'

'That front door.'

'No, I could not get it open.'

'But you saw the superintendent open it the very first time?'

'Yes, that is true.'

'Close the door and go out into the street, and open it without any difficulty?'

'But I could not open it because the bolt was on it.'

'But the key?'

'I said the key slipped back.'

'You never told him that.'

'I do not know whether I told him that,' said Wallace, 'but I tell you that.'

Oliver, re-examining, did not linger long.

'When you were playing the violin with your wife, were you accustomed to do it when you were naked in a mackintosh; was that your habit?'

Wallace looked nonplussed. 'What was that?'

'To play naked in a mackintosh?'

Wallace stared at Oliver and shook his head. 'I have never played naked in my life,' was the shocked reply.

Evidence came next from the two expert medical witnesses, Professor James Dible and Dr Robert Coope, followed by evidence about the critical point of timing from five youngsters: Allison Wildman, who swore that he had seen Alan Close on the Wallaces' doorstep at 'about twenty-three minutes to seven' because 'I passed Holy Trinity Church clock at twenty-five to seven, and it takes me two minutes to walk to Wolverton Street.' Elsie Wright, who swore Close had said he had seen Mrs Wallace alive 'at a quarter to seven'. Douglas Metcalf, who confirmed '. . . a quarter to seven'. Kenneth Caird, who agreed 'a quarter to seven'. And finally Harold Jones, who thrust a newspaper into the Wallaces' letterbox at 'about twenty-five minutes to seven'.

*　　*　　*

Oliver's final task of the day was to produce witnesses to rebut the evidence of PC Rothwell. Louisa Harrison, asked if Wallace had appeared upset when he called on the day of the killing, replied, 'He was joking with me.' Amy Lawrence testified, 'He was the same as usual.' And Margaret Martin remembered him as, 'Calm, and the same in appearance.'

'That is the case, my lord,' said Oliver.

'I think,' the judge said, glancing at the clock, 'the speeches had better be made tomorrow morning.'

4

S OON AFTER MIDNIGHT on Saturday 25 April spectators for the final act of the Wallace drama began to gather outside St George's Hall. At the head of the queue were two navvies who had come straight from work in the Mersey Tunnel. By 4.30 a.m. the line was more than forty people long. By 8 a.m. it stretched along William Brown Street and into St John's Gardens. At nine-thirty, the rain began.

Half an hour later, with the judge, jury, prisoner and everyone else in place in court, Oliver rose to make his closing speech for the defence.

Oliver identified two factors in the case which, he said, were essential in determining guilt. Who sent the telephone message? And at what time had the prosecution proved that Mrs Wallace was killed? Turning to the jury, he said, 'Ask yourselves whether, on the evidence for the prosecution, you can possibly say that Wallace sent the telephone message.' But on the second factor, time of death, Oliver was somewhat less stark. He pointed out that there were two branches of evidence: one medical, and the other that of the milk boy, Alan Close.

The medical evidence, said Oliver, was so ambiguous as to be almost completely useless as a factor in determining the time of the crime. 'Rigor mortis, taken alone, is a hopelessly fallible test; it is not a test at all,' he declared. 'There is an error of at least an hour either way; and that is how I ask you to treat it. I accept quite candidly that, upon the medical evidence, the death might have taken place at such a time as Wallace might have been there, but I submit to you that, looking at the whole of the facts, it is not a bit more likely to have taken place then than after Wallace had gone.'

On the evidence of Alan Close, Oliver said it was significant that within twenty-four hours of the crime, when Close had no interest either way, the police had elicited from him the information that he had last seen Mrs Wallace alive at a quarter to seven. Close had told this to other people and they were so impressed that they urged him to go to the police to eliminate Wallace.

For nearly an hour the quietly spoken Oliver rounded up the evidence, reminding the jury at the close of his speech that the burden of proof was entirely on the Crown. 'You have got a crime here,' he said, 'without a motive. You have got a man here whose affection for his wife cannot be doubted . . .

'Finally, if I may say so, it is not enough that you should think it possible that he did this – not merely enough, but it is not nearly enough. On looking at the two stories, you may say: "Well, the story of the defence does not sound very likely, but the story of the prosecution does not sound very likely either." And if that be the state of your minds, then he is entitled to be acquitted. I suggest that this should be the state of your minds: The story for the defence is not very likely, but at least it is consistent with all the facts. The story for the prosecution sounds impossible.'

Edward Hemmerde rose to make the closing speech for the Crown. Straight away he focused on the two crucial guilt factors mentioned by Oliver. On the identity of the telephone caller Hemmerde knew that his ground was treacherous. In the absence of irrefutable proof the prosecutor turned to sophistry: 'My learned friend said "How did the Recorder get the fact that nobody knew or could have known he was going to be there [the City Café]? He must have got it from the police." I did not, I got it from his client . . .

'Inspector Gold said: "I asked him if he knew anyone who knew he was going to the club" and "Had he told anyone he was going?" To that Wallace said: "No, I had not told anyone I was going and cannot think of anyone who knew I was going."'

A fine point, but in fact a spurious one. Anyone who had glanced at the club noticeboard in the weeks before the murder would have seen that Wallace was expected at the City Café on the night before the murder, because he was scheduled to play in a tournament match. Beattie had told the man on the phone that he expected Wallace shortly. And any unknown caller could have watched Wallace leave home for the City Café at the appointed hour and in the right direction.

Despite his earlier promise, it was not until the closing section of his speech that Hemmerde addressed himself to the question of the time of death, something which, in Hemmerde's view, was 'easily established'.

'The man who had made his plans, whether the boy was seen at 6.30 or 6.35 talking to this woman, had, between that time and 6.49, practically twenty minutes . . . I say there is ample time for it.'

Hemmerde had been speaking for a good seventy minutes when, at last, he reached his climactic peroration. 'You can only convict this man,' he told the jury, 'if you are satisfied beyond all reasonable doubt on all these facts . . . You cannot convict him unless you are perfectly clear, beyond all reasonable doubt, that these matters to which I have been drawing your attention point with almost irresistible emphasis to the conclusion that he is guilty. If you do not think so, of course it will be your duty to acquit him.

'I hope nothing that has fallen from me at all, in my opening speech or in this my final speech, has led you to suppose anything of the sort. I am not entitled, I hope, to over-emphasise inconsistencies or coincidences in this case, but I am bound to suggest to you, on behalf of the Crown, that the evidence connecting this man with that message is strong evidence; that the evidence of what that man did when he came back to the house is strong evidence that he was not acting then as an innocent man; and I also ask you, having regard to what happened when he saw Mr Beattie on that night of the twenty-second, when he said: "They have cleared me"; and Mr Beattie replied: "I am glad to hear it", what did he mean by that? Is that the attitude of a man who has known he is under suspicion, and is looking out as to how he is to meet the case; or who is unjustly under suspicion, and is doing his best to meet the case which is made against him?

'I am sorry to have detained you so long,' Hemmerde concluded, 'but in a case of this length I have felt it my duty to lay before you in considerable detail what I submit is the case for the Crown.'

It was getting on for midday when Hemmerde resumed his seat and the attention of the court shifted to the scarlet-robed figure seated at the centre of the judicial bench. Mr Justice Wright's summing up lasted nearly an hour and a half and greatly boosted the chances of Wallace securing an acquittal; it was pragmatic, workmanlike and totally scrupulous. It began with a scathing dismissal of Professor MacFall's assertion that this was a murder of frenzy. 'In that case,' the judge ruled, 'there is no question of insanity to consider.'

Next, he gave a warning to the jury against judging the case not on the evidence but on what they had read, heard and thought in the weeks before the trial: 'Members of the jury, you, I believe, are living more or less in this neighbourhood. I come here as a stranger and know nothing about the case until I come into the court or look at the depositions, and I need not warn you that you must approach this matter without any preconceived notions at all. Your business here is to listen to the evidence, and to consider the evidence, and nothing else.'

The judge moved on to comment on the nature of the case, describing the killing as 'almost unexampled in the annals of crime' with nothing specific pointing either to the murderer or his motive. As for the evidence, it was circumstantial, the kind that 'may vary in value almost infinitely'.

'The real test of the value of circumstantial evidence is: Does it exclude every reasonable possibility? I can even put it higher,' said the judge: 'Does it exclude other theories or possibilities? If you cannot put the evidence against the accused man beyond a probability and nothing more, if that is a probability which is not inconsistent with there being other reasonable possibilities, then it is impossible for a jury to say: "We are satisfied beyond reasonable doubt that the charge is made out against the accused man."

'Then again, the question is not: Who did this crime? The question is: Did the prisoner do it? – or rather, to put it more accurately: Is it proved beyond all reasonable doubt that the prisoner did it?

'It is a fallacy to say: "If the prisoner did not do it, who did?" It is a fallacy to look at it and say: "It is very difficult to think the prisoner did not do it"; and it may be equally difficult to think that the prisoner did do it.

'The prosecution have to discharge the onus cast upon them of establishing the guilt of the prisoner, and must go far beyond suspicion or surmise, or even probability unless the probability is such as to amount to a practical certainty.'

These clear warning signs to the jury were followed by a meticulous review of the evidence, including, of course, a reference to the time factor, in Mr Justice Wright's view 'the most vital part of the case'.

To the jury he cautioned: 'If you think the times are so short as either to make it impossible that the prisoner should have done the act, or anyhow to make it very improbable, then that would be a very strong element in your conclusion on the real question in the case . . . If you find on a crucial point like this that the element of time is so restricted and so narrow as to make it very improbable even if not impossible, for the person to have done what it is said he did, then that would assist you in coming to a conclusion as to his guilt or otherwise.'

The judge was plainly unimpressed with the criticisms of Wallace's various actions on his return home. He thought the business of Wallace going upstairs first instead of making straight for the murder room of little account, as was the fact that in the parlour Wallace had lit the right-hand instead of the left-hand gas jet. What was more, said the judge, 'It is difficult to see that any idea can be obtained of his guilt from the mere fact that he did not step on the body, or step in the blood.'

Then Mr Justice Wright returned to the question at issue: was there any doubt that it was Wallace who had murdered his wife? 'You may think: "Well, someone did it." Human nature is very strange. You may have a man send a bogus message, and having sent the bogus message, even if he did not see the prisoner actually leave the house, he might go to the house, ring the bell or knock at the door, and be admitted by Mrs Wallace. If she had been told, as the prisoner said, that the prisoner was seeking an interview with Qualtrough, and if he was admitted, he would soon find out that he was not in the house; on the other hand, if he found he was in the house, he could go away . . .

'However you regard the matter, the whole crime was so skilfully devised and so skilfully executed, and there is such an absence of any trace to incriminate anybody, as to make it very difficult to say, although it is entirely a matter for you, that it can be brought home to anybody in particular.

'If there was an unknown murderer, he has covered up his traces. Can you say it is absolutely impossible that there was no such person?

'But putting that aside as not being the real question, can you say, taking all this evidence as a whole, bearing in mind the strength of the case put forward by the police and by the prosecution, that you are satisfied beyond reasonable doubt that it was the hand of the prisoner, and no other hand, that murdered this woman?

'If you are not so satisfied, if it is not proved, whatever your feelings may be, whatever your surmises or suspicions or prejudices may be, if it is not established to your reasonable satisfaction as a matter of evidence, as a matter of fact, of legal evidence and legal proof, then it is your duty to find the prisoner not guilty.

'Of course, if you are satisfied, equally it is your duty to find him guilty.

'But it is your duty to decide on the evidence which has been given before you during these three days, and, whatever your verdict is, that is the acid test which you must apply.

'Will you consider your verdict and say whether you find the prisoner guilty or not guilty?'

5

I T SEEMED, SAID the *Liverpool Echo* that night, like a stage play in a real-life setting. The principal characters were all keyed up to the highest possible pitch of anxiety and excitement.

With two exceptions.

Mr Justice Wright, who during his summing up never once raised his voice beyond a pitch adequate for the jury's hearing.

And Wallace himself, 'the only other person in court who seemed perfectly oblivious to what was going on'. His customary attitude – arms folded, head slightly on one side as though with weariness – remained unchanged. Only when the judge began his summing up did Wallace betray any sign that he was more than an ordinary spectator. He leaned forward more intently, his right arm doubled up beneath him on the rail of the dock, his fist clasped beneath his chin, listening closely to all that the judge said.

The low voice ceased; there was an audible sigh in the court; the jury retired. Counsel for the prosecution and for the defence left the places into which they had sunk, exhausted, after their long addresses; the prisoner's white head disappeared down the narrow stairway leading to the cells beneath.

At the foot of the steps leading to the cells Wallace awaited the verdict with seeming indifference. Chatting to one of the warders, then with Hector Munro, he never for one moment appeared to lose his composure. He began to clean his spectacles, breathing on one lens, then the other, and polishing them with his handkerchief. One tiny speck of dirt seemed to give him trouble; the more Wallace rubbed it, the more it seemed to stick fast. Puff, polish . . . puff, polish . . . after each sequence Wallace held the glasses up for inspection, but still he was not satisfied. At last, after the umpteenth polishing, he held them aloft, saw they were clear, and put them on.

And at that moment the jury returned into court. It was twenty-five past two. They had been absent for an hour.

With the judge and his retinue in place, Wallace was led up into the dock. He was carrying his hat and coat. 'Optimistic, eh?' murmured one of the warders flanking him. Wallace stood motionless, hands clasped behind his back.

The jury filed in. Only one man stole a furtive glance at Wallace. Eleven jurors sat down. The foreman remained standing.

The Clerk of Assize spoke. 'Gentlemen of the jury, are you agreed upon your verdict?'

'We are.'

'Do you find the prisoner at the bar guilty or not guilty?'

'Guilty.'

At once, the tension was shattered by a gasp of astonishment that sounded like a roar from the spectators. Court officials called for silence. The clerk turned to Wallace. 'You have been convicted of murder upon the verdict of the jury,' he said.

'Have you anything to say why sentence of death should not be passed according to law?'

Firmly, Wallace replied, 'I am not guilty. I don't want to say anything else.'

The black cap, ancient and awesome symbol of judicial despatch and used by every judge as he sentenced a prisoner to death, was placed on the head of Mr Justice Wright. Slowly and quietly, he spoke. 'William Herbert Wallace, the jury after a very careful hearing have found you guilty of the murder of your wife. For the crime of murder, by the law of this country, there is only one sentence, and that sentence I now pass upon you.'

Wallace was duly sentenced to death by hanging. Then, still displaying no emotion, he turned and walked down the steps to the cells, his hands still clasped behind his back.

6

W ITHIN AN HOUR of the verdict Mr Justice Wright left St
George's Hall to the accompaniment of a fanfare from
the Assize trumpeters. He was driven to the Judges' Lodgings
in Newsham Park to pack his bags. Wallace also left the court,
hustled out of a side entrance by warders and driven to Walton
Gaol in a Black Maria. At the prison he was ordered to strip
naked and change into the special grey uniform reserved for
prisoners awaiting execution. As he did so he was crying uncon-
trollably. Still weeping, he was led along a passage to the
condemned cell.

All over Liverpool the newsboys were on the streets, their
cries echoing in the sad, slow dusk: 'Wallace verdict . . . Wallace
to hang . . .' The news was even flashed on to the screens of the
city's cinemas. And by opening time the verdict was the talk of
the town. It continued to generate controversy in the days that
followed. Indeed, as the *Liverpool Echo* remarked, public interest in the case, great as it was throughout the trial, swelled
enormously once the verdict was known.

The *Echo*, and every other local newspaper for that matter,
was swamped with correspondence about the case, most of it

bitterly disputing the verdict. 'Heaven defend me from a jury of my fellow countrymen and countrywomen,' wrote someone who had attended the entire trial. 'It is possible even,' wrote another who was present, 'that such an obvious and fatal disqualification as deafness may be present, in greater or lesser degree, in or more members of the jury.' Norman Torry, a writer from Rock Ferry in Cheshire, proposed a fund should be launched to finance an appeal. 'I . . . like the hundreds of other spectators, was aghast at the finding of the jury . . .' he wrote. 'If a man is to be convicted on such flimsy evidence and in the face of the strong and reasonable doubt surrounding every point, the jury system stands condemned.'

While Wallace languished in the death cell public attention on Merseyside shifted towards the ten men and two women who had tried him from the cosy, comatose anonymity of the jury box. 'Had the jury been mixing with the public at large they would have *felt*, almost, the view that while there was a general *belief* that Wallace was guilty, there was equally general belief that the evidence was not strong enough to put the issue beyond doubt in the minds of men and women,' declared one local columnist. 'The press box view generally was that the verdict would be not guilty. The court generally was frankly surprised, and of twenty-eight people in a club not one expected the verdict . . .'

There was little doubt that Wallace had wound up in front of a sleepy and prejudiced jury. After the committal hearing, reported extensively in all the local daily newspapers circulating in Merseyside and south-west Lancashire, it occurred to Hector Munro that he might seek a *certiorari*, to have the case tried in another part of the country. But he had been assured by the prosecution that none of the jurors would be drawn from Liverpool, and that the risk of pre-trial prejudice would be minimal. For the rest of his life Munro regretted accepting that assurance. It soon became clear that the one-sided account of the murder of Julia Wallace had circulated far and wide during the committal; the fact that the jurors at the trial came from as far away as Southport, St Helens, Runcorn and Widnes made not a scrap of difference.

On the morning after the verdict Wallace was served with the traditional first breakfast of the condemned man: bacon and eggs. He was visited by the prison governor and told that the date for his execution had been fixed for Tuesday 12 May. A prisoner under sentence of death was allowed a number of special privileges, and Wallace was permitted to send out for his violin and his chess set. These occupied him during the long days that ensued. Meanwhile, Munro and Roland Oliver were busily preparing for the appeal. They set down ten grounds, of which only the first really carried any weight: that the verdict was unreasonable and could not be supported having regard to the evidence. The whole of the evidence was consistent with Wallace's innocence and the prosecution never discharged the burden of proving that he and no one else was guilty.

This was tantamount to asking the Appeal Court to rule, in quashing the verdict, that the Liverpool jury were fools, or at least that they had made a dreadful mistake. This had never happened since the establishment of the Court of Criminal Appeal in 1907. So, a ruling in Wallace's favour would make legal history. And while Wallace himself was quietly confident of success, his lawyers – Oliver, Scholefield Allen and Munro

William Herbert Wallace as a young man.

Julia Wallace.

29 Wolverton Street, fifty years after the killing. *(Michael Green)*

Back entry used by Wallace on the night of the murder, little changed since 1931.
(Michael Green)

The Wallaces' kitchen, pictured on the night of the murder, with the tea things and evening newspaper still on the table. The home-made cabinet which was damaged by the killer can be seen to the left of the range, beneath Wallace's books. *(Police file)*

The City Café, meeting place of the Liverpool Central Chess Club, pictured a few days after the murder, with the notice board and telephone kiosk flanking the doorway. *(Police file)*

The notice board, with the second-class championship fixtures clearly showing that Wallace was expected at the café on the night of 19 January. *(Police file)*

2ⁿᵈ Class Championship.

1ˢᵗ Prize 10/-   2ⁿᵈ Prize 5/-

Mondays.

		NOV		DEC		JAN	FEB
		10	24	8	15	5	19	21
1	Chandler F.C.		9	3D	4	5	6	7
2	Ellis T.	7L	1	x	3	4	5	
3	Lampitt E.	6W	7	1D	2	x	4	8
4	McCarthy	5	6	2	W	2	3	x
5	Moore T.	4	x	0	1	2	3	
6	Wallace W.H.	3L	4	5	x	7	1	2
7	Walsh J.	2W	3	W	6	1	>	1

Underlined take Black.

LIVERPOOL MURDER CHARGE

FEB 1931

MRS. WALLACE'S HUSBAND ARRESTED

TO APPEAR IN COURT TO-DAY

C.I.D. APPEAL TO AN UNKNOWN MAN

Liverpool police officers last night arrested William Herbert Wallace (52), insurance agent, who will to-day be charged at the police court with the murder of his wife, Julia Wallace, at Wolverton-street, Richmond Park, Anfield, Liverpool, on January 20th last.

Mrs. Wallace was found dead at her home at 29, Wolverton-street, with her head battered.

The chief of the Liverpool C.I.D. appeals to a stockily-built m... who was seen in the street in Richmond Park about 8.35 on the night of the tragedy talking to another man to come forward.

William Herbert Wallace (52), insurance agent, will appear in Dale-street, Liverpool, Police Court to-day charged with the wilful murder of his wife, Julia, aged about fifty-two, at 29, Wolverton-street, Richmond Park, Anfield, Liverpool, on January 20th.

At seven o'clock last night Superintendent Hubert Moore, Superintendent Thomas, and Inspector Gold drove in a car to a house in Sefton Park where Wallace has been residing temporarily with relatives, and arrested him. He was taken to the Main Bridewell, where he was charged, and detained overnight.

Superintendent Moore, Chief of the Liverpool C.I.D. made a further state...

Mrs. Wallace's battered body was found in the front room of her house. Pictures and walls had been splashed with blood. Although robbery was a suggested motive, only £4 was missing. The police ascertained that on the night before the tragedy someone with a deep gruff voice, who said his name was "Qualtrough," telephoned a Liverpool café arranging an appointment with Wallace at an address in Sefton Park.

No weapon could be found. It was assumed that the assailant must have been spattered with blood, but all that could be found was a blood-stained and partly-singed raincoat near the body. The most minute microscopical examination failed to disclose any...

Wallace's arrest reported by the *Liverpool Daily Post and Mercury*. *(Liverpool Daily Post)*

(top left) Superintendent Hubert Moore, head of Liverpool CID. *(Liverpool Daily Post and Echo)*

Three leading legal figures at Wallace's trial, Mr Justice Wright *(top right)*, Roland Oliver KC for the Defence *(above left)* and Prosecuting Counsel Edward Hemmerde KC *(above right)*. *(Pictures courtesy of Jonathan Goodman)*

Wallace's original instructions to his solicitor Hector Munro. Note the shaky signature and incorrect year. *(Derek Johnston, courtesy of Donald Munro)*

Wallace's conviction reported in the *Liverpool Echo*. *(Liverpool Echo)*

Professor John Edward Whitley MacFall, pathologist, one of the chief witnesses for the prosecution. *(Liverpool Daily Post and Echo)*

Wallace being congratulated by his solicitor Hector Munro after the appeal in London, watched by *(from left)* Munro's first wife, three of Wallace's supporters, Munro's clerk Norman Wheeler, and Wallace's brother Joseph. *(Derek Johnston, courtesy of Donald Munro)*

Richard Gordon Parry.
(From police files, now in the Richard Whittington-Egan Collection)

Atkinson's Garage in the 1920s.

John Parkes in 1981. *(Michael Green)*

Atkinson's Garage in 1981. *(Michael Green)*

Lily Lloyd enthroned in a play staged at Lister Drive School, Liverpool, in the early 1920s, with Gordon Parry at her feet *(right)*.

Who Killed Julia? on the air from Radio City, 20 January 1981, *(from left)* Dr Charles St Hill, R. H. Montgomery, Jonathan Goodman, Philip Chadwick, Ray Jackson and the author. *(Michael Green)*

Some of the panel relax after transmission. *(Michael Green)*

William Herbert Wallace after his ordeal, a broken man. He was to live only a few months after this photograph was taken. *(Liverpool Daily Post and Echo)*

– thought his chances slim. Privately, they were prepared for the worst.

On Friday 15 May, Wallace, escorted by a group of plain-clothes police officers and warders, travelled to London by train for the appeal, which had been fixed for the following Monday. Wallace spent the weekend at Pentonville Prison, locked in the condemned cell, now clad in the blue uniform of the appellant. But this time his optimism had waned. 'I was a prey to the deepest dejection,' he confided in his diary. 'I had little hope that my appeal would succeed. I knew if my appeal was dismissed, my chance of a reprieve was slight.'

Wallace knew nothing of the moves being made on his behalf in Liverpool as the day of his appeal approached. On Sunday 17 May, at the great Anglican Cathedral that over-looked the city, worshippers were praying for Wallace's safe deliverance. It was the idea of the Vice-Dean, Canon Dwelly, who, in his capacity as Sheriff's Chaplain, had sat alongside Mr Justice Wright at Wallace's trial. He had composed this one special prayer, described as 'intercessions extraordinary', to be said at every service:

'You shall pray for them that are set by God's mercy to secure the administration of true Justice in our land. Particularly this day you shall pray for His Majesty's Judges of Appeal, that they may be guided in true judgement. And you shall pray for the learned counsels of our Sovereign Lord the King, that they may be faithful to the Christian injunction of the apostle Paul:

' "Judge nothing until God brings to light hidden things of darkness and makes manifest the counsels of the heart."

'And you shall pray for the people of this County Palatine, that their confidence in the fair dealings of their fellow-man may be restored, and that truth and justice, religion and piety may be established among us. Finally, you shall pray for all who await the judgement of their fellow-man, and commit them to the perfect justice of Almighty God.'

Asked about this extraordinary move, the Anglican Bishop of Liverpool, Dr David, said, 'There is a good deal of anxiety in this city about the case, and we gave people an opportunity to ask for Divine Judgement to be performed. I do not think it is unusual, but right, that people should pray like this.'

7

ON MONDAY 18 May, 1931, the Court of Criminal Appeal in London was packed. Wallace stepped into the court from an opening at the rear of the dock and took his seat between two warders. The public gallery – the biggest in the Law Courts – was full to capacity. The spectators had waited impatiently for nearly an hour while the court dealt with an unsuccessful appeal by a Cypriot man against his conviction for the killing of a London waitress. Now, as Wallace's tall figure came into view, there was a stir in the court. Dressed in a sombre suit, he stood impressively before the judges, clad in their scarlet robes and white wigs: the Lord Chief Justice, Lord Hewart, flanked on one side by Mr Justice Branson and on the other by Mr Justice Hawke. The hubbub died away, there was some slight coughing from the gallery, and clearing of throats from the well of the court as Mr Roland Oliver KC rose to his feet, turned, indicated to Wallace to sit down, and then addressed the court.

Once again, the fight for Wallace's life was on.

Oliver explained that the main ground of the appeal might be put in various ways. It might be said that the prosecution at the trial never sustained the onus of proof, that the evidence, taken as a whole, was consistent with guilt OR with innocence. Or it might be said that as the prosecution were relying on circumstantial evidence, such evidence must, at least, be sufficient to exclude the possibility of someone other than Wallace having murdered his wife. Whatever formula was used, Oliver declared, the real ground of the appeal was that a man who might well be innocent had been convicted of murder and sentenced to death.

There was a pause as Oliver glanced down at his notes.

On the table in front of him lay a transcript of Mr Justice Wright's summing-up speech at the Assizes, a sheaf of typewritten pages heavily annotated. Quoting a passage from it. Oliver suggested that if the statement of law given by the judge was correct, the case should never have gone to the jury.

'There was certainly no eye witness of the murder, except the murderer and the murdered woman. The evidence was, therefore, purely circumstantial. Mr Justice Wright directed the jury on the value of such evidence – and I wish to adopt that direction.'

Once again Oliver glanced down at his notes.

'Mr Justice Wright said the real test of the value of circumstantial evidence was whether it excluded every reasonable possibility of anyone else except the accused having committed the murder. If the circumstances in this case, as I hope to persuade the court, were such that they did NOT exclude every reasonable possibility, then the jury ought not to have found – ought not to have been ALLOWED to find – the appellant guilty.'

Oliver had made his first telling point. The Lord Chief Justice leaned forward and spoke for the first time. 'You say that the case ought to have been withdrawn from the jury?'

'Yes. I am saying that.'

Lord Hewart looked puzzled. 'But no submission of that kind was made to the judge.'

'No.'

Oliver was now arguing on the hoof. 'With the jury I had before me I did not wish to make that submission. I assumed that if the judge had been of that opinion, he himself would have withdrawn the case.'

Hewart nodded. The point, it seemed, was Oliver's.

The court now settled down to hear the story of how Wallace had received the Qualtrough telephone message, how he had sought in vain for a non-existent address, and how he had returned home to find his wife murdered.

Dealing with the absence of bloodstained clothing, Oliver claimed it would have been impossible for a guilty Wallace to have washed or destroyed his clothes in the fifteen minutes available between 6.30 and 6.45. 'At the trial,' he went on, 'the prosecution for the first time suggested that the assailant was naked, but was covered with a mackintosh. That showed how the hopeless difficulty about the clothing had impressed itself upon the prosecution.' And for Oliver, the solution was simple: 'The fact that the mackintosh was burned on the right side, and that Mrs Wallace's skirt was burned, also, was consistent with her having put the mackintosh over her shoulders when opening the Wolverton Street door to the man who had decoyed the husband away, and fallen on the gas fire when she was attacked.'

Oliver moved on. He spoke now about the jury, and the way the jurors had been infected by reports of the committal hearings at the police court. The case had been a nine days' wonder in Liverpool, and with reports from the police court being lapped up by thousands of people it was certain that most, if not all, the jurors had steeped themselves in the prosecution case, little dreaming that they would ever be summoned to serve on the trial jury. 'It is certain,' Oliver stressed, 'that some of them must have expressed strong views one way or the other before they knew they would be trying the accused. It is obvious that some of the jurors must have had their minds biased one way or the other, and did not decide only upon the evidence they heard.'

And what of the relationship between Wallace and his wife? There had been witnesses called to show that they were a happy and devoted couple, and Wallace's own diaries, which obviously contained his most secret thoughts, did not suggest that their relations were otherwise than perfect.

And motive, what of that? Wallace had money in the bank, and was in no financial trouble, and there was no suggestion that there was another woman in the case. But someone else might have had a motive to murder Mrs Wallace: the fact that Wallace himself may have possibly had money in the house. In fact, only about £4 was missing.

Oliver glanced at his papers again. It was time to slip into a higher gear.

'I make a serious complaint,' Oliver declared, looking up at the judges, 'regarding a part of the evidence of Professor MacFall, the police surgeon. For no motive, except to try to get this man convicted, the Professor went out of his way to force upon the court' – and Oliver made the word 'force' fizz around the room – 'and jury, the view that the blows which killed this woman were struck by a frenzied man who was insane.'

The Lord Chief Justice stirred again. Suppose for a moment, he murmured, that MacFall was right? How did the theory point to Wallace more than to somebody else?

Oliver seemed wrongfooted here. 'The person who did this murder,' he began, 'had planned it, and what this witness was obviously trying to do was to let the jury know that . . .'

'I was not putting the point against you,' Hewart interrupted.

'I appreciate that,' Oliver said, recovering his form, 'and I would suggest that the whole of this was most mischievous. The police did press the case. I suggest that this was introduced in a spirit of malevolence.'

Eyes and heads turned, and lips were pursed in surprise. Everyone was now looking straight at Oliver.

'No,' he added, hurriedly, 'malevolence would be wrong. I withdraw that, and substitute zeal.'

A climax was past, only to be followed by a second. As Oliver began to argue that his client's guilt could not be deduced from his demeanour in the house on the murder night, Wallace sat, his chin resting on his right hand, closely following every word.

'There are certain facts which are absolutely crucial,' Oliver declared. 'The first one is: who sent the telephone message, or, rather, did the prosecution prove that the appellant sent the telephone message of the nineteenth? If he did, he is guilty; if he did not, he is innocent. It was absolutely crucial.

'The second vital fact is this: at which time was Mrs Wallace last seen alive?' Oliver submitted there were many reputable witnesses who could have given evidence that she was seen alive considerably later than six-thirty, but the police did not call them. Instead, they had chosen to stand on the evidence of one little milk boy, whose evidence depended totally on his reliability when he said that going round with the milk he noticed the time by the Holy Trinity Church clock. It had been left to the defence to call the other evidence. 'The prosecution,' Oliver continued, his voice rising to a crescendo, 'never got within arm's length of what is called proof. At every stage of the case all the prosecution did was to say: "You might have done . . . It is consistent with your having done."

'Surely,' he thundered, 'I am entitled to insist that the prosecution prove their case!'

Oliver pursued the question of the milk boy, Alan Close. Within twenty-four hours of the murder he had told three other people that he had seen Mrs Wallace alive at about a quarter to seven. A newspaper pushed through the letterbox at about half past six was later found open on the table. Was it suggested, asked Oliver, that after committing the murder Wallace had taken the paper and laid it there?

'I have to suggest that in this case, the jury were inflamed against the appellant by the way in which it was pressed. It was conducted in an oppressive fashion. If your lordships are in any doubt as to whether there was a miscarriage of justice or not, that is a matter to which weight must be given.'

Next, Oliver turned to the evidence concerning the time at which Mrs Wallace was last seen alive, evidence which he claimed showed that Close had reached 29 Wolverton Street 'later than half past six'. He also dealt with the tram tests carried out by the police – 'young, athletic people' – to find out how long it took them to cover the route which Wallace said he took to the tram stop in Lodge Lane. The police covered the distance in between seventeen and twenty minutes. One officer, following a different route, did it in fifteen.

'Were the jury intended to understand that Wallace, an elderly man, rushed straight from the horrible murder of his wife, without waiting to cleanse himself or his clothing, and jumped straight on a tram?' he asked. And Oliver reminded the court that the time at which he reached the Lodge Lane tram stop had been fixed at 7.06 p.m. ('as near as could be') and that Wallace must have left home at 6.45 p.m. ('or thereabouts').

And what about the time of the killing? All the prosecution could say was that Mrs Wallace might possibly have been alive at the time when Wallace was in the house. 'That,' said Oliver, 'does not even begin to go in the direction of proof.'

In Oliver's submission, 'What one looks for in this case and completely fails to find is any piece of evidence which is not consistent with innocence.

'If that be the result of the investigation of the evidence, then – in my submission – this verdict is unreasonable and cannot be supported, having regard to the evidence. There is grave danger that there may have been a miscarriage of justice. This court has, on many occasions, upset the verdicts of juries on that very ground.

'A verdict which shocks the sense of justice cannot stand,' said Oliver.

His speech lasted nearly four hours, and at the close Oliver apologised for taking so much time, explaining that he was compelled to go into every matter. 'You cannot have a man convicted of murder on this sort of thing,' he added.

* * *

On the second day of the appeal, Tuesday 19 May, it was the turn of Edward Hemmerde for the prosecution. He began by answering Oliver's criticisms of the previous day, saying he could not see where Oliver had got his idea that the jury were 'not particularly friendly' or 'prejudiced'. It was deliberately arranged, said Hemmerde, that the jury should not be chosen from the city of Liverpool. The jurors came from Widnes, Southport and Warrington. 'It was,' he explained, 'a jury of the county of Lancaster.' And turning to Oliver's comments on the police, Hemmerde declared, 'It was said that the police had coached witnesses, that the witnesses had been brought into line, and that the police had suppressed witnesses . . . I want to say here and now that as far as the police are concerned, I took charge of this case at least a week before and if this case was pressed, I pressed it.'

He added, 'I take full responsibility for everything that was done in this case, and the police had nothing whatever to do with the conduct of it.'

Hemmerde, like Oliver, spoke for four hours. All three judges had questions for him about the mysterious telephone call. Mr Justice Branson asked what evidence there was that Wallace had sent the bogus message himself. 'There is no direct evidence,' Hemmerde admitted. 'There couldn't be any if a man chose to make a bogus call on himself.'

The Lord Chief Justice asked, 'Are you not really saying that if it be *assumed* that this man committed the murder, other circumstances fit in with that clearly?'

To which Hemmerde replied that a mass of detail pointed to the fact that the caller was Wallace, and that the jury 'when they considered what the man did afterwards . . . were brought irresistibly to the conclusion that it all fitted together like a jigsaw puzzle.'

While all this was going on Wallace himself was sitting in a side gallery, leaning forward on the rail, cupping his hand behind his ear. But as Hemmerde's lengthy submission drew to a close he began to fidget nervously, and his apparent composure began to slip as his own counsel, Roland Oliver, rose to reply, briefly, to some of Hemmerde's points.

At half past three Oliver resumed his seat. And then, something happened which surprised everyone: the judges retired to consider their decision, the first time for many years that this had happened. As they trooped out of the court Wallace was led from the gallery to a corridor outside, his face now quite ashen.

But while the principal characters had left, in the well of the court the spectators were growing in number. 'It was crowded to suffocation,' wrote the man from the *Liverpool Daily Post*, 'numerous barristers from other courts adding themselves to the congestion as time went on. There was a loud buzz of conversation, but the tense feeling did not die away. There was many a reference to the anxiety that the appellant must be feeling.

'It was after 4.15 when there was a cry of "Silence" in the court, and there was silence upon the instant. The judges came in and bowed low in response to the rising of the court to its feet; and when all were seated, the appellant was ushered in. Now he looked tired and worn, and once or twice swayed slightly, but his eyes were fixed upon the Lord Chief Justice, and only once did he lower his head.'

For a full minute, nothing happened. Then, Lord Hewart began the judgment.

'The appellant, William Herbert Wallace, was charged at the Assizes in Liverpool with the murder of his wife on January twentieth. In the result he was convicted and on April twenty-fifth last he was sentenced to death. He now appeals against that conviction.

'Three facts are obvious. The first is that at the conclusion of the case for the Crown, no submission was made on behalf of the appellant that there was no case to go to the jury. The second fact which seems to be obvious is that the evidence was summed up by the learned judge with complete fairness and accuracy, and it would not have been at all surprising if the result had been an acquittal of the prisoner. The third obvious fact is that the case is eminently one of difficulty and doubt.

'Now, the whole of the material evidence has been closely and critically examined before us and it does not appear to me to be necessary to discuss it again. Suffice it to say that we are not concerned here with suspicion, however grave, or with theories, however ingenious. Section four of the Criminal Appeal Act of 1907 provides that the Court of Criminal Appeal shall allow the appeal if they think that the verdict of the jury should be set aside on the ground that it cannot be supported having regard to the evidence.'

Here, Lord Hewart paused to moisten his lips.

'The conclusion to which we have arrived,' he murmured with infinite lack of urgency, 'is that the case against the appellant, which we have carefully and anxiously considered . . .'

A pause.

'. . . and discussed . . .'

Pause again.

'. . . was not proved with that certainty which is necessary in order to justify a verdict of guilty.'

It was as though the whole court had begun to sway.

'And therefore it is our duty to take the course indicated by the section of the statute to which I have referred. The result is that this appeal will be allowed . . .'

A noise in court: sharp gasps and the scampering feet of the newspaper copy boys.

'. . . and this conviction quashed.'

A burst of applause, stifled on the instant. 'One just caught a bright gleam in the eyes of Wallace, who had been standing there looking deathly pale as he went through the minutes of the uttermost limits of his ordeal,' the *Daily Post* reported. 'The police in the side gallery with him smiled at him and indicated that he might withdraw, and he turned and went out of court a free man. The judges were still on the bench. They had finished their work, and the majesty of the law seemed to see nothing and hear nothing of the commotion that had now arisen.

'Outside, for some minutes, a crowd gathered, waiting to see Wallace go away. There was not long to wait. He came out putting on his bowler hat from underneath which a long wisp of his white hair appeared. He could not speak. There was the making of a smile on his face, but it looked like the smile that a man whose nerves are dreadfully frayed tried to put on in response to the greetings of people who have not been so far along the road of anxiety.

'When he came to the street gates, one of his friends cried, "Call a taxi. Don't go into the Strand." Wallace stood still. He was still barely smiling, and hardly seemed to know what was being said or done. A taxi was called, and he was rushed into it.

'For a moment it held up a bus, and the passengers looked out, casually wondering why there was a rather excited crowd around a taxi in the Strand.'

News of the Appeal Court judgment flashed around Liverpool within the hour. At the Prudential offices in Dale Street there was jubilation; at the Sefton Park home of Mrs Amy Wallace a *Liverpool Echo* reporter dashed to the door with the news. 'I am so glad,' said Wallace's sister-in-law. 'We have always believed in his innocence.' Edwin, her son, came into the room, and said he was thrilled.

That evening at Lime Street station an enthusiastic crowd of Wallace's relations and friends gathered to meet the train from London carrying lawyers Scholefield Allen and Hector Munro. 'I believe in his innocence,' declared Munro, 'as all the people who have been in close touch with him do.' Superintendent Hubert Moore, Inspector Herbert Gold and other police officers who had travelled home on the same train slipped away unquoted.

Wallace remained in London overnight with his brother Joseph, having been escorted from the court by a reporter from the *Daily Dispatch*. Next morning, the newspaper carried an extensive 'interview' with Wallace:

'No tongue can speak the emotion I feel. When the warder motioned me to stand up and hear the verdict I prayed that strength would come to me to show nothing of the tumult that was in my heart . . . I said to myself again and again: "Forget hope"; then . . . I cannot tell you the great rush of feeling that came to me.

'Then we sat cramped together in the crowded taxi – every jar of the gears or squeak of the brakes, heavenly music; the discordant sound of voices and street noises, the music of choirs and celestial musicians; that is the song in my soul.

'That is the song which, even while I look at you and you cannot hear, is singing in my heart. That is the song which is making me ache to see Liverpool. But how can you know what I am feeling? Man, you must be hurled to hell to know what it is to be hoisted to heaven.'

The following morning Wallace took an early stroll in Piccadilly and visited the Prudential headquarters in Holborn. In Liverpool details emerged of the public subscription launched to help finance Wallace's defence. It had cost in the region of £1,300 but only about £200 had been raised. Prudential staff had subscribed between £450 and £500, and the company itself had made money available to defray Wallace's costs.

In Fleet Street and elsewhere leader writers had been quick to spot the significance of the appeal. *The Times* said the case 'offers a striking example of the efficiency of the Court of Criminal Appeal, and of its value as a protection against the errors which even the justest intentions and the most scrupulous care are not always able to prevent'.

The *Daily Telegraph* took a different view: 'It [the appeal finding] has created the presumption that there is still at liberty a monster of wickedness who, in addition to planning and carrying out a cold-blooded and brutal murder, sought by a cunning device – that of the fraudulent telephone call, to which the prosecution attached so much importance – to direct suspicion upon his victim's husband. That is a matter to which the attention of the police authorities concerned is urgently directed by the outcome of this extraordinary prosecution.'

The response from the Liverpool police came the following day, coinciding with the resumed inquest into the death of Julia Wallace. The proceedings took less than two minutes. Coroner Cecil Mort told Hector Munro, 'I am going to close this inquest formally, in accordance with the Coroners' [Amendment] Act. I have received a notification from the Court of Criminal Appeal with regard to the proceedings of that court, saying that a conviction had been quashed . . .'

Shortly afterwards, the police in Liverpool stated officially that they would not reopen investigations into the circumstances of Mrs Wallace's death.

8

I T WAS SEVERAL days before Wallace returned to Liverpool.
First, he took a short holiday with his brother in the Lake
District. Despite the advice of Hector Munro, who had heard
about a renewed hate campaign against Wallace, he returned to
live at Wolverton Street and resumed his insurance rounds in
Clubmoor. For several weeks he endured the taunts and rail-
ings of people who before the murder had welcomed him into
their homes. Now, it seemed, everyone was against him.
Despite the overturning of the verdict on appeal, Wallace –
although a free man – remained a prisoner of suspicion. 'Find
all the neighbours up against me,' Wallace wrote in his diary in
June. 'They are the rottenest crowd I ever struck. Mean and
paltry brained. I feel it a wicked insult to Julia. How she would
have scorned the whole thing!'

At last, he could stand it no longer. Using money saved
during a series of libel actions against a number of newspapers,
Wallace bought a small bungalow in Meadowside Road,
Bromborough, a suburb across the Mersey from Liverpool in
Wirral. It was called The Summer House. There he was looked
after by an old friend, Annie Mason. 'My dear Julia would have

absolutely revelled in this house and garden,' wrote Wallace, 'and it hurts me to realise that this is her long wanted house, and now she is not here to enjoy its peace and beauty.'

Although Wallace had left Anfield, and had been moved from street collections to an office job at the Prudential head office in Dale Street, he remained a haunted man. 'The last few days,' he wrote in September, 'I have been depressed thinking of my dear Julia. I'm afraid this will be a very lonely winter for me. I seem to miss her more and more, and cannot drive the thought of her cruel end out of my mind.'

If the winter of 1931 was lonely, then the following winter was both lonely and anguished. Wallace's chronic kidney complaint had given him increasing pain in the closing months of 1932. On 9 February 1933 an ambulance took him to Clatterbridge Hospital, a few miles from his home. Wallace knew he would never return. As soon as he arrived at the hospital he made a will. Surgeons operated and for two weeks Wallace rallied. But on the evening of Saturday 25 February he lapsed into delirium. At midnight he lost consciousness. And at 3 a.m. he died.

At his bedside were the Master of the Infirmary and a night nurse. 'It is authoritatively stated,' said the local newspaper, the *Birkenhead News*, 'that at no time during his last illness did he make any statement having any material bearing upon the tragedy of his wife's death.'

The following day, Wallace's nephew Edwin arrived from Glasgow, where he was studying medicine, to arrange the funeral.

Crowds of sightseers tramped through the grim gates of Anfield Cemetery and made the long trek to the grave of Julia

Wallace. But finding the grave unopened, and the inscription unaltered, they tramped out again. However, when the cemetery closed at dusk a team of gravediggers worked on and by the light of flares began to open the grave. Early the following morning they had finished.

At nine o'clock on Wednesday 1 March a cortège of cars appeared from a side drive, moving slowly through the cemetery, led by a hearse carrying Wallace's coffin. After a service at the undertaker's private chapel the cars carrying the dozen or so mourners moved to the graveside. A full committal was conducted by a local Anglican curate, and Wallace was laid to rest alongside his murdered wife.

Grouped around the grave on that keen spring morning were Wallace's nephew; Hector Munro and his clerk Norman Wheeler; Caird, the chess-playing grocer; and a man from the Prudential. There were just four wreaths. By far the biggest, from Annie Mason, bore the inscription 'Peace after sorrow, from the housekeeper, with deepest sympathy.'

IV

*The Case against
Richard Gordon Parry*

WILLIAM HERBERT WALLACE died a broken man. And an innocent one.

The name of Julia Wallace's killer was given to me nearly half a century after the case, in a telephone call to my office at Radio City in Liverpool. It came from a man who worked with Wallace at the offices of the Prudential Insurance Company.

'We all knew that Wallace was an innocent man,' said the caller. 'And we all know who did it.'

'Oh,' I replied, 'who? Can you remember the name?'

'Remember?' said the man on the phone. 'I'll never forget it. His name was Gordon Parry.'

Richard Gordon Parry was twenty-two years old when Julia Wallace was murdered. From the outset of the investigation in January 1931 his was the top name in the frame. The police claimed to have subjected Parry to the most rigorous investigation, even to the point of examining the seams of his clothes for traces of blood. In the course of the inquiry detectives established that Parry had the motive, the means and the opportunity to commit the murder. They knew of his criminal propensities, which had emerged during his wayward childhood. They knew he had been exposed to his employers as a common thief. They knew that, unlike Wallace, Parry was an accomplished amateur actor. And that, unlike Wallace, he had the use of a motor car.

Weighed in the balance, the evidence against Gordon Parry was every bit as circumstantial as that pressed against Wallace. But two crucial points appear to have weighed in Parry's favour: he had what the police claimed to have been an unshakable alibi for the night of the crime. And, just as valuable to Parry, he had friends in high places. The decision to charge Wallace with murdering his wife may well have been the result of a cover-up as criminal as the killing itself. If so, the cover-up extends into two main areas of civic life in Liverpool fifty years ago, the police force and the city Corporation.

Officials of both must have connived at a monstrous conspiracy not only to pervert the course of justice, but also to send a bewildered and shattered man to the very brink of the scaffold. The whole shabby episode reflects only discredit on those involved. The real facts about what happened behind the grimy blinds of 29 Wolverton Street on the night Julia Wallace died were well known in certain Liverpool circles within days, if not hours, of the killing. But the facts were concealed with infinite care, and lay buried for fifty years. Despite the best endeavours of Wallace himself and, down the years, a succession of authors, the full story of the crime came to light only after a chance conversation, and a decision by a local radio station to make a rather unusual programme.

* * *

Shoestring I am not. Followers of the television series featuring Trevor Eve as the intrepid 'private ear' will be largely unfamiliar with the methods employed in investigating and researching a piece of historical documentary such as the Wallace case. Where Eddie Shoestring munches ham rolls on windy street corners, the real radio investigator is more likely to take his lunch in the canteen at the city library, where he's spent the morning spinning through hundreds of pages of old newspapers, reproduced on a dusty screen using the microfiche retrieval system. His eyes will ache, his patience will be wearing thin, and he will wonder why libraries are kept so infernally hot, even in the middle of summer. But he is unlikely to be required to drive fifty miles at high speed through the night to defuse a ticking parcel, or wake from a drugged sleep bound and gagged in the galley of a cabin cruiser. This is not to say that the investigation of the Wallace case which I undertook for Radio City in the winter of 1980–1 was without its moments of high drama and excitement. But such moments were the peaks between the long, deep troughs of slogging, methodical drudgery, when the job seemed to have all the glamour of a filing clerk's.

At first the Wallace project seemed like a very good programme idea, and nothing more. The seeds were sown in the autumn of 1980 when, as News Editor, I was in charge of the newsroom at Radio City. A bright young producer in the station's general programmes department, Michael Green, wandered across to my desk one afternoon, bringing with him a book he had picked up, quite by chance, in a secondhand bookshop. It was *Murderer: Scot-Free* by an American, Robert F. Hussey. 'It's about an old Liverpool murder,' said Green. 'The Wallace case. Heard of it?'

I had heard of it. Some years before I too had stumbled across a book on Wallace, also in a secondhand bookshop. I could remember neither the title nor the author, and my recollection of the story was very hazy. Mike Green reminded me of the outline of the case, and urged me to read Hussey's book. 'According to this,' he said, 'there's supposed to have been a mystery suspect who's possibly still alive.

'It would make an amazing programme.'

I borrowed the book, read it, and retrieved from a box in my cellar the faded copy of John Rowland's *The Wallace Case*, which I had picked up for coppers in the mid-seventies. Mike Green was right. There were the makings of a very good programme indeed. Journalists are always on the lookout for 'pegs' on which to hang a story, and it struck me that the following January would mark the fiftieth anniversary of the Wallace murder. A perfect 'peg'. But what about the best way of approaching a programme such as this? And, more importantly, what of this idea that the killer might still be alive? And living in Liverpool?

I mentioned the idea to Radio City's then Programme Controller, David Maker. He suggested that a drama-documentary would create the most effective format for the programme, and agreed with me that, where possible, we should use interviews with people still living who had played a part in the Wallace drama fifty years before. Finding such people would be quite a task; for one thing there would be those who would not want to get involved, others whose memories would be defective, and others still who had simply disappeared without trace. And there was the inescapable fact that most of the witnesses, police officers and lawyers would now be dead.

And what of this so-called mystery suspect? Neither Hussey nor Rowland had supplied a name. Where were we going to find a nameless man in an unspecified place who would admit to being suspected of such an infamous murder in another age? Once again, chance took a hand.

Just as I was leaving the newsroom one evening the telephone buzzed on the newsdesk. It was not one of the unlisted numbers, and I hesitated before answering. I picked up the receiver.

'I hear you're looking at the Wallace murder.'

'Yes.'

'I worked with Wallace at the Pru. We all knew that Wallace was an innocent man. And we all know who did it.'

'Oh, who? Can you remember the name?'

'Remember? I'll never forget it.'

So we had a name. Gordon Parry. The caller was Hal Brown, who had telephoned in response to an appeal for information on the Wallace case which I had made on Radio City a few days before. A number of listeners contacted me as a result of that broadcast: one, living in suburban Liverpool, put me in touch with Lilian Kelly, the young switchboard operator who in 1931 had connected the man in the call box with the chess club on the night before the crime. She was now in her seventies, and living in New York. 'I remember the case well,' she told me on a crackly transatlantic telephone link. 'The voice? It was a perfectly normal man's voice, nothing peculiar about it, very calm, no sign of agitation or nervousness.' A woman from Anfield rang to say that one of the lads who had persuaded Alan Close to go to the police was not only still alive but living now where he had lived in 1931, in Redbourn Street, a few steps from the top of Wolverton Street. His name was Douglas Metcalf. He was not on the telephone so rather than wait to make contact by letter I paid him a visit there and then. Within twenty minutes I was on his doorstep, trying in vain to get an answer. The woman next door heard my knocking and said that Metcalf kept irregular hours, working shifts. I scribbled my number on the back of a card and posted it through Metcalf's door. Driving back into town along West Derby Road my spirits rose. Within hours of making the radio appeal we had found two of the people at the heart of the Wallace drama. We had the makings of an extraordinarily authentic programme.

Hal Brown's call about Gordon Parry came a day or two later. It was the point at which the Wallace project really took off, ceased to be just another radio documentary, and assumed for me the nature of a crusade. I was at once excited at the prospect of tracing Parry, of confronting him, and (I had better admit it now) wringing a confession from him. But the elation was tempered with some apprehension. I was still a long way from tracking Parry down. And even supposing I managed to find him, how would he react to being challenged? On this, as on several other important aspects of the case, I was going to need some help.

Almost every celebrated murder has its own oracle, and with Wallace the oracle is without doubt the author and crime historian Jonathan Goodman. His masterful dissection of the case in *The Killing of Julia Wallace* has been the standard textbook for Wallace scholars for fifteen years. Goodman became interested in the Wallace murder in the sixties, when he was working at the

Liverpool Playhouse. He was the first to frame a case against Gordon Parry, but for legal reasons Parry is referred to in his book only as Mr X. I first contacted Goodman at his London home before receiving the call about Parry from Hal Brown. Goodman and I spoke on the telephone at some length about the case, but I found him reluctant to talk about his Mr X.

'You'll excuse me for not being more forthcoming,' he explained, 'but I've had some bad experiences with journalists and I need to protect my interests.' Goodman told me that, quite apart from the obvious risk of libel, he had suppressed the name of his Mr X to protect the man's family. I began to ponder the ethical problems posed by naming Mr X. 'Can they be weighed against those associated with putting an innocent man on trial for his life?' I wrote that night in a letter to Goodman.

Over the days that followed the radio programme began to take shape in my mind. By mid-October I had set out the broad outline in a formal programme proposal. 'Surprisingly,' I wrote, 'a good number of people involved in the affair are still alive, traceable and ready to talk.'

Then out of the blue came the call from Hal Brown naming Parry. Once again, I called Jonathan Goodman. Yes, Gordon Parry was his Mr X.

'Where is he now?' I asked.

Pause.

'Somewhere between Liverpool and London.'

Goodman's circumspection was understandable. But at the time it seemed simply unhelpful. Parry would be an old man, and time was short.

At first Hal Brown too was reluctant to talk at any length about Parry. He rejected my offer to call at his home to interview him 'because my wife knew Parry and gets upset just thinking about him'. Instead, Hal Brown called at Radio City a few days later. After some cajoling he agreed to record the following, an interview that was to form one of the most haunting sequences in the programme:

'He [Parry] was a suave, smooth type of young fellow, very good-looking, and he'd been responsible for quite a few misdemeanours, apparently. Altogether, my colleagues and I felt that there could probably have been a far better case made against Parry than against Wallace himself.

'I remember one day during Wallace's trial I was working in the Prudential stationery store and I was surprised to see Parry coming into the office . . . And he asked me for some stationery. I refused, and said: "Anyhow, I should have thought you'd have been up at St George's Hall." Parry turned to me with a horrible look on his face and said: "What do you mean by that?" And I said I meant that, knowing Wallace, Parry would have been up there. I'll never forget the look on his face.'

Hal Brown's recall after fifty years was remarkable: 'I remember being terribly shocked when I heard of the murder and that Mr Wallace had been arrested. Because to me and to most of his colleagues, he was absolutely the wrong type to do a thing like that. One particular thing that stuck in my mind was knowing that Wallace only had one kidney. He wouldn't have been able to move very quickly. In fact, he didn't. He was a slow mover. And to think he could have possibly raced around Liverpool creating an alibi for himself was just unthinkable.'

Following Wallace's discharge at the Appeal Court and his reinstatement with the Pru, Brown got to know Wallace rather better. They shared an office at the back of the Prudential building in Dale Street. Almost every post brought more hate mail. Wallace would say to his young colleague, 'Brownie, read through these for me and just give me the ones you think I should see.'

'Of course,' said Hal Brown, 'most were vindictive and vile. Very few were sympathetic.'

Hal Brown recalled the last time he saw Wallace. 'It was when it was necessary for him to go to hospital for a check-up on his remaining kidney. And I remember seeing him standing by the door looking rather bewildered and lost.

'And I said, "Hello, Mr Wallace."

'"Just a moment, Brownie," said Wallace.

'I went over, and he said, "The specialists have told me that if I have an operation on my one kidney I could live for a couple of years, and that if I don't, I won't last more than six weeks. What would you do, Brownie?"

'I said he couldn't expect me to make such a decision. Wallace agreed. "No, I'm sorry, I didn't mean to give you that job. But I've decided. I've nothing to live for now. I'm not going to have an operation."

'And that was the last I saw of him. A short time after that, he died.'

Late in October I visited Wallace's solicitor, Hector Munro, in London. He and his second wife welcomed me at their small flat in Swiss Cottage. Frail, slight, and rather hard of hearing, Munro received me in his study where he had set up a small table for his notes. And an ashtray, into which he flicked the ash of interminable cigarettes. His manner was brisk for a man in his eighties, and he took a keen interest in my plans for the programme. About Wallace he said much, but about Parry very little, referring me always to Goodman's book. The purpose of this initial visit to Munro was to reconnoitre; because of his age I was unsure about whether he would be an effective interviewee. But his mind was clearly in good shape and, as we chatted over coffee, I realised that he would make a very valuable and authentic contribution. Munro agreed to see me again, and in the meantime gave me permission to study the case files which, I discovered, were still stored at Munro's offices in Liverpool.

F ROM ONE OF the four large tatty envelopes piled on the
table I carefully pulled a sheaf of typewritten documents. I
was sitting where Hector Munro's son Donald had left me, in
the partners' dining room at Campbell Davis and Co., over-
looking Dale Street in central Liverpool. 'Help yourself,'
Donald Munro had said.

I rifled gingerly through the piles of yellowing typescript.
These documents were copies of the various written statements
made by Wallace to the police during the murder investigation.
They were filed in chronological order, beginning with the
statement volunteered by Wallace to Inspector Herbert Gold at
about midnight on the murder night. It was headed: Anfield
Detective Office, Tuesday 20th January 1931. The statement
covered four foolscap pages. I was familiar with the contents
because the statement had been reproduced in Jonathan
Goodman's book. But the fifth sheet in the file made me catch
my breath. It was headed: Dale Street Detective Office, 22.1.31,
and was longer than the first statement, running to five pages.

'William Herbert Wallace further states: –' it began. 'Mr
Gordon R. Parry, of Derwent Road, Stoneycroft, is a friend of

my late wife and myself. He is now an agent for the Gresham Insurance Coy, but I'm not quite sure of the company.

'He was employed by the Prudential up to about 12 or 15 months ago, and he then resigned to improve his position. Although nothing was known officially to the company detrimental to his financial affairs, it was known that he had collected premiums which he did not pay in and his Supt Mr Crewe of Green Lane, Allerton, told me that he went to Parry's parents who paid about £30 to cover the deficiency. Mr Crewe's office is at 2 Gt Nelson Street. Parry is a single man about 22 yrs of age. I have known him about three years and he was with my company about three years. I was ill with Bronchitis in December in 1928 and Parry did part of my collecting for about two or three days a week for about three weeks. I discovered slight discrepancies and spoke to him about it. He was short of small amounts when paying in and he had not entered all the amounts collected in the book. When I spoke to him he said it was an oversight and that he was sorry and he put the matter right. Previous to Parry doing my work he had called at my house once on business and left a letter for me which he wrote in my front room. I was not in at the time but my wife let him in. While he was doing my work in Dec, 1928 he called very frequently to see me about business, and he was well acquainted with our domestic arrangements. He had been in the parlour and kitchen frequently, and had been upstairs in the middle bedroom a number of times to see me while I was in bed. I do not think he had called to see me after I resumed duty in Jan 1929, but if he had called my wife would have had no hesitation in admitting him. I have often seen him since he has been working for his new company and have spoken to him. About last November I was in the City Café one evening, I think it was on a Thursday, playing chess, and I saw Parry there. He was by himself walking across the room. I said "Good evening" and he returned my greeting. I think that was the last time I saw him. He is a member of an Amateur Dramatic Society which holds its meetings at the City Café on Thursday evenings. I do not think he drinks. He is engaged to a Miss Lloyd, 7, Missouri Road, Clubmoor. He would be on a weekly salary from his company plus a commission on business and his earnings would be about £4 a week.

'There was another man named Marsden who also did part of the work for me while I was ill in Dec 1928. I do not know his address. He was an agent for the Prudential Coy for two or three years and left before he did my work. Parry recommended him. I have heard that Marsden left the Prudential on account of financial irregularities. While he was working for me he often came to my house to see me on business. He also knew the interior arrangements of my house. I have seen Marsden several times since he worked for me. I do not know if he is working now and I do not know anything about his private affairs. If he had called at my house my wife would have asked him in. Both Parry and Marsden knew the arrangements of my business with regard to the system of paying in money collected to the Head Office, Dale Street. There is a definite order of the Company's that money must be paid in in [sic] Wednesday's [sic] but this is not strictly enforced and I paid in on Thursdays usually. I have had the cash box from which the money was stolen for about 16 years. I always put the company's money in that box, and it was always kept on the top of the bookcase in the kitchen during the day time. At night I always took it upstairs to my bedroom. Parry and Marsden knew I kept the money in the box because while they worked for me I always put the money into it when they called to pay over to me their collections. They had both seen me take it down and put it back to the top of the bookcase in the kitchen often. Marsden is about 28 years of age, about 5 ft 6/7ins, brown hair, and fairly well dressed. Parry is about 5ft 10ins, slimmish build, dark hair, rather foppish appearance, well dressed and wears spats, very plausible . . .

'I forgot to mention that I believe Mr Parry owns a motor car or has the use of one, because I was talking to him about Xmas time in Missouri Road and he had a car then which he was driving. He gave me one of his Company's calendars . . .

'I have now found by the calendar that Mr Parry's employers are the Standard Life Assurance Coy, whose head office is at 3, George Street, Edinburgh.'

I had to read the statement twice more to convince myself that I understood its drift. Parry . . . slight discrepancies . . . well acquainted with our domestic arrangements . . . been in the parlour and kitchen frequently . . . knew I kept money in the box . . . very plausible. Less than forty-eight hours after the murder, here was Wallace plainly putting the finger on Parry, providing the police with a lot of material about his background and suggesting a possible motive: shortage of money.

Elsewhere in the files were bundles of statements, handwritten by some long-dead solicitor's clerk, from various witnesses, numerous lists, photographs, reports and notes, together with a full transcript of the trial. But the Parry statement was sensational. With the permission of Donald Munro, I photocopied the sheets and took them back to my office. That afternoon, I set out on the trail of Mr Gordon R. Parry, of Derwent Road, Stoneycroft.

3

A<small>T FIRST THE</small> trail went quite cold. The 1931 Liverpool
street directory listed a William Fraser Vaughan Parry
at 28 Derwent Road. I took this to be Parry's father, and
spent several days in the libraries in Liverpool and Birkenhead
establishing his identity. He turned out to be a juvenile
employment officer with Birkenhead Corporation, who had
died in 1933. Of a son called Gordon there was no trace.
Widening the search I traced a Gordon R. Parry, living in
the early thirties in the village of Saughall Massie in Wirral.
I was sure I had hit on the right man for this curious reason:
I had just finished reading Jonathan Goodman's Wallace-
inspired novel *The Last Sentence* in which Gordon Parry is
flimsily disguised as George Palermo. The name of Gordon
Parry's house in Saughall Massie was Palermo. I assumed
that Goodman had played a nifty trick in choosing Palermo
as the 'cover' for Parry. I dashed to the address but the house
was deserted. An elderly woman next door told me she
remembered a neighbour called Gordon Parry, but he had
been a ship's officer and had had nothing to do with
insurance.

Another red herring, another frustration.

Meanwhile I had invited Jonathan Goodman to act as consultant to Radio City's Wallace programme, but we had yet to agree terms for his help. Naturally, until a deal was struck, Goodman remained reticent about Parry's current whereabouts. In fact, he seemed a trifle uneasy about my own efforts to track down Parry unaided. During the first week in November I wrote to him making a formal offer in return for his file on Gordon Parry. My own search for Parry continued as I awaited Goodman's reply.

Then, at last, things began to move.

The Wallace team – Producer Mike Green, Programme Controller David Maker and Senior Producer Wally Scott – reasoned that Parry must have acquired a criminal record, a legacy of his alleged embezzling activities even before January 1931. Through police contacts we managed to obtain a copy of Parry's computer printout, or at least that belonging to the only Liverpool-born Gordon Parry who fitted the bill: one Richard Gordon Parry, born in Liverpool in 1909 (making him, as Wallace himself had said, twenty-two years of age in 1931). After listing convictions for various offences in Liverpool, London and the south of England, the record then showed a gap of nearly forty years. But at the bottom was a single line recording a drink-driving conviction in 1974. The offence had occurred in North Wales. Tantalisingly, the printout made no mention of Parry's current address. So I turned to the North Wales telephone directory and ran my finger down the columns of Parrys.

Eight subscribers were listed as R. G. Parry. Then, in the very back of my mind, I remembered something that

Goodman had said, teasingly perhaps, in one of our early conversations about Mr X: something about living on top of a hill or mountain, something or somewhere inaccessible. Two of the R. G. Parrys listed had addresses which included the word 'hill'. One was in Blaenau Ffestiniog slate-quarrying country and unlikely, I felt, as the last refuge of R. M. Qualtrough. The other hill-dwelling R. G. Parry was the last on the list. I could hardly believe it. If this was the man, then Parry was living only sixty-odd miles from Liverpool, and less than ten miles from the town where I had grown up and where my family still lived. Parry's address was on Waterloo Hill in the tiny village of Llangernyw, in the Vale of Clwyd, south of Colwyn Bay.

After countless hours poring over books, guides and old directories, I knew that at last I had got my man. 'I've tracked down Parry,' I told David Maker that night. 'I'm going to see him.'

'If you're not back by sundown I'll send the bloodhounds after you,' was the jokey reply.

The excitement I felt at having almost certainly traced the right Parry was mingled with apprehension at the thought of confronting a man whom I suspected of being a very nasty character indeed. I need not have worried.

The next morning we heard again from our police contact.

'About that chap Parry,' he said. 'There's something I forgot to tell you.'

'What?' I asked, not quite knowing what was coming.

'I'm sorry, I should have told you yesterday.'

'Well?' I said, impatiently.
'Did you know Parry?'
'No, I'm trying to trace him, that's all.'
'Well, you're too late. He's dead.'

4

I WAS TOO LATE – but only just. Parry had died in April 1980, just seven months earlier. Despite the setback I determined to try to piece together his last years, to see if any friends or relations could shed some light on his role in the Wallace story. Two slender possibilities remained: a deathbed confession, or a dramatic revelation in his will.

As a young newspaperman I trained in North Wales and got to know the Roberts family who ran a firm of undertakers in Colwyn Bay. The undertaker's parlour is as much a part of the cub reporter's beat as the police station and the local vicarage. So I telephoned Graham Roberts. 'How do I find out who buried someone who died in Llangernyw last year?' I asked.

'That'll probably be Gwilym Davies,' said Graham. 'What was the dead person's name?'

'Parry. Richard Gordon Parry.'

Silence at the end of the line.

'Did you say Richard Parry – Dick Parry?'

'Well, I understood he was known as Gordon.'

'Hang on. I'm passing you over to Phil.'

Philip Roberts was Graham's younger brother. In a moment he came on the line. 'What's all this about asking after Dick Parry?'

I explained why I was asking.

'You won't believe this,' Philip said.

'Go on,' I muttered, somewhat resignedly.

'I knew this chap, knew him quite well as a matter of fact. I called him Dick. He died last spring. We both drank in the same pub, The Marine in Old Colwyn.'

I listened, could not speak.

'Dick was one hell of a character. Used to get a lot of people's backs up. Had an incredibly arrogant manner on the telephone. Bit of a handicap really because that was his job: switchboard operator.'

I found my voice. 'What, with the GPO?'

'No. At the hospital in Colwyn Bay.'

This was almost surreal. The man I suspected of being R. M. Qualtrough, the sinister telephone caller in Liverpool, had earned a living as a switchboard operator.

I explained to Philip Roberts that I needed to find out as much as possible about Parry's later life, and the circumstances surrounding his death. 'Yes,' said Philip, 'I remember now. There was some mystery attached to it.'

The next few hours were spent telephoning various people and officials in North Wales. The Llangernyw undertaker, Gwilym Davies, told me that the funeral at Colwyn Bay Crematorium had been paid for by Parry's daughter, who lived 'down south'. As for the mystery surrounding Parry's death, that was soon cleared up. It seemed he had lain dead in bed for two days before being discovered by the village constable, alerted by neighbours who saw that Parry's milk had not been taken in. Although there had been no inquest, a post mortem had shown that he had died of a heart attack. He was seventy-one. An official at the coroner's office read me the notes on the death certificate written by Parry's daughter, to the effect that her father had been a heavy smoker and an alcoholic.

The daughter had also explained that she was the child of her father's second wife. On his remarriage Parry had worked in London as a GPO telephone operator. When he moved to North Wales in 1968 he had worked as a switchboard operator at various hospitals in the North Clwyd area. Since 1976, and the death of his wife, Parry had lived alone in his remote hilltop cottage. Down the mountain, in Llangernyw, Parry had been a familiar figure in both the village pubs, The Stag and The Bridge.

This mass of detail, gathered in one hectic afternoon, was my reward for the earlier frustrations and dead ends. But more was to come.

On 7 November, I received from Jonathan Goodman a letter confirming his acceptance of the consultancy arrangement for the radio documentary, together with a copy of Wallace's statement implicating Parry. This, of course, I had already seen at Munro's office in Liverpool. But Goodman also enclosed an account of an interview he had conducted with Parry in 1966, when Goodman was researching his book. This extraordinary encounter had taken place on the doorstep of Parry's home in south London. It had been witnessed by Goodman's friend, author and journalist Richard Whittington-Egan. In the course of a conversation lasting nearly half an hour, Parry had 'let slip that he often went to tea at Wallace's house, where Julia accompanied him singing on the piano'. (Wallace was quite unaware of these musical afternoons. As Goodman pointed out, Wallace would surely have mentioned them in the statement in which he kept referring to Parry.)

Jonathan Goodman's letter was full of surprises. I knew of Parry's reported romance with Miss Lloyd of Missouri Road, but I did not know that two years after the murder and after Wallace's death, Parry jilted the young lady. Neither did I know that Miss Lloyd had been responsible for supplying Parry with an alibi for the night of the killing.

Then came Goodman's knock-out blow. Miss Lloyd, jilted by Parry, 'went to Hector Munro offering to swear an affidavit saying that the alibi she had given Parry for the night of the crime was a fabrication: quite untrue – and, indeed, quite impossible (as the police could have discovered if they had taken the trouble), as she worked as a pianist in a Clubmoor cinema and was there the whole of that night.

'Munro decided that, as Wallace was dead, nothing would be served by raking up the case,' said Goodman.

All this was beginning to look complicated, so I sat down and summarised the main points against Parry as we now knew them:

- Parry, a petty crook, fabricated an alibi for the night of the murder, an alibi corroborated by his girlfriend, Miss Lloyd, whom he later jilted.
- After the break-up with Parry, Miss Lloyd offered to swear that the alibi was false, but the offer was never taken up.
- Parry, who knew details of the Wallaces' domestic set-up, took part in clandestine musical afternoons with Julia, without Wallace's knowledge.

- Parry was habitually short of money, knew Wallace's collecting routine, and had the use of a car.
- Parry was a member of an amateur dramatic society which met at the City Café on Thursday evenings. It was at the City Café that Wallace's forthcoming chess fixtures were advertised on the noticeboard.

A run of disappointments with several aspects of the Parry investigation led to yet another let-down: the contents of Parry's will, a copy of which arrived in mid-November. Far from containing a dramatic revelation or confession, it was as humdrum a document as it was possible to be, in which Parry merely made over all his possessions to his daughter. In August 1980 the will had been proved at just over £18,000.

After much heart-searching I decided that I would have to contact Parry's daughter direct. I had obtained her name and address, and telephoned her at her home in southern England. She was a most pleasant-sounding woman in her early thirties. I explained that her father's name had cropped up during my researches into an old Liverpool murder, but she had not even heard of the Wallace case, let alone her father's alleged involvement in it. I then wrote to her at some length, giving details of what I knew, in the hope that something might jog her memory. It was some weeks before I had a response, and when it came it was from her husband. He said my letter had upset his wife 'who knew nothing about the case or her father's involvement'. Parry, he said, had been 'secretive, a bit of a recluse' and, to some extent, 'the black sheep of the family'. Parry's daughter had had very little to do with him.

On Parry's death his son-in-law had been through his papers, but there had been nothing of interest; he had kept very little. He had also spoken to Parry's younger brother and sister. They too knew nothing of the case. They had refused to speak to me, preferring to 'let sleeping dogs lie'.

One by one, we were running out of breaks. Parry's later years seemed every bit as mysterious as his activities in Anfield in 1931. It seemed that the definitive last word from Parry would be his remarks to Jonathan Goodman written up directly after the doorstep encounter fifteen years earlier by his fellow criminologist, Richard Whittington-Egan.

'We found him a bland, plausible man who was not made in any way uncomfortable by our questioning. He has grey hair, smoothed sleekly back, and a neat-clipped military-style moustache. He appears to be in very robust health, wiry and well-preserved for his age. He is of reasonably powerful build, has noticeably large hands, and a loose, damp and rather fleshy handshake. His eyes, which are of that bold blue which is traditionally associated with "sex-maniacs", are penetrating and alternately shifty and too-candid. He exhibits a certain lack of affect. He engenders an air of spurious authority of the kind that one encounters in the knowing, self-possessed and self-satisfied kind of jailbird. It was an air of authority that made us think of the type of ex-army non-commissioned officer who becomes a commissionaire.

'He also exudes a false trowel-laid-on charm, which can easily beguile, but is as bogus as the bonhomie of a car salesman. This manner masks, in our opinion, considerable firmness, even ruthlessness. He would be a nasty man to cross. We would sum him up as a tricky, position-shifting individual of the con-man type. He is evasive, manipulative, sharp, on the ball and very clever. He is quite well-spoken, and throughout the interview kept a self-satisfied and inappropriate smile on his face.

'He hinted that, if he chose, he could reveal much about Wallace, whom he described as "a very strange man" and implied that he was sexually odd. He further said he knew why Wallace might have killed his wife, and added that he could think of no one else who would have been likely to do so. He emphasised that women clients from whom Wallace collected insurance payments were afraid of him and that they did not like to admit him to their house. Again, he explained that Wallace was a "very peculiar-looking man – and immensely tall."

'Julia Wallace he described as a "very sweet, charming woman".

'Parry believes, he says, that Wallace murdered her.

'Parry vigorously denies that Wallace named him as his prime suspect. He claims that all Wallace said was that he (Parry) was the person whom Mrs Wallace would be most likely to admit to the house.

'Parry was not unpleasant, but he was adamant in his refusal to talk about his part in the Wallace case . . . He was quite ready to admit that, as a young man, he was what he called "a tearaway". But he makes little of the various criminal charges against him. Just youthful high spirits. No real harm done. "It was very awkward for me having my little misdemeanours dragged up at the time of the case," he remarked.

'He agreed that he had stolen various sums of money, and concurred immediately and wholeheartedly with the proposition which we put forward that he had simply been "a young man with tastes that exceeded his unaided financial capacity to indulge them".

'The police, he said, were in and out of his home in Liverpool by the minute for two days at the time of the investigation. But they finally seemed satisfied as to his innocence when he was able to produce some people with whom he had spent the evening of the murder "arranging a birthday celebration". (This was considered interesting and perhaps significant in view of the fact that Mr Qualtrough spoke on the telephone of being busy with his daughter's twenty-first birthday party. Remember, Parry was an amateur actor, a member of a Merseyside dramatic society, and had he been impersonating Qualtrough on the telephone that bit about the birthday party would have been just the sort of haphazard embroidery that a "method" actor might well add to his performance to lend atmosphere and verisimilitude. Also, Parry's acting ability might lend him the confidence to believe that he could adequately disguise his voice on the telephone.)

'Parry said he used to sing as a young man, and would often go to tea to Wallace's house, where Julia would accompany his singing on the piano or violin. Wallace knew nothing of this.

'He REFUSED to talk about the Wallace case – "not if you were to offer me to £2,000" – because, he said, he had promised his father that he would not talk to anyone about it.

'He REFUSED to divulge Miss Lloyd's Christian name. He did, however, let it slip that he is still in touch with her and that she is now living in Llandudno. But he would not say where.

'He DID NOT REMEMBER if he was in Breck Road (close to Wolverton Street) on the night of the murder having the batteries of his car recharged, although this information was given to Jonathan Goodman by his father.

'He said – that the worry of it all shortened his mother's life;

'– that the incident broke up his engagement to Miss Lloyd;

'– that he "quite liked" Wallace;

'– that Mr Crewe, the Prudential superintendent, was utterly convinced of Wallace's guilt (this we know to be untrue);

'– that he was in the army after 1931.

'We were surprised to find that he knew of the deaths of Crewe, Close (the milk boy) and Dr Edwin Wallace (the latter was Wallace's nephew and his death was not at all widely reported). This suggests to us the probability that Parry watches everything that appears in connection with the mystery.

'Our impression was that Parry was the type of man who, manifestly, could have committed the crime.

' "I won't discuss it at all," he told us, and his manner made it plain that there was nothing we could do to influence him. Without saying as much, he gave us the impression that he had fooled "better people" than us. There was an air of slightly insolent, slightly amused and contemptuous superiority about him.'

Goodman and Whittington-Egan left Parry on his doorstep utterly convinced that they had just met a murderer.

5

O NE OF THE many curiosities in the Parry interview was his reluctance to talk about his former girlfriend, Miss Lloyd. Almost from the outset of our radio investigation it was clear that one of the few people who held the key to the Wallace mystery, apart from Parry himself, was the woman known in Liverpool half a century before as Lily Lloyd. (The forename was supplied without difficulty by Hal Brown.) Her name first cropped up in Wallace's statement of 22 January 1931 which first put the CID on the trail of Gordon Parry. 'He is engaged to a Miss Lloyd, 7, Missouri Road, Clubmoor,' declared Wallace.

We realised at once that the odds of Lily Lloyd still being alive were very good indeed; we knew that in 1931 Parry was just twenty-two years old, so it was a fair bet that his girlfriend would either be roughly the same age or even younger. That would mean that she would now be aged about seventy. Even though Parry himself was dead, if we could locate Lily Lloyd to check the story of the demolished alibi (and her reasons for destroying it) our case against Parry would be considerably strengthened. How, we wondered, could we locate a woman now presumably known by a different (married) name in a city the size of Liverpool half a century after losing her trail? Parry had said she had moved to Llandudno, but somehow this just didn't ring true. The Wallace team were discussing the problem of finding the lady in the bar next door to the radio station when Senior Producer Wally Scott hit on the answer. 'We'll appeal on Billy's show,' he said.

In Liverpool, Billy Butler is an institution. Ex-beat group musician and shipping clerk, he had built up an enormous following for his daily local radio show with its homespun flavour and neighbourly dimensions. Wally's hunch was correct. Within an hour of Bill appealing on the air for information about 'a lady called Lily Lloyd from Missouri Road who played piano in a cinema in Clubmoor in the early thirties' I had found her. A woman who had known her forty years before telephoned us with Lily Lloyd's married name and present address. On their retirement the couple had moved away from Liverpool. But, as far as she knew, Lily Lloyd was almost certainly still alive.

For some days we debated the best method of approaching Lily Lloyd; now an elderly, possibly infirm woman, for whom a romance with Gordon Parry might well hold bitter memories. One option was to turn up on her doorstep, unannounced, but programme budgets are tight and normally will not stretch to financing potential wild goose chases. For one thing, Lily Lloyd might have died; there was a chance that she wasn't the right woman anyway; and even if she was, there was a greater risk still that she would refuse to talk.

At last, in the middle of November, I telephoned her. Under the Independent Broadcasting Authority's code of broadcasting practice I couldn't do what I wanted to do: record the conversation without Lily Lloyd's prior approval. So I had to rely on my shorthand notes, made in the presence of Programme Director David Maker, in case they were disputed later.

Lily Lloyd answered the telephone and responded to some opening conversational gambits in a pleasant, educated voice. I explained that I was calling from Liverpool, and had traced her through an old friend. At first we spoke about her days as a cinema pianist, which she recalled with evident pleasure. Then I turned the talk to the Wallace case. And to Gordon Parry. At once her manner changed and she became withdrawn and taciturn. From my notes I compiled the following record of the interview:

'In January 1931 I was going out with Gordon Parry, but we were not engaged. I gave a statement to the police investigating the Wallace murder, but it was only partly true. This was because I only saw Gordon *later* on the night of the crime. I can't remember how much later.

'I have made that part of my life a closed book. To reopen it now would cause me terrible distress.

'I was very, very much in love with Gordon and he with me. He was a very charming, handsome and talented young man, and I was terribly upset when the relationship ended.

'There were only ever two men in my life,' she went on, 'Gordon, my young love, and my husband, with whom love blossomed.

'I knew Gordon had died last April, and that his wife had died some years ago.'

And finally she said, 'To remember all this fifty years on causes me great pain. But I will say this: I can't possibly believe that Gordon did this murder, and he certainly never confided in me anything that suggested he might have done.

'The episode is closed, and it belongs to me alone.'

Lily Lloyd refused to record an interview, or to see me in person. A letter following up the phone conversation went unanswered. By late November we had discovered that in retirement Lily Lloyd had become well known in local public life. And she was certainly unshakable in her refusal to take the matter further. So we had, at least, established that Parry was without the alibi he had claimed for the crucial hours of the killing, even though the woman whom he met shortly after the killing believed him to be innocent. In the *Who Killed Julia?* programme Jonathan Goodman gave me his assessment of Lily Lloyd's testimony:

'Considering the lady's present exalted position in society, I don't find it in the least surprising that she gives Parry a character reference. She's hardly likely to admit that she had a romance with someone despite the fact that she knew him to be a rogue. The important thing is that she confirms that she assisted Parry to fabricate an alibi. And it's reasonable to assume that Parry asked her to do this before he was interviewed by the police: a distinctly odd action by an innocent man – and a dangerous one.

'It's surely disgraceful that the police made no effort to check the so-called alibi, proof here that they weren't interested in any suspect other than Wallace.'

Lily Lloyd had confirmed to me that she offered to swear an affidavit to Hector Munro depriving Parry of his crucial alibi. But on this central point Munro's memory proved sadly defective. With Goodman, I paid a second visit to Munro's London flat a few days after the Lily Lloyd phone call, and on the question of the affidavit offer, Munro would say only, 'My recollection is very feeble. I don't remember that at all.'

6

Time was now running short, Christmas was approaching and I had booked a much-needed holiday abroad for the first two weeks in January. I wanted to complete the research by Christmas so that Producer Bill Morrison could pull the programme together in time for my return. Michael Green had been making good progress in his search for other surviving witnesses. As well as Douglas Metcalf, who had finally responded to my note dropped through his letterbox and who gave us a lot of much-needed encouragement, we had located two other youngsters who had figured in the story: Allison Wildman and Harold Jones, both of whom had vivid recollections of the case and their roles in it.

In early December I spent a memorable evening at the Liverpool home of Dr Charles St Hill, who had recently retired as Home Office Pathologist for the Merseyside area. Not only did he impress me with his comprehensive knowledge of the case, but I found that he was totally convinced that Wallace was an innocent man. 'The complete absence of blood on Wallace is enough to convince me,' he said. 'I don't think it's possible for any man to carry out that sort of assault in which blood was spattered all round the walls without getting at least traces on himself. And in fact at the trial MacFall admitted that Wallace's head and face should have been heavily contaminated with blood.'

Dr St Hill agreed to take part in the programme as one of a panel of five experts. Also taking part would be Jonathan Goodman, Philip Chadwick (a solicitor from Sheffield who became fascinated by the case after reading Jonathan Goodman's book), Ray Jackson, the former head of Merseyside CID (who took a dim view of the police work in the case but who remained unconvinced by the case against Parry), and Robert Montgomery, a Liverpool barrister who for years had maintained that Wallace was guilty, and who had 'prosecuted' the case against him at a mock trial held in 1977 by the Merseyside Medico-Legal Society.

'For a start,' said Montgomery, 'look at the reasons for the telephone call. If the object was theft, it wasn't necessary to emphasise to the supervisor that the telephone seemed to be out of order when it wasn't; that the telephone caller was starting the alibi *at that point*. If the motive was murder and the murderer wasn't Wallace, he didn't need to get Wallace out of the house the next day; he could have murdered Mrs Wallace while her husband was out at the chess club.'

I finished the programme script in a furious two-week burst of activity. I sent the draft to Lesley Clive, an experienced radio writer from Wirral, who inserted the drama sequences and honed up my faltering narrative. The final product was emerging at last: a powerful drama-documentary telling the story of the crime, the trial and the appeal, using, where we could, the voices of authentic participants, with key sequences dramatised using professional actors and actresses. By the turn of the year we had assembled our case. No one on the programme team doubted that we had got it right. But would the public verdict be the same?

We accepted without question that in a case so old it would be quite impossible to assemble wholly convincing evidence against any particular suspect. Despite that we were faced with two central questions: if the police had kept an open mind about the identity of the killer, and pursued all the leads with the same diligence, would Gordon Parry's alibi really have held water? And should William Herbert Wallace or Richard Gordon Parry have been standing in that dock at the Liverpool Spring Assizes in April 1931?

These fundamental questions raised a third: why did the Liverpool police not show a keener interest in Parry at the very start of the investigation?

When the CID examined Parry's file at police headquarters they would have seen that he had had his first brush with the law while still in short trousers. He was convicted at the juvenile court of damaging property. 'Each day on his way to and from school, he pulled down a boundary wall at the front of houses in the course of erection,' recalled the court clerk Henry Harris when interviewed by Jonathan Goodman in the sixties. 'It was being done so regularly that the builders decided to keep watch, and Parry was caught in the act. I think the damage was considerable . . . I do know that, thereafter, he was a great source of sorrow and anxiety to his parents because of his evil tendencies . . .'

The file would have shown that Richard Gordon Parry was born on 12 January 1909 in Liverpool. His father was a treasury official with Liverpool Corporation, and the family lived at a pleasant villa-style house in Woburn Hill in the comfortable suburb of Stoneycroft. The boy attended Lister Drive School a few hundred yards away. Young Parry's record would have indicated the punishment meted out by the court, but Henry Harris could not recollect it when he recalled the case some fifty years later. It may or may not have been supplemented (as was customary in middle-class households then) by a good hiding from his father, William John Parry. Whether it was or not, it seems to have had little corrective effect. Gordon Parry's demolition job was to mark the start of a long and varied criminal career.

At school Parry apparently made little impression. But he was a handsome, sturdy youth, and his striking appearance helped him to a place in the school dramatic society. It was as a fledgling amateur actor that he first took an interest in a stunningly attractive girl a year or two younger than he was, Lily Lloyd. The couple started courting. Gordon left school to begin work as an apprentice insurance salesman with the Prudential, but found that the meagre wages, supplemented by what commission he could earn, scarcely allowed him to indulge his extravagant taste for good living, wine, women and motor cars. So he began to steal money, the money he had collected from the working people of Liverpool who scraped together a few pence a week to buy themselves a modicum of protection in the event of sudden misfortune.

When Parry was in his late teens and apprenticed with the Pru he met William Herbert Wallace. The relationship was never exactly a friendship: the two men came from totally different family backgrounds and age groups (Parry was thirty years younger than Wallace). As far as we know, the two men first met in December 1928 when Wallace was sick, and Parry took over part of his round. As well as familiarising himself with the Wallaces' domestic arrangements Parry at this time struck up an acquaintance with Julia Wallace, whom he thought sweet and charming. While Parry was doing the rounds of Clubmoor, Wallace, checking the books in his sickbed, began to notice slight discrepancies. Wallace spoke to Parry about the matter. It seems that Parry was short of small amounts when paying in, and hadn't entered all the sums collected in the book. Confronted with this, Parry apologised and claimed it was an oversight. He made up the shortfall himself, out of his own pocket. Later, Wallace learned that this was not the first time that Parry had had his fingers in the Prudential till. Some months before Parry had been found to be short in the amounts he was paying in at the company's head office in Liverpool. It seemed he had been pocketing certain amounts himself. Eventually the deficiencies came to the attention of the Prudential superintendent, Joseph Crewe. Rather than sack Parry, Crewe evidently decided instead that he would speak to the young man's parents about the matter.

Crewe explained what had been going on, and that the money would have to be made up. Parry's father evidently decided to smooth things over on his son's behalf, because it was Parry the elder who made up the deficiency. The sum involved – £30 – was quite a substantial amount in those days: Gordon Parry's own earnings (salary and commission) amounted to only £4 a week. His father, on the other hand, was well placed to offer help on financial matters, being employed in the City Treasury. How embarrassing it would have been for a man not yet at the peak of a promising career in public administration to have his son exposed as a petty embezzler. Thirty pounds probably seemed a pretty cheap settlement to keep the family name unblemished. And unblemished it stayed until this second episode involving William Herbert Wallace.

It is fair to assume that Wallace mentioned these fresh discrepancies to other colleagues at the Prudential. Whether he did or not, Parry was building up quite a reputation as a man who couldn't be trusted. There is no record of any further deficiencies concerning Parry, but we know that he left the Prudential towards the end of 1929. Officially, he resigned to improve his position. Unofficially, the word was that Parry had been caught thieving again, and had been told to quit or be fired.

Most of this serves to cast young Parry in a pretty poor light. Wallace knew all about Parry's chequered past, and told it to the Liverpool CID in his lengthy statement made just two days after the murder. Plainly, Wallace felt that Parry had both motive and opportunity to murder his wife: a young man – 'very plausible' – who would have been let into the house by Mrs Wallace, who would have known how much money should have been there for the taking. Not only that, but he knew the exact location of the cashbox in which the money was kept, and which had been found – minus about £4 – when Wallace returned from his fruitless search for Qualtrough.

Faced with all this new information, it is hard to understand why the police showed such scant interest in keeping Parry firmly fixed in the frame. According to Jonathan Goodman, 'It seems they interviewed Parry, who said he'd spent the evening with Lily Lloyd. This apparently satisfied the police, who didn't bother to check it further.' Police zeal may also have cooled as soon as they realised that Gordon Parry was well connected in Liverpool. In later years his father would be promoted to the post of Assistant City Treasurer.

William Parry spent the whole of his working life in the service of Liverpool Corporation, and held a part-time post as a lecturer in public administration at the Liverpool City School of Commerce. He was a founder member of the Liverpool branch of the local government officers' union, NALGO. And William Parry was not Gordon's only illustrious relation in high places. His father's cousin, George H. Parry, was the city's Chief Librarian, and in 1931 at the pinnacle of his life's achievements. Indeed, such was his impact on Liverpool's cultural scene that when he died in 1933 his life and works were commemorated at a service in Liverpool Cathedral.

'Clearly,' says Goodman, 'the police would have had to employ every ounce of tact in checking out Parry's alibi. It's one thing to investigate a man suspected of petty thieving. But quite another to check out an alibi for murder.'

Exactly what the police did do is a matter of private, not public, record. As mentioned in the Introduction to this book, the file on the murder of Julia Wallace is locked away in the archives of Merseyside Police. The Chief Constable, Mr Kenneth Oxford, has twice refused me permission to examine its contents, which should have contained any statements and notes written down in connection with Gordon Parry and Lily Lloyd.

There is one further curiosity about Parry's role in the investigation, which may or may not have persuaded the police to look elsewhere for a suspect. Superintendent Hubert Moore would almost certainly have known Parry's father personally, not just through the normal civic and public channels, but through someone very close to both men. William Parry's typist was a young girl called Imelda Moore, daughter of none other than Superintendent Moore himself.

A vexing feature of the Parry dimension in the Wallace case was the offer by Lily Lloyd to swear an affidavit to the effect that the alibi she had given Parry on the murder night was quite untrue and, indeed, impossible (as the police could have discovered for themselves, had they only taken the trouble). Wallace's solicitor, Hector Munro, explained the failure of the defence team to secure this vital affidavit when I interviewed him in early 1981: 'Wallace was dead by the time Miss Lloyd came to see me, and I had no client. A solicitor in England doesn't act without instructions or just out of the blue. I was very busy and had finished with that case. We were satisfied with getting Wallace off. We had no material at all on which to base a complaint about what the police had done. We thought they had actually checked the alibi of the people whom Wallace said had possibly done the murder.

'There was nothing I could do about it.'

Although Lily Lloyd never went on the record to render Parry's alibi worthless, the fact that she offered to do so is surely just as conclusive. When I traced her in 1980 she admitted to me that she lied when she said that Parry had spent the evening of the murder with her. In her words, the statement she gave to the police a few days after the killing was only partly true, in that although she had spent part of the evening with Parry, it was the *later* part. She cannot remember how much later. But it is plain that it was late enough to rob Parry of the alibi he claimed for the early part of the evening, to cover the time of the killing.

In the years following the Wallace case Parry was in and out of court on several occasions, as recorded in the newspapers of the day. From the *Liverpool Echo* in February 1932: 'Councillor Herbert Owen found Parry sitting in his car in North John Street. When asked what he was doing, Parry said: "Sorry, that's my car in front." He went to the other car, and produced some keys. On failing to open the door he started to move away. Owen informed a constable, and Parry agreed to go to the detective office, but bolted. The PC followed, blowing his whistle, and Parry was tripped by a tram inspector in Dale Street and arrested. Outside the bridewell in Cheapside, he threw himself on the floor and had to be carried inside. Parry was fined £5 with £6 costs.'

From the *Aldershot News*, September 1934: 'Richard Gordon Parry charged with two others with taking and driving away a motor car without consent, jailed for three months with hard labour.'

From the *Willesden Chronicle*, July 1935: 'Richard Gordon Parry, salesman, bound over for fraudulently embezzling the sum of £2 7s 3d received by him for his employers. Accused pleaded guilty, bound over for a year.'

This catalogue of petty crime becomes startlingly less petty on Parry's return from London in the mid-thirties. In May 1936 Parry appeared in court at Prescot near Liverpool accused of assaulting a girl he had met in a bar. The girl's story was that

Parry had offered to drive her home, but instead drove off to Rainhill where he assaulted her. Parry denied the charge, and said it was totally ridiculous. And although the outcome of the case was not reported, it is almost certain that Parry was sent for trial at the Liverpool Summer Assizes. But there appears to have been no press coverage of the case. Either it was just too sordid, or it was squeezed out by a sensational civil case which was tried at the same court involving the late Mrs Mirabel Topham and the then directors of Aintree Racecourse.

Parry was twice married, and had a daughter by his second wife. The family later moved to London and it was there in 1966 that Jonathan Goodman interviewed him. (Goodman located him via William Parry, who was still living in Liverpool. Parry senior died a short time later.)

By Christmas 1980 the case against Gordon Parry hinged on several key points.

He had a twin motive: a grudge against Wallace, who had reported him for cooking the insurance books; and a desperate shortage of money, the kind of money he thought he would find in the cashbox. He had opportunity: Julia Wallace would have let him into the house. And – most unusually in those days – Parry had a car, or at least the use of one. Whoever committed the murder would have been drenched in blood, and a car would seem the most practical way of making an escape.

The telephone caller Qualtrough was the murderer, and the caller would have had to put on a pretty convincing act. Parry was an amateur actor, a member of a dramatic society which met, like the Central Chess Club, at the City Café where Wallace's chess fixtures were posted up for anyone to see.

If the police had kept an open mind about the identity of the killer, and pursued all the leads with the same diligence, would Parry's alibi really have held up? And should William Herbert Wallace or Richard Gordon Parry have been standing in the dock at the Liverpool Spring Assizes in April 1931?

7

TUESDAY 20 JANUARY, 1981, was a fine, brisk winter's day in Liverpool. I spent the morning in the newsroom at Radio City, sketching out the live discussion which would follow the taped programme that evening, and checking over the studio with the engineers. At half past twelve I was at Lime Street station to meet Jonathan Goodman and Philip Chadwick, the solicitor from Sheffield who would support Goodman's case against Parry. After lunch, where we were joined by Producer Michael Green, the four of us strolled through the city centre to North John Street and the basement which, half a century earlier, had housed the City Café. We stood at the foot of the stairs leading down from the street. One by one we peered through the windows of the double doors that led to the old café, just managing through the gloom to pick out part of the pseudo half timbering tacked across the plaster walls. We said little, content to stand in the dusty old stairwell with our thoughts.

Later, in the watery sunshine, Goodman, Green and Chadwick decided to visit Wolverton Street while I returned to the office to deal with any last-minute problems. I found that the *Liverpool Echo* had run a big feature on the programme, and that people were already starting to call on the phone-in lines, wanting to book a place in the discussion. On his return from Anfield, Goodman and I were interviewed by Peter Levy on his *City Extra* programme, prompting still more calls. It was clear that the station had a major hit on its hands; all the pre-programme publicity had paid off. But would the programme itself and its extraordinary hypothesis live up to it? Nerves began to play unkind tricks. What had I got myself into? What would be the reaction of Parry's family? How could I possibly defend myself against charges of defaming a dead man?

What if Wallace *had* done it after all?

Just before six o'clock the telephone on my desk rang.

'Are you doing this Wallace programme tonight?' The man's voice at the other end of the line was thick Liverpudlian, and not unfriendly. 'I've just seen the piece in the *Echo* tonight.'

'Oh yes?'

'Is your Mr X really Mr P?'

'Yes.'

'Parry?'

'Yes.'

'What d'you know about the car?'

My mind was racing. 'What car?'

'The car Parry used.'

'I can't prove he did have a car.'

'Well, he did. How would you fancy talking to someone who saw the car straight after the murder?'

'You're joking, of course.'

'No I'm not,' the man continued. 'I can put you in touch with the bloke that washed the car out after Parry done the murder.'

'How quickly?' I glanced over my shoulder at the newsroom clock. Just on six.

'Aye, well, it'll take a bit of time.'

'Tonight?'

'No way.'

I reached for a pad and a pen. 'What's your name?' The caller said his name was Thompson, and gave a number in the Walton district of Liverpool. 'I've got to go,' I said, scarcely bothering to conceal the exasperation I felt. 'I'll call you later.'

Upstairs, Programme Controller David Maker had been entertaining the guests. 'I've just had a very odd phone call,' I said, pouring out a stiff whisky.

'Snap,' Maker said.

I looked at him, puzzled. 'From a man called Thompson?'

Maker shook his head. 'He didn't say what his name was. But I got the impression he was a relation of Parry.'

'Oh, Christ.'

'He was very annoyed. He'd seen the piece in the *Echo*. He kept on saying something about a man called Nuttall, that we'd been getting a lot of duff information from him.'

'I've never heard of Nuttall.'

At that moment I was beginning to wish I had never heard of William Herbert Wallace.

Of course it was too late for second thoughts. At half past six, precisely fifty years since Julia Wallace was last seen alive, our programme *Who Killed Julia?* went on the air. We heard the first hour over drinks in the second-floor conference room. Then I ushered Goodman, Chadwick, St Hill and Jackson into the lift and down to the studio.

The discussion that followed the taped section of the programme gave the five experts an opportunity to put forward their own thoughts and theories on the identity of the killer. But it was the subsequent phone-in section that yielded most. A man from Bebington claimed that Parry was notoriously untrustworthy as an insurance salesman. 'While I was away at sea,' he recalled, 'he conned my mother into handing over my insurance cards. I knew he had a vicious character: he was a dual personality and I knew he could fight. So I took a friend with me to his home in case there were any fisticuffs to get my cards back, which I did. He also conned Lily Lloyd's mother into an insurance policy, and into handing over her engagement ring.'

Ted Holmes, calling from Liverpool, was the House Manager at the Clubmoor Cinema where Lily Lloyd was employed as a pianist. He described Parry as an unscrupulous con man. 'I'm convinced he would have murdered anyone for money. He was an inveterate liar, and twisted me over an insurance policy.'

At this point I took up the questioning. 'Can you say for certain whether Miss Lloyd was, as she now says, playing the piano that night at the Clubmoor Cinema?'

'That I couldn't tell you,' said Mr Holmes, 'but while she was working there, Parry would come each evening to collect her while they were courting.'

'What time would she normally finish playing the piano?'

'She used to play during the break when the orchestra went for a drink. Somewhere between nine thirty and ten.'

'So you're saying it was Parry's practice to pick up his then girlfriend Lily Lloyd from the cinema between nine thirty and ten o'clock?'

'Yes, or between eight thirty and nine o'clock, I'm not quite certain.'

'What time would she start work?'

'I'd say about half past seven, eight o'clock.'

Proving, as Jonathan Goodman observed, that she was there between about half past seven and nine o'clock, the important period for the alibi.

But Ray Jackson, the former detective, was unimpressed. 'All the evidence so far is to prove that Parry was a con man. Just because the man was a fraud, or inclined to be one, doesn't mean to say he would commit murder.'

Barrister Montgomery agreed. 'He may have been a con man, but that doesn't mean to say he's going to murder for a few pounds.'

The next caller was Mr Russell Johnston who, to our astonishment, turned out to be the grandson of Wallace's neighbours, Jack and Florence Johnston. He thought the evidence against Parry no more damning than the evidence presented against Wallace. And on the business of the musical afternoons said to have been arranged illicitly between Parry and Mrs Wallace, Mr Johnston was positively sceptical. 'My mother, who had recently married and was living with her in-laws at 31 Wolverton Street, can't recall hearing any piano playing or singing in the afternoons during the period leading up to the murder.'

Jonathan Goodman commented that Parry may have been talking about making sweet music in a different way. 'But certainly this was what he told us, and without any prompting.'

Philip Chadwick asked Mr Johnston whether his grandparents had thought Wallace was guilty. 'I can't comment because I never really discussed it with them,' he said, 'but I did discuss it with my mother. She was so intimate with the Wallaces that on the morning of the murder, she was cleaning the upper bay window of 31 Wolverton Street and can remember waving to Mrs Wallace in the next bay. And my mother's always been convinced that Wallace was the murderer. One of the reasons was that after my grandfather had gone to fetch the police, my father came home from work and asked where his parents were. My father went round and found that my grandmother was in the middle kitchen, while Wallace himself was standing in the back kitchen cutting up meat for the cat in a very casual, rather cold manner.'

Ray Jackson, while conceding that the murder inquiry had its flaws, nevertheless remained sceptical about the case against Parry. 'His alibi should have been checked out at the time and – if it was false – proved to be so. Having done that, the police would have regarded him as a suspect – but nothing more.

'You've certainly no more evidence against Parry than you have against Wallace. In my view, there's more evidence against Wallace than there is against Parry.'

The programme over, we moved upstairs from the studio to the conference room for more drinks. But I was in no mood for socialising. Rudely, I excused myself and drove straight home to bed, exhausted. The following morning I found that the newspapers had been generous in their coverage of the programme. 50 YEAR MURDER 'SOLVED' said the headline in the *Daily Telegraph*: 'baffling murder case, which made legal history, was "reopened" and possibly solved last night with an answer to the question which had intrigued criminologists for fifty years – "who killed Julia Wallace?" . . . Last night, fifty years to the day that Mrs Wallace was murdered, Radio City, Liverpool's independent radio station, named the man they believe should have stood trial for the crime which aroused enormous interest in 1931. Months of patient "detective" work by a team of investigators has led them to the conclusion that Richard Gordon Parry, the son of a former assistant treasurer with Liverpool Corporation and a visitor to the Wallace home, was the culprit . . .'

The local morning paper, the *Liverpool Daily Post*, was more sceptical: 'The fifty-year-old guessing game of just who killed Julia Wallace continued last night after a radio station named their prime suspect . . .'

Press coverage of the programme continued for several days. The *North Wales Weekly News*, which circulates in the Llangernyw area, splashed its own story a couple of days after the broadcast: 'Village shocked by "murder" story after fifty years.' The story began: 'Villagers in Llangernyw were fond of Mr Richard Parry. They thought he was a kind and helpful member of their community. But this week their memories of the man who died in April last year received a sharp shock, because on Tuesday night Mr Parry was named as a possible killer . . .'

After outlining the background to the murder and the programme, the piece went on: 'But Llangernyw people have refused to believe that this was the same Mr Parry they knew and respected. The landlady at a local pub, The Bridge Inn, Mrs Gillian Gee, said she had known Mr Parry for three years since he and his wife came to live in the area. "I know people change, but I can't believe we're talking about the same man," she said yesterday. Mrs Gee said Mr Parry had been kind and helpful. However, he was very lonely and because of this he spent a lot of time in the pub chatting to regular customers. "He had been very lonely since his wife died two years ago. He was very fond of her. He came to The Bridge just for company. He helped clean up and repair things.

' "Even though he was getting a bit doddery he still kept an active interest in what was going on around him. He was a very nice old gentleman, very well educated and well spoken," added Mrs Gee.

'The landlady of The Stag Inn, Mrs Dorothy Wood, said Mr Parry was "quite a character" and was a regular there. He smoked Woodbine cigarettes and the landlady used to order this brand specially for him. He did all his own laundry and was always clean and tidy.'

The *Liverpool Daily Post*, meanwhile, indulged in a gentle knocking job. 'Residents in the peaceful North Wales village of Llangernyw were stunned and sceptical yesterday after an allegation that one of their most respected residents could have been a murderer . . . "It's very hard to believe, really," said former telephonist Mr R. P. Jones of Abergele Road. He worked with Mr Parry on the switchboard at Abergele Hospital for six years. "He was a bit dictatorial and sure of himself but always a gentleman. He was well educated and very self-assured," he recalled.

'But one woman, who declined to be named, dismissed the allegation as a stunt. "How can someone get away with it for fifty years?" she asked. "I worked with him for a good few years at the hospital and I don't believe it for a minute."

'Mrs Edith Jones questioned the propriety of hanging a dead man. "He's not here to defend himself and it seems an unfair way of finding him guilty," she said.'

The outcry reached a climax with a story run in the *Abergele Visitor* newspaper the following day, headed MURDER STORY IS RAPPED BY SISTER – FAMILY SHOCKED AND APPALLED BY CLAIMS.

'The sister of a dead man suddenly accused of a fifty-year-old murder has hit out at the people who made the allegations. Mrs Joan Smith said the family were appalled and distressed that the allegations should be made a year after the death of her brother, Mr Richard Parry of Llangernyw. Mrs Smith revealed that Mr Parry's daughter had not even known until now that her father was questioned at the time of the murder of Julia Wallace fifty years ago.

'Mrs Smith, now living at Beckenham, Kent, said: "We think these new allegations are dreadful, not for us, because we're a generation that knew what had happened, but for the next – his daughter knew nothing about it."

'Mrs Smith said: "Obviously the Press have a great deal of money, and obviously they've taken legal advice about what they can say and do legally. So they're not going to say anything which they can be taken up on. It's been very distressing and we think the best thing now is simply to do nothing."'

The same theme was developed a few days later by the *Liverpool Echo*: 'A radio programme which branded a dead man over the murder of Julia Wallace in Liverpool has been attacked by his family as a "horrible and baseless character assassination".' The story quoted Mrs Joan Smith describing the allegations made in the programme as monstrous. ' "It says little for justice that such things can be said about a person after he, or she, is dead. And that, under the present law, relatives are unable to bring any kind of action against the accuser," she said.

'Mrs Smith points out that the time of the Wallace murder was a period of great distress to her family. Her brother, she said, was thoroughly investigated by the police, as were a considerable number of other people. His alibi was checked out and forensic experts even took the seams out of his clothes and gloves for tests. After an exhaustive investigation, Mr Parry, who had not been in contact with the Wallaces in the two years prior to the crime, was completely cleared of implication, Mrs Smith said . . . She criticised the documentary's producers for not contacting members of the family, who knew the extent of the investigation.'

This was incorrect. I had specifically asked Parry's daughter and her husband for facilities to contact other members of the family, but had been told that none of them wished to comment, preferring to 'let sleeping dogs lie'. And it was simply untrue to claim, as Mrs Smith claimed, that Parry had not been in contact with the Wallaces in the two years before the crime, or that 'a considerable number of other people in Liverpool' had been thoroughly investigated by the police.

The first assertion does not square with Wallace's recollection of meeting Parry twice in late 1930, once at the City Café, and again in Missouri Road, Clubmoor. As for the second, who were these 'other people'? Leaving aside the inevitable cranks who always confess to well-publicised murders, there is no evidence to indicate the existence of any serious suspects other than Parry and Wallace.

*   *   *

While the post-programme debate continued in the local press, Michael Green and I were taking stock. Had we pushed the Wallace story as far as we could? Certainly we were well pleased with the programme and the way in which we had rekindled the Wallace controversy. For the most part the debate we stimulated was serious and constructive: I was invited to speak to a group of Merseyside police officers at the force's training school who were studying the Wallace case as part of their instruction in detection methods.

And as the days passed I was becoming more convinced than ever that our programme had got it right, that Parry was our man or at least a more credible suspect than Wallace. The doubts that had crowded my mind on the night of the broadcast began to evaporate. Scores of letters from listeners – most appreciative and supporting the programme's argument – served to confirm my growing conviction about Gordon Parry's role in the Wallace affair. More than ever I was sure that Parry should have been the man in the dock. And I was certain that Parry must have had the use of a motor car.

I discussed this point at length with Michael Green. First of all there was the murder itself. The killer had managed to slip away from Wolverton Street unnoticed. If it was Parry, he had returned to his home in Woburn Hill, Stoneycroft, about a mile away, completely undetected despite the probability that his clothes were heavily bloodstained. If the crime had been premeditated, then it made sense to use a car and to park it nearby. Then there was Parry's interview with Jonathan Goodman. Parry had clearly been ruffled when challenged by Goodman about his alibi for the murder night. He said that his car had broken down in Breck Road. Green was convinced that

Parry was lying on this point, but had inadvertently let a half-truth slip out. He had unwittingly revealed two important facts: that he owned a car, or had the use of one, at the time of the murder; and that he had been using a car on the murder night.

Green checked with the local authority in Liverpool and with the licensing office in Swansea. Both said there were no records of car ownership dating back as far as 1931. So he filed it away in his head, along with other half-supported theories.

I, meanwhile, was turning my attention to the business of the telephone call received shortly before the transmission of *Who Killed Julia?* The caller had given me a telephone number and the name Thompson, but had said little else. But something he had said stuck in my mind. And the more I thought about it, the more tantalised I became.

'You might stumble across it yourselves,' Thompson had said.

I spoke to the man Thompson on several occasions in late January and early February. In essence his story was that he could put me in touch with a man who had washed down Parry's car on the night Julia Wallace was murdered, and who had found a bloodstained glove inside the vehicle. According to Thompson, the car cleaner was not only still alive, but lucid and ready to talk. Thompson kept insisting that it was not him but a friend who would lead us to this crucial missing witness. This served to complicate the financial arrangements which Thompson was anxious to finalise: he wanted £200 in exchange for the name and number of the mysterious go-between. In the absence of any guarantees about the veracity of the story, or the menial state of either the go-between or the car cleaner, I offered £50. Thompson would have none of it. 'You and I both know it's worth more than that,' he kept telling me. 'Anyway,' he added enigmatically, 'you may find out for yourselves.'

After each successive phone call, Michael Green and I felt increasingly sceptical about the existence of this so-called 'friend' – the go-between. My feeling was that Thompson had stumbled on the story, probably in the course of idle pub talk, and the general hoo-ha about the Wallace programme had encouraged him to formulate a business proposition concerning the information, information which he knew (or thought he knew) I would pay for handsomely. But we differed on the price. 'You've been watching too much television,' I told Thompson during one of our telephone conversations. 'Fifty pounds is a very fair fee.'

'My pal thinks it's worth more,' Thompson replied.

He and I never met. But I was forming a mental picture of a slightly menacing figure inhabiting the twilit Liverpool underworld with its cheap talk and shady deals. Both Michael Green and I were becoming more and more peeved that, after all our hard work, someone like Thompson could, in effect, try to blackmail us into paying for information. So, after the challenge of exposing Gordon Parry came a second challenge: to find the mysterious car cleaner for ourselves.

If we could do that, and prove that his story was true, the case against Gordon Parry would be clinched.

V

Conspiracy of Silence

MICHAEL GREEN TURNED detective, and began with the assumption that Gordon Parry used a car on the night Julia Wallace was murdered. Parry himself, interviewed on his doorstep by Jonathan Goodman and Richard Whittington-Egan, had claimed that his car had broken down in Breck Road. Green studied a map of the Anfield area and visited the Picton library in Liverpool to compile a list of garages operating in or around Anfield in 1931. To Green, Thompson's cryptic tease could only mean that the garage where Parry was supposed to have had his bloodstained car washed down was still in business somewhere. But where? Green checked the list of garages printed in the 1931 Liverpool trades directory against the garages listed in the 1981 Liverpool telephone directory. He checked both names and addresses, in case the garage in question had changed hands. He spent several fruitless evenings touring the Breck Road area in his car, but none of the garages still in business seemed to fit the bill. So, back in the office, he sat down and did some hard thinking.

If Parry was living in Woburn Hill at the time of the murder, he thought, it made more sense for the garage to be near his home, probably on Green Lane. Green returned to the library and compiled a new list. He found several garages listed in the Green Lane area in 1931, and he began to check each one in turn. He soon discovered that Green Lane had been renumbered, probably after the Second World War, but he managed to identify original sites by dividing the streets into blocks. One garage had become a bakery, and the others had disappeared completely – except one on the corner of Green Lane and Rockbank Road. This was easy to pinpoint because there was a church on the opposite corner. This place seemed to fit the description exactly. It had a workshop and was only five streets away from Woburn Hill. Green talked to the staff and telephoned the owner. Nothing.

'I went home disappointed,' Green recalls, 'and turned again to the old street directory. OK, I told myself, where do I go from here?'

Green tried to imagine what things would have been like in the thirties. Fewer cars, he thought, therefore fewer garages. The murder of Julia Wallace occurred in the evening. So if Parry had visited his local garage it must have been open at around eight or nine o'clock at night. This seemed odd, or at least unusual. Unless the garage had a special reason to be open at such a late hour. Why should it be open at night?

Then, without warning, a brilliant thought came to him. What if the garage doubled as a taxi business? 'I started to get really excited,' says Green. 'This, it seemed, could be the key I was looking for. I turned to the directory again and checked through the trades section for 1931. There was a firm called Atkinson's Taxis and Motor Engineers at 1a Moscow Drive, just two streets from Woburn Hill. It was too much to hope that it was still listed in the 1981 phone book. Good God – it was there! In black and white! The same name and the same address!'

The next morning Green parked his car outside Atkinson's in Moscow Drive, Stoneycroft. It looked to have hardly changed since the thirties. He got out of the car and walked into the office. 'I'm from Radio City,' he explained. 'We're looking into a famous murder which happened in 1931. I don't suppose you know anything about a bloodstained car which is supposed to have been brought in to a local garage on the night of the murder?'

'It was here,' said a voice from behind. Green turned. A man in shirtsleeves was leaning against the office wall. He introduced himself as Gordon Atkinson, one of the brothers still running the family business.

Over a steaming mug of tea Gordon Atkinson told Michael Green the story told to him by his father. Of how Gordon Parry had roared into the garage on the night of the Wallace murder and demanded to have his car hosed down. Of how the night cleaner, in fear of his life, had done Parry's bidding. Of how the cleaner had come across the bloodstained evidence of Parry's atrocity. Of the conspiracy of silence that had witnessed the ordeal of William Herbert Wallace half a century earlier.

'The cleaner,' said Green, unable to contain himself any longer. 'Who was he? Is he still alive?'

'His name is John Parkes,' said Gordon Atkinson, 'and he lives just around the corner from here.'

Five minutes later Michael Green was knocking at the door of a small terraced house in Guernsey Road. There was no reply. A neighbour, spotting the dapper bespectacled stranger, told Green that John Parkes had recently been admitted to hospital for a minor operation. He did not know when Parkes would be home again. But he gave Green the name of Parkes's son, who worked at Walton Prison. 'Having come so far,' says Green, 'I didn't want to leave it a day longer, especially as John Parkes was an old man and evidently not in good health. That evening I went round to the hospital, found the ward and spoke to the nurse on duty. She showed me the old man asleep in his bed, and gave me his son's telephone number.'

Green hurried back to his flat in Sefton Park and telephoned John Parkes junior. He explained why he was calling, and why it was vital that Parkes should give permission for an interview with his elderly father. Without hesitation, Parkes agreed. 'Sure,' he said, 'go tomorrow.'

2

SEFTON GENERAL HOSPITAL sprawls behind Toxteth Park Cemetery in a flyblown area of Liverpool squeezed on to the map between the dismal terraced streets of Wavertree and the faded grandeur of Sefton Park. Green coaxed his car through the late lunchtime traffic clogging the city centre, up the hill past the university to the traffic lights at the junction of Lodge Lane and Smithdown Road. Neither of us had spoken since leaving the office; now, waiting at the lights, we craned our necks, looking for the ghosts of trams and men who had ridden them from this very spot half a century before. Our route took us where Wallace had ridden, south along Smithdown Road, past the ends of streets that must have changed very little since that night in January 1931 when he too stared impassively at the names fleeting past: Webb Street, Scholar Street, Mulliner Street. Here on the fringe of the inner city traffic had thinned out and we picked up a little speed, past the wall of the cemetery to our right, to the lights and the turning to the right through the hospital gates.

We parked the car and looked round, half expecting trouble. Had Thompson got wind of our appointment? A couple of nurses came sniggering out of a doorway and pulled their capes tight around them. A car engine fired into life from a distant part of the hospital complex. We grinned and got out. I unloaded the heavy black Uher tape recorder from the boot, checked that the microphone was clipped securely to the shoulder strap, and grabbed three reels of tape from the small pile strewn amid the tool kit and odd pieces of junk. Slamming the boot lid, I turned and walked to where Green was standing by the ugly opaque plastic double doors that led to the wards. Just as we started towards them, someone – a man – shouted to us from behind, 'Oi!'

We stopped in our tracks and turned, not really knowing who or what to expect.

'Can't you read?'

One of the hospital orderlies had appeared from nowhere and was jabbing his finger angrily at a notice on the wall where the car was parked. Unmistakably it said: Ambulances only.

'All right,' said Green.

'See you inside,' I said.

The pair of us wandered down the corridor, slowly at first, as strangers in hospitals tend to, studying the plastic direction notices and sniffing the hospital smell. A woman in a dressing gown shuffled past and looked suspiciously at the tape recorder slung over my shoulder. We turned left and climbed some stairs, still looking, still listening for some sign that the game was up. From miles away, it seemed, came unfamiliar noises, the kind of noises only ever heard in hospitals: squeaks, rumbles, bangings that reverberate for longer than you expect.

'Here it is.'

We had arrived on a landing with a door marked Ward 10. Green led the way, looking for the Sister. In another wave of panic I piled the recording equipment on a chair and checked the ward lavatory; from down the hall I could hear a muttered conversation. Satisfied that no one was waiting for us in the toilet I rejoined Green, who was standing with a staff nurse in front of a pair of double doors leading to the ward. Through the circular windows a man was shuffling towards us, helped by a nurse.

'That's him! It's got to be!' Green whispered excitedly.

The staff nurse smiled. 'That's Mr Parkes. We've arranged to put him in a side ward for you.' She indicated a door to the left.

I opened the door and poked my head round it. Two very old women glared at me. The staff nurse pushed past and into the room. 'Now then, ladies, we mustn't hold up these gentlemen from Radio City, or you'll never get your requests played.' She shooed them out and they hobbled away, mumbling. I dumped the Uher on a chair at the side of a single bed and walked to another chair placed at the front of it. As I sat down, John Parkes tottered into the room.

He was wearing an old red dressing gown and slippers. Underneath, a pair of faded pyjamas. His white hair was cut short, and he had a squint. We introduced ourselves, and the nurse who had helped him up from the main ward sat him on the bed and swung his legs up so that Parkes, propped up by a couple of pillows, could be as comfortable as possible.

Green moved towards the chair where the Uher lay and began setting up. My immediate anxiety was that Parkes should clearly understand who we were, why we were there, and what he could expect from us in return. I explained that we were from Radio City, that we had both been involved in a programme about the Wallace murder case, and that we understood he had some information that would be of interest to us.

'Aye, I have that.' His voice had just the suggestion of quavering. I glanced at Green, who was nearly ready with the Uher.

'Don't say anything yet, Mr Parkes,' I said. I turned to the two nurses who were hovering in the corner. 'Can we have a few minutes on our own with him?'

The nurses smiled. 'Try not to tire him out,' said the staff nurse, closing the door behind her.

I could see that Green was ready to record. 'Could Mike just sit on the side of the bed? He's got a little tape recorder and we'd like to record what it is you've got to say.'

It struck me that I had been speaking in a raised voice, assuming a man so frail to be at least partially deaf.

'Can you hear us all right?' asked Green.

'Oh aye, I can hear you fine.'

Green fiddled with the Uher, adjusting the sound level. 'Mike will ask you questions and I'll just sit and listen,' I added, nodding to Green. He made another adjustment to the tape recorder, then pressed the buttons that would set the machine running.

'Mr Parkes, can I take you back fifty years to January 1931? Can you tell us where you were at this time, where you were living and where you were working?'

I held my breath. Parkes seemed to squint into the middle distance, pursing his lips. For a second or two there was dead silence. Then, in a rather high-pitched, hoarse voice, he began to tell his amazing story.

3

IN January 1931 John Parkes was twenty-four and living with his mother in a cottage in Tynwald Hill, Stoneycroft. He was working as a cleaner and general dogsbody for £2 a week at an all-night garage in nearby Moscow Drive, not far from its junction with Green Lane. This was Atkinson's Taxis and Motor Engineers, which was – and still is – known as Atkinson's Garage. The owner, Mr William Atkinson, had three sons: Wilfred, Harold and Arthur. All the Atkinson menfolk worked in the business, and John Parkes, because of his age and the fact that he lived just a stone's throw away, was considered very much one of the family. They called him 'Pukka'. He was well thought of by the Atkinsons, a good worker, honest, industrious and punctual. Young Parkes worked nights. His hours were roughly from 11 p.m. to 9 a.m. Life as an all-night garage hand was no soft touch, but in 1931 one man in four in Liverpool was out of work and John Parkes was grateful for the security afforded in the service of Atkinson's Garage. It was a big place for those days, and a busy one. As well as the business generated by private customers the firm operated a fleet of taxis and these would need constant maintenance, service and cleaning. At night the garage became something of a social centre for some of the customers. The Atkinsons had a flat above the garage, and certain clients would often drop by for a late-night drink or a chat in the kitchen. Some of the clients were welcome there. Others were not. Among this last group was Richard Gordon Parry.

Dapper and suave, he was known in the neighbourhood as something of a wide boy. John Parkes had known Parry for several years. They had been at school together in Lister Drive but the relationship had never quite fused into a friendship. Somehow, though, their paths continued to cross and whether he liked it or not John Parkes could not help but get to know Parry as well as anyone.

'I knew him very well,' said Parkes. 'I knew him at school, I knew him off school. I knew him exceptionally well. I'd describe him as a lady's man. He always went round with a dress suit on and a collar, always very smartly dressed. Once in the garage, he asked, "Do you like me?" I said, "I don't trust you." I told him that straight to his face.'

Parkes was far from being the only man in Liverpool to entertain a distrust of Gordon Parry. In fact, it was hard to find anyone who did trust him. Parkes's opinion of Parry was not just based on tittle-tattle or hearsay, but on personal experience. It was Parry's habit to visit the garage late at night, climbing the stairs to the little kitchen on the first floor. Parkes recalled quite clearly:

'He was in insurance, and trying to get business, but at the same time his mind was on other things. He was wanting money *badly* and he tried to rob the sons of the garage. He was caught going through the wardrobe where one of the sons kept money. And after that the boss said to the sons and me, "Close the door of a night, and don't let him in. Things are not safe."'

Parry's parents were comparatively well-to-do; Parry idolised his father, and in return it seems the father indulged his son. Somehow (possibly it was a gift from his father) Gordon Parry had acquired a car. This must have done wonders for his flashy image with women, but it had a disastrous effect on the state of Parry's finances. John Parkes remembered the car, and the trouble it caused.

'I think it was a little Swift,' he said. 'As a matter of fact, Atkinson's overhauled the engine for him and never got paid, because Parry hadn't got the money to pay. They had great difficulty getting the money off him.'

On the evening of Tuesday 20 January, 1931, John Parkes left his home in Tynwald Hill as usual and made his way through a back entry to Atkinson's Garage. It would have been between 11 p.m. and 11.30 p.m. Among the regular night-time callers who were welcome at the garage was a local beat bobby called Ken Wallace. It happened that PC Wallace called on John Parkes that night because he had some news: that of the murder earlier that evening in Wolverton Street, Anfield.

'He came into the garage,' Parkes recalled, 'and said there'd been a bit of trouble in Wolverton Street. I said "Why?" and he said a murder had been committed and that Mr Wallace had been charged with it.'

Parkes said, 'Wallace? That's Parry's friend.'

'That's right,' said the constable.

But PC Wallace, like the crowd that had gathered outside 29 Wolverton Street, had got hold of the wrong end of the stick. Wallace had not been charged with the murder; he had not been charged with anything. Superintendent Moore himself had only arrived at the scene at 10 p.m., and wouldn't arrest Wallace for another thirteen days. Certainly, the *rumour* was that Wallace had been charged, but as with so many fine points of detail in the Wallace case, the fact of the matter was completely the opposite.

John Parkes, on the other hand, was nearer the truth. Wallace wasn't exactly Parry's friend, but he was certainly an acquaintance. John Parkes must have mused upon the possibilities as PC Wallace said good night and moved off along his beat. But any musings were brought to an abrupt halt with the arrival some time later of Gordon Parry himself. What was to follow was the core of John Parkes's story. He told it in his own words, as he remembered it, more than half a century on:

'Later that night or early morning, Parry came in with his car. I was busy in the garage washing some cars down, and he said he wanted me to wash his car. His car was clean as far as I could see. But I got the high-pressure hose and went all over the car, underneath, inside, everywhere.

'As I was doing this I saw a glove inside a box in the car and I pulled it out to stop it getting wringing wet. Parry snatched it off me. It was covered in blood. And Parry said to me: "If the police found that – it would hang me!" Well, I was a bit dubious about things, and then he started rambling again about a bar which he'd hidden outside a doctor's house in Priory Road. He said he'd dropped it down a grid outside the house.

'He was in an agitated state, I could tell that by what he said. And when I was washing the car down, I knew *why* I was washing it and I didn't dare say anything, I realised my washing the car down had washed all the evidence away, but the evidence was there on the glove – blood on the glove – and Parry saying that would hang him, and talking about the bar where he'd hidden it . . . I remember all that as clear as daylight.'

It is necessary to look at this story in some detail. Because if it is true, it is the most damaging evidence against Parry. Was John Parkes really saying that as well as washing the outside of the car, he had sluiced down the inside as well?

'Definitely. Without any shadow of a doubt. Every particle of the car was washed, where normally one wouldn't bother. And he stood over me as I did it telling me what to do. I saw the glove jutting out of this box and I only pulled it out because had I played the hose on it, it would have been saturated. Parry just snatched it away and said, "If the police get hold of that, it would hang me." And I realised then that he wanted me to swill the box out, and the glove with it. But I didn't. I got the glove out before I started.'

The glove was a leather mitt – 'and I think it had a little tear in it,' said Parkes. He was wearing high thigh boots to protect his trousers from splashing water 'and any bloodstains off the car would have just gone straight down the grid.'

The washing completed, Parry gave John Parkes five shillings for his trouble and, not long afterwards, drove off into the night. 'Some nights Parry would stay until three or four in the morning before going home, but on this particular night he just chatted for a bit and then went.'

Parkes admitted that he was 'a bit worried' about what Parry had told him. The following morning, before going off shift, he confided in his boss, William Atkinson. Atkinson's advice to Parkes was simple: Don't have anything to do with it. Parkes also admitted taking five shillings off Parry, money which rightly belonged to the garage. 'Keep it,' said Atkinson.

'What if Wallace is convicted of killing his wife?' asked Parkes. 'We'll have to tell the police.' Atkinson agreed. And when, four months later, Wallace was found guilty at Liverpool Assizes, Atkinson kept his word. He telephoned Superintendent Moore at the CID office.

Moore took brief details over the telephone, then drove out to Stoneycroft to interview John Parkes in person. He listened as Parkes poured out his story of Parry's late-night visit, the washing of the car, and the discovery of the bloodstained glove. He sat stony-faced as the young garage hand repeated Parry's panic-stricken disclosure about the whereabouts of the iron bar he had used to bludgeon Julia Wallace to death, the bar he had dropped down a grid outside a doctor's surgery in Priory Road.

Moore's response to the evidence of John Parkes was curt and dismissive. 'Pooh-pooh,' he spluttered. 'You must have made a mistake.'

Parkes, feeling that his duty as a citizen had been discharged after his interview with Moore, then felt free to confide his amazing story to friends. Their reaction was unanimous. 'What you've said has saved Wallace's neck,' they said, 'because now there's doubt in the case.'

But how, Mike Green and I wondered, half a century later, could John Parkes be absolutely certain that this happened as he says it did, within hours of the killing of Mrs Wallace? Parkes laughed softly, shifting slightly on the bed to get comfortable. 'I'm as sure as I'm talking to you now,' he said. And the pair of us believed him.

There was another crucial point. If Parkes's story was correct, and Parry had arrived at the garage just hours after the murder, why were there no bloodstains on his clothes? Parkes knew the answer to that. It seemed that some time before the murder, probably only a few days, Parry had borrowed a long oilskin cape and a pair of thigh-length waders from some people living in the district, telling them he was planning a fishing trip. Neither the cape nor the waders were ever returned to their owners.

'While I was washing the car, I knew what I was doing. It's no use my saying anything else,' Parkes said. 'I realised I was washing away the evidence. But there was nothing I could do. I was too afraid to stop, because I knew Parry was a dangerous man. And when I found the glove, it made me even more afraid. I thought, "By jingo, I'll have to be careful here!" And then he told me all about where he'd hidden the weapon. Well, I couldn't have picked that up by conjecture, could I?'

Parkes was talking faster now, and excitedly. 'Parry was in a state of insanity . . . he had to do something . . . had to tell somebody . . . and he told me everything. Now, if I'd been a bit more wide awake, I'd have got more out of him. He would have told me more. But Parry was only concerned with getting that car washed down thoroughly.'

On the Qualtrough masquerade, John Parkes was convinced of Parry's capacity for such a subterfuge: 'He was such a liar! He could spin a yarn and get away with it. He had this habit of coming up into the kitchen over the garage, picking the phone up and calling people he didn't know, and talking to them. And, of course, Parry was in this dramatic society. And it was nothing for him to alter his voice.

'He could alter his voice like you changing a shilling!'

*   *   *

Parry evidently came perilously close to confessing the killing of Julia Wallace within hours of committing the murder. It may have been that Parry needed to unburden his guilt by telling someone – anyone – about it. But in the days that followed, any guilt that Parry felt would have been tinged with fear, the fear that Parkes might have told his story to the police. Realising this, Parkes himself began to worry about his safety. His fears grew some time later when Parry reappeared at the garage. This time he was not alone.

'After the murder, and his virtual confession to me,' said Parkes, 'Parry came round with another chap. And after that, the Atkinsons advised me to change my route to work, in case anything nasty happened.'

Why, in 1931, did the police not take the testimony of John Parkes more seriously? It is plain that the CID regarded Gordon Parry as a prime suspect in the days following the killing of Julia Wallace: both Parry and his sister had spoken of a rigorous and painstaking investigation involving extensive forensic tests. It now seems obvious that Parry's true part in the affair was concealed by a tragic conspiracy of silence, a conspiracy born out of fear at Atkinson's Garage, and among the people in Stoneycroft who knew that Parry had borrowed oilskins, ostensibly for a fishing trip. (They included a driver for a local grocery store and a policeman.) All of them had kept quiet. Not one had been pricked by conscience to come forward, even as Wallace was brought, quietly protesting his innocence, to the brink of the scaffold. John Parkes explained.

'They didn't want to get involved. The driver from the grocer's knew, but he didn't want to get involved; the policeman knew, and he didn't want to get involved. If someone had only backed me up I could have cleared Wallace. He would never even have been convicted.

'The blood on the glove alone was enough.'

The old man was getting tired. He had told us his story, and assured us that he understood the grave implications it contained. 'I realise fully,' he said, 'and I wish I had realised the implications at the time. Parry had given me all the evidence, talked to me, told me to wash his car down, and I saw the blood and heard about the bar down the grid. But I was afraid of anything happening.'

John Parkes had a simple explanation for keeping his story quiet until now, fifty years after the murder. 'Once I knew that Wallace's neck was saved [after the appeal] I let it die down. But it's always been on my mind all along. I can remember the facts so vividly. I think Wallace was an innocent man and he should never have been convicted. And I think Superintendent Moore made an absolute mess of that case . . . an absolute mess of it.'

It was getting late. Green and I thanked old John Parkes for his time as we packed up our equipment. Presently, the ward sister appeared, helped the old man off the bed and led him shuffling back to his ward. Michael Green and I hurried out of the hospital and into the car park. Where an hour before we had stolen furtive glances at strangers in case they turned out to be saboteurs, now we felt only elation. Now we knew the case against Gordon Parry was clinched.

We raced back into town to replay the taped interview in the studio. At once we made plans for a follow-up programme, to be called *Conspiracy of Silence*, featuring the exclusive interview with 'the missing witness'. Michael Green and I set out to interview two members of the Atkinson family, each of whom, in their way, backed up the amazing story of John Parkes. First we spoke to the widow of Wilf Atkinson, one of the brothers helping to run the garage in 1931. We found Mrs Dolly Atkinson living quietly in a small bungalow about ten miles from Liverpool.

'I remember Mr Parkes telling me and my husband about being forced to wash the car. He told us all about it the morning after. I've known Mr Parkes for many years, and he certainly wouldn't make up a story like that.'

Mrs Atkinson's son Gordon now runs the family business with his brother David. Gordon Atkinson was told the story of Parry's car by his father, and has no reason to doubt that it is true. When Michael Green and I returned to Atkinson's Garage to meet him for an interview, Gordon Atkinson led us into the old garage workshop, dark, cluttered, and seemingly little changed since 1931. He flashed a torch up on to one of the beams. 'Look up there,' he said. We peered up into the roof space and there, as it had remained down the years, was the metal arm from which used to run the swinging hose, the apparatus with which John Parkes had washed away the blood of Gordon Parry's victim so many years before.

4

SHORTLY AFTER INTERVIEWING John Parkes in early February 1981 the Wallace team decided to contact Lily Lloyd once more. We felt that we now had enough fresh evidence to justify such a move, although we all knew that a second approach stood little chance of success. Rather than risk rebuff on the telephone, or another unanswered letter, we opted for a bold stroke. We sent Radio City's chief crime reporter, a hard-nosed young Liverpool Irishman called Kieran Devaney, to see her. If he couldn't get her talking, we reasoned, no one could.

Devaney was despatched to the small town where Lily Lloyd lives in a lonely bungalow on a windswept cliff overlooking a bay. Leaving his taxi and driver waiting out of sight, he set off to walk the hundred yards to her home in pouring rain. By the time Devaney had climbed the steps to the front door he was soaked through.

The door was answered by a small old lady. From her dress and her features Devaney thought that in her time she had obviously been 'a good-looker'. 'Excuse me,' he said, 'are you Lily Lloyd?'

'Goodness,' she exclaimed, 'no one has called me that for years.'

Devaney apologised for disturbing her. He explained he had come to see her about the Wallace murder. She seemed shaken and began to close the door, saying, 'I don't want to talk about that. It's all a long time ago. I've put it out of my mind now. It hurts me even to think about it.'

Devaney explained that he knew about her affair with Gordon Parry, and about the events at Atkinson's Garage. He said that it seemed she had helped to fabricate Parry's alibi. But Lily Lloyd refused to be drawn. 'I've made a new life for myself here,' she said. 'I don't want to be disturbed.'

It was obvious to Devaney that Lily Lloyd knew of the latest developments in the case, and of the broadcast of *Who Killed Julia?* Standing on her doorstep, rain now trickling down his neck, Devaney knew it was hopeless. He told her that in all probability she was the only person still alive who knew what happened to Julia Wallace on the night she died. 'If I'm the only person who knows the truth,' she said, finally, 'then I'll take it with me to my grave.'

And with that she closed the door.

That night Devaney tried several times to telephone Lily Lloyd from his hotel. There was no reply. The following day he paid a second visit to the house. The curtain twitched, but the door stayed shut.

When Devaney climbed down the steps to the road below, the taxi driver was waiting at the bottom. He had driven the hundred yards from where Devaney had left him in the hope that the taxi man would not see which house he had visited.

'I'm just curious,' said the driver.

On the return journey Devaney told the taxi man the purpose of his visit, and that he was researching a programme about something that had happened in Liverpool fifty years before.

'You've come about the murder of Julia Wallace,' said the old-timer. 'I used to live near Wolverton Street as a child, and I was there at the time of the killing.

'I've known Mrs —— for years. But I never realised she was Lily Lloyd.'

The extraordinary and haunting story of John Parkes was broadcast on Radio City on 26 February 1981. The programme had been edited, written and produced in just three days. On the day before the programme was transmitted I received a short letter from Merseyside Police, in response to a further request to see their file on the Wallace case. The request was turned down. Deputy Chief Constable Peter Wright added, 'In view of the controversy aroused by your previous programme it would be inappropriate for police records to be released as a basis for further public debate.'

WHAT COULD THE Wallace murder file contain that the police are still so anxious to conceal? Evidence of a bungled, inefficient and blinkered investigation by the CID? Statements from Gordon Parry and Lily Lloyd, together with notes of interviews conducted with them? Knowing as I do now that the file is manifestly incomplete, I wonder whether it might ever have been possible to demonstrate the existence of an extraordinary cover-up, and to identify the architects of a monstrous subterfuge at which officials of both the Liverpool Police and Liverpool Corporation connived? Of course I cannot even begin to prove it, but it may just be possible that young Gordon Parry was the hapless fall-guy in a plot to conceal some kind of fraudulence involving his father at the City Treasury. It is a tantalising thought. Suppose Gordon Parry had let slip some indiscretion concerning such a fraud to Julia Wallace in the course of one of their 'musical afternoons'. Suppose Julia had mentioned it to her husband, and that he, in turn, had confronted young Parry and threatened to expose his father. Gordon Parry may have reported the leak to his parent. William Parry would have reasoned that both the Wallaces knew too much, and may have charged his son, the source of the leak, with the task of eliminating the problem. The rest we know. At the start of the investigation into Julia Wallace's murder, Gordon Parry's name was gently removed from consideration, conceivably as the result of pressure from his father. William Parry, after all, did have connections.

In September 1933 Gordon Parry's uncle, George H. Parry, died. Uncle George had worked in the Liverpool library service for nearly forty-five years, becoming Chief Librarian in 1929. A week after his death, the Dean of Liverpool, Canon Dwelly, conducted a memorial service at Liverpool Cathedral. The Lord Mayor was represented, and all manner of nabobs and nobodies from the Corporation turned up, including the Town Clerk. The Assistant Chief Constable went along. So did the City Analyst, W. H. Roberts. And there, representing the Chief Constable himself, was none other than Detective Chief Superintendent Hubert Moore.

William Parry retired as Assistant City Treasurer for Liverpool in July 1950. All the obituaries following his death in 1966 mentioned the fact that Mr Parry had organised the first issue of ration books to the citizens of Liverpool during the Second World War. He left two sons and four daughters. Could he have died in the knowledge that his son Gordon had kept his promise never to discuss his part in the Wallace affair?

While much new information about Gordon Parry has come to light, many grey areas remain. When I interviewed Hector Munro in late 1980, his memory and recollection of the Parry dimension proved sadly defective. Jonathan Goodman and I tried as best we could to persuade Munro to open up on the subject of Parry, but with little success. For one thing, he was unhappy from a legal point of view about speculating over Parry in case surviving relatives were to seek redress through the courts. Munro had a vague idea that Parry wrote an article for *John Bull* magazine after the case entitled 'I am the man Wallace accused', but neither Goodman nor I can find it.

In a letter to Goodman in November 1980, Munro pointed out that during Wallace's trial the police gave evidence that they had investigated 'all the cases where Wallace alleged that some other person might have committed the crime, and . . . informed the jury that they were satisfied that such allegations were unfounded. The defence had no information to enable cross-examination to be directed to the issue . . .

'As for my late client,' wrote Munro, 'I have always, as you know, believed that his conviction was entirely unsupported by evidence; nor do I believe that he might have been guilty . . . To me, it seems that, even if Parry's alibi could now be shaken, this would not prove guilt of the murder, whatever might be thought by some of the public.

'All I could say would be that Wallace always believed that Parry was guilty, and my recollection is that he had some kind of brush with Parry in a Liverpool street, after the quashing of the verdict . . . It would seem wrong that at this distance of time anyone should unwittingly be allowed to admit supporting an alibi which may have been unfounded if examined more closely than was done by the police.'

Whatever secrets about Parry were known to Hector Munro, they remained intact to the end. In February 1981, a few days before the broadcast of *Conspiracy of Silence*, Munro died in hospital.

6

LOOKING AT THE case now assembled against Gordon Parry, some critics have detected a certain lack of vigour on Munro's part in investigating Parry's role in the Wallace affair. The fact is, of course, that it was no part of Munro's remit. His job was simply to secure an acquittal for Wallace. Against all the odds he did. In my view, the conduct of the defence by both Munro and Roland Oliver was above reproach. But at the very outset of the murder inquiry Wallace was not the prime suspect. It has been assumed down the years that talk of a mystery man – a Mr X – has been over-emphasised by successive writers and researchers. The fact is that from the first day of the investigation until its elimination something like a week later, the top name in the frame was that of Gordon Parry. Everyone has assumed, as I did, that only when Wallace blurted Parry's name to the police in his statement on the evening of Thursday 22 January, 1931, did Parry even figure in the story. Not true. It seems that Wallace gave Parry's name to the police much earlier. In fact, on the murder night itself.

In the spring of 1981, Harry Bailey, son of the detective sergeant involved in the case, confirmed this to me. 'My father told me that Parry was the prime suspect,' said Bailey. 'The police were on to him straight away, turning over his house and his car, which they stripped down at Old Swan. But Parry had an alibi – and it was unshakable.'

Jonathan Goodman, in his account of the case, records a conversation shortly after the trial between Bailey and Sydney Scholefield Allen. 'When I retire,' Bailey reportedly said, 'I'll tell you something about the investigation that will interest you immensely.' But it seems the two men never met again. What was it that Bailey thought would be of such interest? Was it Parry's role in the case? Or something more peripheral, such as the state of one of the detectives in the murder house on the night of the killing, Inspector Herbert Gold.

'Gold was drunk when he arrived at Wolverton Street,' Harry Bailey told me. It was about 10.30 p.m. on the murder night. 'My father, who was sober, had ordered a uniformed bobby guarding the foot of the stairs not to let anyone pass. For some reason the instruction was ignored or forgotten because Gold lurched into the house and went straight upstairs to use the lavatory. How much blood was washed away in the subsequent flushing is impossible to say – possibly none at all, since neither PC Williams nor Hubert Moore noticed any on their odysseys around the house with Wallace. But in grabbing the handle of the lavatory chain to flush the toilet, Gold obliterated the finger-prints of arguably the last person to grasp it: the murderer.'

Subsequent tests revealed two sets of prints: those of Gold and those of William Herbert Wallace.

Wallace was not the only person to point the finger of suspicion at young Gordon Parry. Munro's files on the case contain the following anonymous letter, which plainly although obliquely refers to Parry as 'the youth':

'Dear Sir,

'I trust you will pardon me for not desiring my identity to be known in connection with the writing of this letter, as I have my occupation to think of. I therefore do hope that the letter will not be shewn to a third party for any reason.

'It must be clearly understood that I do not propose to make any definite accusation against any person concerning the case with which you are dealing. All I wish to make to you is a suggestion or two concerning one person.

'Attached to this letter I forward a visiting card, the original owner of the card you will observe is the name of a young lady, but I would direct your attention to the person's handwriting on the back of the card, in pencil. His address is also stated. The card was given to me some two years ago or more when the youth wished to give me his address for business purposes.

'The youth named was, up to a short time ago, an employee of the same Company as Mr W. H. Wallace and I know him exceedingly well, I have been given to understand that while Mr Wallace was incapacitated from work through illness not long ago the youth was assisting in the collection of premiums for Mr Wallace. It is safely assumed that he knew the late Mrs Wallace very, very well. I also understand that he at that time visited the home of Mr Wallace frequently.

'The youth although not now employed by the office concerned has it is suggested been recently asking present agents for the loan of money. You will observe by the printed address on the visiting card that the lady resided at Clubmoor at the time the card was given to me. She was then, and I presume now, the companion of the youth concerned and named on the other side of the card. She then worked as a pianist at a cinema in or about that district close to the home of Mrs Wallace.

'Collection of premiums of most agents almost always finishes on Tuesday evenings each week. It is suggested that an ex-employee must of course be aware of the fact. Could not the real motive of such a crime in the first instance be robbery? If the person was known to the woman and invited into the house and the home was burgled, would not the woman, if alive, be in a position to say the name of the person who called? This of course could not be done in the circumstances which we now know. Mrs Wallace has gone.

'Some employees of the Company would and could I suggest give you an account of the suspicions which surrounded the youth named on the card, when he was working with them. I suggest that a new line of inquiry should be adopted by the police. I suggest that certain inquiries should be made concerning the whereabouts of this youth at the time of the telephone message on that previous night of the tragedy and also at the time the crime was committed on the Tuesday night.

'The youth is known to me and I have seen him since he left the employ of the Company. He possesses a motor car, or perhaps I should say, drives one. He may say that he was out of town on that night, but that of course must be proved if the police were to make inquiries.

'Yes, I know still more concerning the youth and happenings which occurred during his employ in the insurance business, but I consider it not my duty to inform any person of such suspicions. It is the duty of any other person or persons under whose authority he worked.

'Mr Wallace was also known to me. I only knew him as a perfect gentleman and businessman. I know that he was far from being in good health. Finally, I feel and express to you that in my humble opinion Mr Wallace could not possibly have the physical strength to do the deed of which he is accused, neither could he have the reasoning power to premeditate such a crime on his own wife.'

Whoever wrote this letter, it certainly was not Wallace. It is undated, but evidently written after his arrest, because it is addressed to Hector Munro. The writer used a typewriter, an instrument not normally available to prisoners on remand at Walton Gaol. It goes without saying that a copy of the letter would have been forwarded to the police without delay.

7

I CAN QUITE SEE that in many ways it seems a pity to spoil a perfectly good mystery by claiming to have solved it. In my own defence, I have to point again to the fact that I am by no means the first to make such a claim. As we have seen, the line of accusers stretches all the way back to Wallace himself. Here is the entry from Wallace's personal diary dated 14 September 1931, four months after his release:

'Just as I was going to dinner Parry stopped me and said he wanted to talk to me for a few minutes. It was a desperately awkward position. Eventually I decided not to hear what he had to say. I told him I would talk to him someday and give him something to think about. He must realise that I suspect him of the terrible crime. I fear I let him see clearly what I thought, and it may unfortunately put him on his guard. I wonder if it is any good putting a private detective on to his track in the hope of something coming to light. I am more than half persuaded to try it.'

Wallace never did. Many unpleasant facts have come to light since then, and the case against Parry has been considerably strengthened. But there are those who remain unconvinced.

One, a man called Jimmy Tattersall from the Sefton Park area of Liverpool, telephoned me a few days after the broadcast of *Conspiracy of Silence*. When I met him in a pub on Lodge Lane a day or so later, he was angry and scornful. 'Gordon Parry a killer?' he barked into his beer. 'You're joking, aren't you? He wasn't a violent man at all. In fact, he'd have fainted at the sight of blood.'

We talked for an hour.

'I was a big mate of Parry's in the twenties and thirties,' Tattersall said. 'He was a well-groomed lad, dandified I suppose you'd say. We were at Lister Drive School together. To be honest, I suppose the pair of us were a bit snooty. And a bit toffee-nosed. But when I left school I had to come down to earth, whereas I don't think Gordon really ever did.

'After school I worked for an electrical wholesaler at the top of Stanley Street. Sometimes Gordon and I would meet at a place called the Café Nord, a basement in North John Street, a bit like the old Kardomah. By this time Gordon was courting Lily Lloyd (they'd met at Lister Drive) and I was keen on her sister Daphne. They were both lovely girls.'

From his top pocket Tattersall drew a fragile and yellowing piece of folded newsprint. It was a cutting from the *Daily Mirror*, dated September 1935, and contained a picture of Daphne Lloyd kissing her new husband, an Italian musician named Salvatore Caminata, after their wedding at St Mary's Church in Liverpool's West Derby district. Daphne was indeed a lovely girl. The caption to a similar photograph published in a Liverpool newspaper, and which Tattersall also produced, said Daphne had been a member of the famous Ziegfeld Follies in New York and at the time of her marriage was in cabaret in London.

Tattersall stared at the pictures for several moments.

'Trouble was,' he said, finally breaking his reverie, 'Gordon was always short of money. He'd always be borrowing off me. Mind you I'd always get it back prompt. I always used to have a bit of money on me because I was very careful and never used to waste it.'

With another pint of beer he added, 'Of course, in those days, young people like us didn't go boozing or clubbing it, y'know. There was nothing like that. All the same, we managed to have a pretty good time.' Jimmy Tattersall's sagging face seemed to lighten a little. 'Gordon and I used to take girls walking up the middle of Muirhead Avenue. And we'd take the odd tart to Newsham Park. We both came from respectable families, though, and we had to be careful.'

Although Tattersall had fixed the interview with the idea of repairing some of the damage done to Gordon Parry's character in the course of two radio programmes, I discovered that he was obliging me with a number of facts that squared neatly with many of the anti-Parry points which had hitherto remained a little hazy. Like his habitual lack of money. And his way with women. But what about the crucial point concerning Parry's car? Jimmy Tattersall screwed up his eyes and tried to think back. 'I don't remember that he had his own car,' he said at last. 'But he certainly knew that if he did have one, or the use of one, he could pick up tarts.' ('Tarts' is a pejorative Liverpool expression meaning all nubile women, not just prostitutes. Tattersall never explained precisely what he meant by the word.) 'I had a company car, and felt like a lord,' he said. 'But as for sex,' he added, not that I had asked, 'well, you didn't have to have sex to really fancy a girl. A jump was a bonus, of course, but not the be-all and end-all.'

We spoke at length about the Wallace affair. Throughout, Tattersall dismissed the idea that Parry may have been the killer. 'I remember meeting Wallace once. Parry introduced me to him. This was before the murder, in town somewhere, possibly the City Café. After the killing I remember thinking that Wallace looked much too fragile to murder his wife. And Parry, I remember, said it was very sad that Wallace had been accused of the murder.'

Tattersall willingly let me have the loan of a number of original newspaper cuttings featuring prominently the name of Richard Gordon Parry. All were reports of court cases, and all were familiar to me, except one. It was dated 1932, and appeared in one of the two Liverpool evening papers of the period. Parry had admitted three charges of stealing money from telephone kiosks in Liverpool cafés, and was fined £15. Parry had asked the court to take into consideration two offences of taking away motor cars and two further offences of stealing money from phone boxes. In court, Parry said, 'I now realise the serious nature of the offences and my foolishness.' He pleaded for leniency, and promised that he would never offend again. Of course, it was a promise he never kept.

'Parry wasn't a violent man,' said Jimmy Tattersall before we parted. 'In fact, he'd have run away from a fight. He'd have fainted at the sight of blood. I admit he and I were a couple of bad lads. But there's a difference between pinching money out of phone boxes and pinching cars and killing someone.

'Isn't there?'

* * *

Despite Jimmy Tattersall's attempts at a character reference, there seems little doubt that at the time of the killing Gordon Parry was mobile, broke and angry at Wallace for reporting his professional misdemeanours to his chiefs at the Prudential. These facets of Parry can now be usefully assessed alongside Wallace's own thoughts and suspicions, as set down in Wallace's life story, serialised in the spring of 1932 in *John Bull* magazine:

'Now let me say this.

'I know the murderer.

'. . . He killed Mrs Wallace with such savagery that he is capable of and had reason for attempting to remove me before I complete the only mission I have left in life – to place him in the dock where I stood, and in the condemned cell I occupied.

'I will reconstruct the crime from the knowledge I have since obtained.

'I do not for a moment suggest that because the Court of Criminal Appeal quashed my conviction the police would regard their dignity as publicly hurt if they now arrested the murderer.

'Yet I feel bitter because, since my acquittal, they refuse to give my lawyer or myself any information as to whether, and how far, they have carried on any investigation.

'I must have been well known to the man who took my wife's life.

'In the days that followed Mrs Wallace's death, when I was searching, possibly as intensely as the police, for a clue to the identity of the murderer, my private thoughts were often focused on the man.

'I did not then mentally convict him. I innocently believed that to establish a charge of murder against anyone, justice demanded the known presence of a motive.

'How sorely I was to be disillusioned when my own life was at stake! With what mixed memories of my decision not to implicate this man did I listen to the prosecuting counsel confessing that he could not show any reason why I should commit the murder, yet demanding all the same that I should hang.

'Even after my liberty was given back to me it was some time before I could connect my suspect with the crime. There were many circumstances by which I could deduce his guilt, but my idea of fair play still demanded that I should be able to show his motive for committing the crime.

'Then at last I discovered why he went to my house and killed my wife. He must have known my haunts, and it was easy for him to be sure when I would be at my chess club to receive the telephone message by which he lured me away from the neighbourhood of my home. In the large café which accommodates the club there is posted a list of forthcoming matches, the players, the hour and the date.

'The murder took place on a Tuesday night. Often I had in my house on Tuesdays as much as £100 of my employers' money, which I paid in weekly on Wednesdays.

'He must have got to know this, and also that the money was usually kept in a cashbox and where the box always was.

'When I left the house, he would have been watching to see me depart.

'It was my wife's rigid rule not to admit strangers into the house when she was alone, and to this day it has been a cause for speculation how the man actually made his way inside. He must have been ready with a pretext to be allowed to wait until I returned.

'He followed my wife into the sitting room, and as she bent down and lit the gas-fire he struck her, possibly with a spanner. The implement of murder was never discovered.

'He now had to kill her. To strike her again while she lay on the floor and him standing over her would mean the upward spurting of blood.

'Two strides took him into the lobby, where he had observed my mackintosh hanging, and he held it as a shield between him and her body while he belaboured her to death.

'She must have been felled as soon as she lit the fire and before she could regulate the flow of gas. It would have been at full blaze, and as he bent at the fireplace the flame set alight the mackintosh.

'Then he would see that the bottom edge of her skirt was burning and, throwing the mackintosh down, he must have dragged her away from the fire and on to a part of the coat, leaving her in the position I found her.

'So intimate was the knowledge he had gained of my affairs that I can picture his surprise when he broke open the cupboard and cashbox and found only £4 on a Tuesday night.

'The reason there was only £4 in the house was that at the end of the previous week I had not made my usual heavy insurance collections because I was in bed, as the police satisfied themselves, with a fever. And most of the money I had taken on the other days of the week had been disbursed to health insurance claimants. Of these facts the murderer was not aware.

'Only now do I know that at the time of the crime he was in desperate straits. And I have found that he had been convicted for offences involving money. Today report reaches me that his appearance suggests mental disturbance and deterioration.

'I have no doubt whatever in my mind that he was the man who murdered my poor wife. I think with horror at the very thought of the brutality he displayed . . . If I had ever reason to seek the death of my wife I could not have used such methods as those by which she died. I have been a teacher of science and chemistry, and at the time of the tragedy I had at my command, even in my house, materials by which with a score of methods her end could have been brought about painlessly and without attracting suspicion.

'If I were to die tomorrow I would have only one wish – to see the murderer brought to justice and this terrible stigma removed from me. Revenge will not bring my dear wife back again, but I shall be satisfied if justice is done.'

8

S INCE THE WALLACE programmes were first broadcast on Radio City, and shortly afterwards by the London news and information station LBC, in the early months of 1981, many listeners – including a fair proportion of unbelievers – have said that the real value of the programmes lay in the authentic testimony of the many people we traced who actually had a part to play in the Wallace story. I admit that I was surprised to find so many of these people still alive, ready, willing and able to go on tape with their views, recollections and, in some of the most valuable instances, their evidence. In this last category I group Douglas Metcalf and his surviving friends from Richmond Park in 1931, Allison Wildman and Harold Jones.

My aim in rooting out such people was to have the Wallace programme transcend the usual 'scissors and paste' approach, in other words, simply retelling a fairly well-known story using archive material from press cuttings and books. My feeling is that by reaching back half a century to as many real people as possible the Wallace drama truly lived again. Sometimes we were able to push the story forward a little, but not always.

Sometimes luck was with us, but not always. How was it done? Here are just a couple of examples of how we researched specific aspects of the Wallace story.

Of the four people who spoke to Qualtrough in the course of his telephone call to the Central Chess Club, only one to my knowledge was still alive. Lilian Kelly, now living in New York State, was the operator at the Anfield Telephone Exchange who connected the call. 'The procedure in those days,' she told me, 'was that you lifted the receiver, asked the operator for the number you wanted, the operator connected you and said "Go ahead please", and the caller then pressed button A, which caused the money to be taken and the connection to be made.

'What happened when Qualtrough tried the first time was that he picked up the receiver and spoke to my friend Louisa Alfreds at the exchange and asked for Bank 3581. She made the connection, said "Go ahead please" and moved on to her next call. But a moment later the caller was back on to the exchange, and this time I took the call. He had obviously pressed the wrong button [button B instead of button A] and had cut himself off. The reason I remembered it was because he'd pressed the wrong button, and had paid his money but not received his correspondent. I said to Louisa Alfreds sitting next to me that this man had just been on before. Anyway I tried the Bank number twice. The first time the number was engaged, but the second time it rang.

'When he spoke the voice sounded like a perfectly normal man's voice. There was nothing peculiar about it that I can remember. It was a calm voice, very calm, certainly no sign of agitation or nervousness. I remember exactly what he said to me: "Operator, I have pressed button B but have not had my correspondent yet." Later of course I heard Wallace speak at the trial, but I could not have sworn that it was the same man.'

Of the exchange supervisor, Annie Robertson, and the City Café waitress, Gladys Harley, I can find no trace. And the trail leading to the chess club captain, Samuel Beattie, arguably the most crucial witness in the story, quickly cooled. At the time of the trial Beattie was living in a substantial semi-detached house in Ballantrae Road, Mossley Hill, a salubrious district close to Calderstones Park. From there he travelled daily to his office opposite the Cotton Exchange in central Liverpool, where he worked as a cotton broker's manager.

One of the stories that came my way while researching the case was one to the effect that in the weeks and months following the trial Beattie brooded more and more over the true identity of the man to whom he spoke on that fateful night. The brooding turned to depression, then eventually, the story went, Beattie's mind was overwhelmed with doubt, and he suffered a mental breakdown from which he never recovered. The story may be all or partly fancy, but it was a fact that the company for which he worked ceased trading four years after the Wallace case.

I eventually traced a woman who lived next door to the Beatties shortly after the case. She recalled the family moving to Ballantrae Road from Warbreck Moor on the other side of Liverpool. 'They were a very happy-go-lucky family,' she told me, 'with a great sense of humour, always laughing and enjoying life. They made their own music in the evenings, and very often we would be lulled to sleep by their music.

'If Mr Beattie suffered a nervous breakdown, he showed no sign of this. I never discussed the Wallace case with Mr Beattie, but must have heard later that he had been very distressed at having spoken to the man on the telephone.'

And so the trail to Beattie went cold. There was a suggestion that not long after the trial the family moved to one of the period squares in Toxteth, that Samuel Beattie's daughter had opened a nursing home, either in Liverpool or across the river in Wirral. Of course, the idea that Beattie himself was still alive was, and is, a very long shot indeed. There is no official record in the defence papers as to his age in 1931, but my understanding is that he was well into middle age. I still find it hard to believe that not one writer immediately after the case bothered to press Beattie about his thoughts on the identity of the caller Qualtrough. And sadly I suspect that the chance to do so has long since passed us by.

While some people like the delivery boy Metcalf were comparatively easy to trace, others proved far more elusive. One especially: Florence MacFall, widow of Professor MacFall. I already knew that she was many years younger than her husband; this was confirmed by a wedding-day picture dated 1935 from the files of the *Liverpool Daily Post* and *Echo*. But I could find no trace of her in the telephone directory, and no one at Liverpool University, where Professor MacFall had worked, could help. So I discovered MacFall's last address before his death, a retirement house in a village near Holywell in North Wales. I called there one afternoon in March 1982 and over the garden gate spoke about the MacFalls with the present occupant, a retired headmaster. He knew of the Wallace case, and of my programme, recalling Parry's name with no prompting from me. I asked him to make inquiries with his bank, in the hope that the deeds of the house might lead me in the right direction.

Three weeks later the headmaster called me at work with the name of the solicitors in Warrington who had dealt with the sale of the house after MacFall's death. Of these lawyers there was no trace, but there was one other piece of information: the name and address of MacFall's bank in Liverpool. I called one of the managers and a quick check on the computer showed that the branch still had a customer called Mrs F. M. MacFall. I wrote to her care of the bank, but never received a reply.

I can understand the fears of Mrs MacFall (now an elderly lady) about becoming involved in yet another examination of her late husband's role in such a controversial case. There are probably a score of reasons why she did not respond to my request for an interview. But at the end of the day her refusal to talk to me leaves any rational criticism of the medical aspects of the case completely undefended.

In the original Wallace programme the former Home Office pathologist Dr Charles St Hill argued eloquently against Wallace's complicity in the murder of his wife. First, there was the timing: if Alan Close's first statement that he saw Mrs Wallace alive at 6.45 p.m. was correct, it would have been impossible, St Hill maintained, for Wallace to have murdered her. And there were other reasons for thinking Wallace was innocent.

It was unlikely that someone like Wallace would have foreseen a profusion of splashing blood. The absence of blood on Wallace was a strong point in his favour. If he had pulled his wife's bloodstained head away with his hand, it must have been saturated with blood. And, St Hill argued, there MUST have been traces of blood under the killer's fingernails. No blood had been found either on the cabinet or the cashbox it contained. This was probably because, after murdering Julia Wallace, the thief had pulled on a pair of gloves to hide his fingerprints.

St Hill also pondered the method used for the murder. Wallace was an amateur chemist and of slight physique. Surely, St Hill reasoned, he would have poisoned rather than killed his wife in one of the most brutal ways available. The Qualtrough telephone call had been staged to ensure that it would be traced, casting suspicion on Wallace.

Although to my mind these points amount to an overwhelming case in Wallace's favour, I have since sought a second opinion from one of Britain's most eminent criminal pathologists. Professor Keith Simpson. Nowadays, he told me, no one could rely on the progress of rigor mortis to estimate the time of death, 'for it has been shown to be far too unreliable a basis. Even temperature measurements have to be given at least one hour, probably nearer two, on each side of the probable peak time.

'So MacFall – not himself a specialist in forensic pathology – was wrong to rely on it. Rigor is far too variable in its onset and course. Indeed, sometimes it never follows even the rough rules, and occasionally may never develop at all. Modern practice seldom pays much attention to it – indeed faults lie not only in its irregularities, but also in its detection. It's just done by feel, and plainly very, very unreliable.'

So how should it be done? Professor Simpson says it is when the body's heat loss (under the particular circumstances), the rigor and the eyeball fluid chemistry, and the passage of food into the duodenum ALL coincide, that a significant time can be fixed as the 'peak probability'.

Professor Simpson added, 'MacFall would be strongly cross-examined nowadays, and his fellow pathologists would urge him to be much more wary about giving an exact time. It is one of the really "boggy" areas of forensic medicine.'

In the light of Professor Simpson's comments, I checked back on MacFall's forensic report on Julia Wallace's body, to see if any observation had been made about the passage of food. Only one sentence made any reference at all to the subject. 'The stomach,' wrote MacFall, 'contained about four ounces of semifluid food consisting of currants, raisins and unmasticated lumps of carbohydrate.' These, presumably, were the remains of the meal eaten by Mrs Wallace and her husband before his departure for Menlove Gardens and her encounter with the killer.

Today, the only man left alive who had a central part to play at Wallace's trial is Leslie Walsh, Junior Crown Counsel to the late Edward Hemmerde KC. In 1931 Walsh, like defence solicitor Hector Munro, had just got married. As in Munro's case, it was Walsh's first murder trial. 'I was twenty-seven at the time,' he told me when we spoke in October 1980, 'and, admittedly I was a little green. But there was, and is, no doubt in my mind that Wallace was guilty.'

Walsh lives in retirement with his wife in the pleasant Manchester suburb of Urmston. A small, puckish and affable man, he spent most of his career not at the Bar but sitting as a stipendiary (full-time) magistrate, first in Salford, and briefly later in Greater Manchester. He told me that I was the first journalist ever to approach him for his views on the case, and appeared just a little flattered. We spoke of Jonathan Goodman's scriptural account of the case, *The Killing of Julia Wallace*. On Goodman's assertion that Hemmerde was set on winning the case for the Crown to further his own career, Walsh was scathing.

'Absolute rubbish,' he snorted, over a tray of tea and homemade cakes. 'If that were so why did he leave so much of the spadework to me, his junior barrister and a complete novice at murder trials? I found myself doing a lot of the examination of witnesses – admittedly not the crucial ones – while Hemmerde himself was actually elsewhere in the building in another court appearing on a civil case totally unconnected with this so-called crucial trial. He was often out of the court on this other case, and only seemed to come back to conduct the examination-in-chief of crucial and important witnesses, and to conduct the cross-examination of others.'

On the efficiency of the Liverpool CID he commented, 'I visited the murder house on a couple of occasions and attended, with Hemmerde, a number of pre-trial conferences with Superintendent Moore and other officers. At no time did we, as the prosecution team, feel that the police work was anything other than satisfactory. I can't remember having any qualms whatsoever about their integrity, or quality or capacity. Certainly, Hemmerde didn't.

'Nor,' said Walsh, leaning forward in his chair to make the point, 'was there one word of criticism of the police from the defence.'

Walsh believes implacably in Wallace's guilt. 'Suggestions to the contrary are interesting in themselves,' he said, 'but totally baseless in fact.'

For example, the crucial point about the timing. 'We have the milk boy, Close, saying that he called at the house at 6.30 or maybe 6.45, and that Mrs Wallace came to the door and spoke to him about his cough. I don't think either Hemmerde or I believed that for a minute. The person he spoke to was Wallace. Wallace had forgotten about the milk boy calling, and hadn't expected him. It was Wallace. Wearing one of his wife's dresses.'

But what about the fact that Wallace was well over a foot taller than his wife, wore glasses and had a moustache?

'It was dark, and anyway the encounter probably lasted only a few seconds.'

And Wallace impersonated his wife's voice? I was simply incredulous.

'Yes. You can do it. I can do it.'

Walsh obliged with a brief, fluting obbligato.

'The prosecution couldn't say all that at the trial of course, because Close was a prosecution witness and to have challenged his story would have weakened our case.'

On another point in the evidence he argued that 'Wallace said that on discovering the body of his wife, he walked round it to light the gas at the side of the fire. Yet he had not a single spot of blood on his shoes or clothing, despite the fact that the room was drenched with it. The fact was that the gas was already lit. It would have been impossible to walk into that room and not get blood on your feet, and do what he did without knocking the furniture over. I tried to myself some weeks later, when the bloodstains were still on the carpet. I had to do a little dance to step round from the door to the gas avoiding any blood. And that was with the lights up.'

Leslie Walsh vividly recollects his feelings as the trial progressed. 'Both Hemmerde and I considered it was going well. As for Oliver, for the defence, I wouldn't say he was gloomy, but he was sure the jury would convict. Scholefield Allen, his junior, would never give an opinion. But when we were all in London for the appeal, I asked Allen what he really thought. And he said he thought Wallace was guilty.

'On the third day of the trial, the Friday, I spoke to Oliver during the adjournment for afternoon tea. We were walking up and down the corridor and I asked him what he thought of the case. He said – and I can remember his exact words – he said: "There is no doubt in my mind that Wallace is guilty, and there is no doubt that the jury will convict, but they ought not to."

'Some time after the case I met the trial judge, Mr Justice Wright, at Manchester Assizes. He, too, said he'd been convinced of Wallace's guilt. But he did add that he didn't think the prosecution had proved it.'

There was a twinkle in Walsh's eye. But he is a jolly man, and believes what he says.

Today, a dwindling number of Liverpudlians survive to recount their recollections of the Wallace case. One of them is George Holt, who moved to Anfield at the age of three.

'People who weren't around during the first three decades of the century have no idea of the poverty that existed then. There were no cars or continental holidays: a penny to Seaforth was the fare to the shore.

'One of my earliest memories was of my father taking me to see the German band that used to play on Saturday nights in the summer before the Great War. During these visits I probably caught my first glance of Wolverton Street. It was always a quiet street, with a strange sort of magnified silence.

'When I was young I used to think of Wallace as the tallest man in the world, mainly because he was so terribly thin. The femur is the longest bone in the body, but with Wallace it was the tibia that seemed the longest. Walking, he appeared to put his foot down with a slight stamp, an action executed with thought and not unconsciously.

'In the phone box, Qualtrough was just six strides across Rochester Road from the Cabbage Hall picture house, now Liverpool FC Supporters Club. In those days the cinema was a blaze of light. The running time of a tram from Cabbage Hall to Lord Street was eighteen minutes, then a two-minute walk to the chess club. If, by chance, Wallace had retained his ticket that night, the case could have collapsed. It was nine minutes running time by tram from Cabbage Hall to the time clock at Eastbourne Street in Everton. All trams going into town had to punch that clock. Had the police followed up the tram inquiries, it could not have proved Wallace guilty, of course, but it could have proved him innocent.

'Had the tram passed the time clock before seven thirty, the case against Wallace would have crumbled.

'On the murder afternoon Wallace called on Mrs Brinley Richards, wife of my Uncle Ben. She said he was his normal self. She paid him, he thanked her and said he would see her in three weeks' time.

'In 1959, just before he died, I visited Uncle Ben in hospital and he began to talk about the Wallace case. The point in his mind that cast most doubt on Wallace's guilt was how, if he were the villain, he managed to win his chess match. He agreed that the people of Liverpool had nothing to be proud of in the way they'd treated Wallace. And, on reflection, he now agreed with the Appeal Court judgment. Heaven help us, he said, if a man were to lose his life on such flimsy evidence.

'I thought how wonderful it was to see a sick man at the age of eighty rearranging his mental furniture, when Uncle Ben turned to me with a half-smile and a nod of his head, and added, "But he done it all right!"'

Les Hill is rather younger than George Holt, and remembers more of Gordon Parry than Wallace.

'My family lived next door to the Parrys at the time of the Wallace case. We had very little to do with them to be honest, but I do remember that like his father, Gordon Parry was a loner. He never seemed to have any friends. He and I were at Lister Drive School together. He had a great reputation as an actor and a singer.'

Hill knew that Gordon Parry was an unpleasant character, and recalled his getting into trouble with the police for stealing money from telephone boxes. 'He tried to borrow money as well,' said Hill. 'Stan Oliver, who was a junior detective on the case, remembered Parry going into his [Oliver's] mother's shop in Moscow Drive to try to borrow cash, without success.' Michael Green traced Oliver to South Africa and wrote to him for information. The letter went unanswered.

'As for the murder,' Hill continued, 'I know Parry was questioned. He was interviewed for about three hours at Atkinson's Garage. [Neither Parkes nor the Atkinsons mentioned this interview to either Green or myself.] My father told me many years ago that there was a senior police officer at Old Swan who was absolutely convinced that Parry did the murder.'

Les Hill could not recall Gordon Parry having his own car. He did remember a dark blue car, possibly a Morris Oxford, owned by Parry's father and kept in the road outside the house or in an entry across the road. 'But I know that from time to time Gordon drove his father's car. I saw him.'

In March 1981 a Liverpool Labour MP, Robert Parry, tabled a parliamentary question to the then Home Secretary, William Whitelaw. Mr Parry asked Mr Whitelaw to call for a report from Merseyside's Chief Constable, Kenneth Oxford, on the reasons why he declined to release information held by the police relating to the Wallace murder. And, added Mr Parry, would the Home Secretary make a statement? No, came the reply from the Home Office. This is a matter for the Chief Constable.

I was grateful to Mr Parry for taking up the quest on my behalf, but I cannot say I was surprised at the official response. What did surprise me, though, was the MP's sudden change of stripes just ten days later. According to a report in the *Liverpool Daily Post*, Mr Parry was demanding the police clear the name of his dead (and unrelated) namesake following the Wallace programmes broadcast on Radio City. Mr Parry condemned the radio station for taking the unprecedented step of naming a possible suspect when the man himself was dead and unable to defend himself. 'This must never happen again,' said Mr Parry, adding that he had asked Chief Constable Oxford to make public anything in the Wallace murder file which could clear this man (as distinct from anything which could finally identify Gordon Parry as the killer). Robert Parry's efforts to winkle anything at all out of Mr Oxford or his Wallace murder file met with as little success as my own.

9

I DO NOT SAY that everything we now know about Gordon Parry squares with his having been the killer of Julia Wallace. I admit there are several inconsistencies, even contradictions, but until the Home Office allows access to their file on the case it is not possible to say how many of these can be cleared up and accounted for. But even given such a facility, how does it explain the quite extraordinary assumption that a guilty Parry lived with his appalling secret for almost half a century? Was there no one down the years in whom he confided, with whom he shared his terrible burden? Whether he was guilty or not, I am firmly convinced that the key to the mystery lies with Lily Lloyd. She admits being with Parry during the latter part of the murder night. She would have observed his demeanour, his composure – or lack of it – and his appearance. Did a panicking Parry blurt out the truth, as he appears to have done to a mere acquaintance, the garage hand Parkes? Did he swear her to lifelong secrecy and, when jilted a couple of years later, and having hastened to Wallace's lawyer, did she seek to demolish the faked alibi in a heartbroken fit of pique? It seems we will never know.

Summing up, there are several important points that, in my submission, add up to a damaging case against Gordon Parry:

1. He had two motives, one for a simple robbery, to avenge Wallace's 'treachery' in reporting his accounting discrepancies; and a second for murder, to silence the sole witness of his bungled attempt at theft. Wallace claimed that Parry was hard up at the time of the killing.

2. He had the means: the ability, as an amateur actor, to have disguised his voice convincingly during the telephone call; the use of a car to get to and from Wolverton Street; and access to a murder weapon, either something to hand in the house, or an implement he took there himself.

3. He had opportunity: he knew where Wallace's insurance takings were kept, was virtually assured of being admitted to the house by Mrs Wallace, and knew that Wallace himself would be out of the way long enough to commit robbery without risk of interruption.

4. After the killing, Parry claimed at least three different alibis, the first (reportedly to the police) that he had spent the evening with friends, one of whom, Lily Lloyd, he named; the second (to his father) that he was fixing his car in Breck Road; the third (to Goodman and Whittington-Egan) that he had been arranging a birthday celebration with friends.

5. Parry, named to the police by Wallace, was evidently the strongest initial suspect.

6. His antecedents, a history of pilfering, car stealing and his alleged violent nature, weigh against him.

7. Lily Lloyd stands by her 1933 version of events, admitting that Parry did not join her until late on the murder night, late enough to deprive Parry of an alibi for the time of the killing.

8. The substantial new evidence of John Parkes concerning Parry's visit to Atkinson's Garage, recounted for no reward or inducement other than 'to get it off my mind after all these years'.

It seems to me that there is no more to be done about clearing up the Wallace mystery until such time as the missing documents from the police file are located or the Home Office releases the complete contents. It may or may not contain the solution. It may be that Lily Lloyd will one day relent, break her silence, and settle the matter once and for all. There may be someone else, hitherto unidentified, who can unlock the central secret and who, in the light of this book and the radio programmes from which it developed, may be persuaded to do so.

In 1931, had the Court of Criminal Appeal ruled against Wallace, I am convinced that an innocent man would have gone to the scaffold. In the event, an appalling miscarriage of justice was averted, but only just. Years after the case, Lord Kilmuir, who later became Lord Chancellor, declared that there was no practical possibility of an innocent man being hanged in Britain, and that anyone who thought there was, was moving in the realms of fantasy. Happily, the point is now academic; the likelihood of the death penalty being restored in cases of this kind is extremely remote.

As for Gordon Parry, no one can say for a certainty that had he been tried for the murder of Julia Wallace the result would have been a conviction. Had he denied the charge we can only speculate about the nature of his defence. But I submit that had the evidence available today been produced at the Liverpool Spring Assizes in 1931, the outcome would not have been in doubt. In the event, no one was subsequently charged with the murder, and the case remains, technically, unsolved. To that extent, it was the perfect murder.

Postscript

Today in Anfield the trams and the gaslights are gone, but the shades of Julia and Herbert Wallace may still be found in the windy corners and shop doorways in Breck Road. They move imperceptibly amid the shabby crowds, the ungovernable children scampering across its dreary wastes and pinched perspectives.

The house in Wolverton Street, indeed the street itself, has scarcely changed. Campbell's dance hall, which used to stand at the end of the street, has gone. But that is all. Occasionally, at weekends, a car will turn into the street from Richmond Park and pull up outside number 29. But the people who come in search of the Wallace house are invariably disappointed. The present owners have painted the place peach and cream and smartened up the windows with crisp white nets. The young couple living there discourage visitors. So the Sunday afternoon pilgrims stare at the place for a few moments, then they drive away in search of somewhere to have a cup of tea.

If they drove into the centre of Liverpool it is unlikely that they would notice the site of the old City Café. But the door is still there, beneath a Grecian-style portico, at number 24 North

John Street, and so are the steps that used to lead down to the basement café. Nowadays, someone has opened a record store there, and the telephone kiosk has gone.

In Dale Street, the entrance to the magistrates' court has been modernised and glassed in, but upstairs the courtrooms themselves have changed little in fifty years. Seldom are queues reported for the public seats. Most murder cases these days are as bleak and mundane as the weekly appearances of the Friday-night drunks. But you can still buy the *Echo* at the kiosk next door.

South of the city, in leafy Allerton, Menlove Gardens is still a three-sided affair. Green and cream Atlantean buses will still set you down in Menlove Avenue, near the corner of Menlove Gardens West.

And on an autumn evening with dusk coming on, I walk where Wallace walked, thousands of nights before, each of us in search of ghosts. And across more than half a century, my fingertips touch his.

Appendix 1

Wallace's First Statement to the Police

Anfield Detective Office, Tuesday 20 January, 1931

William Herbert Wallace says: –

I am 52 years and by occupation an Insurance Agent for the Prudential Assurance Co, Dale Street. I have resided at 29 Wolverton Street with my wife Julia (deceased) age, believed 52 years, for the past 16 years. There is no children of the marriage my wife and I have been on the best of terms all our married life. At 10.30 a.m. to-day I left the house, leaving my wife indoors, doing her household duties. I went on my insurance rounds in Clubmoor district. My last call being 177 Lisburn Lane, shortly before 2 p.m. I then took a tram car to Trinity Church, Breck Road, arriving at my house at 2.10 p.m. My wife was then well and I had dinner and left the house at about 3.15 p.m. I then returned to Clubmoor and continued my collections, finishing at about 5.55 p.m. My last call being either 19 or 21 Eastman Road. I boarded a bus at Queen's Drive and Townsend Avenue, alighted at Cabbage Hall and walked up to my house at about 6.5 p.m. I entered my house by the back door, which is my usual practice, and then had tea with my wife, she was quite well and then I left the house at 6.45 p.m. leaving by the back door. I caught a car from Belmont Road and West Derby Road and got off at Lodge Lane and Smithdown Road, and boarded a Smithdown Road car to Penny Lane. I then boarded another car up Menlove Avenue West [*sic*], looking for 25 Menlove Avenue East [*sic*], where I have [*sic*] an appointment with Mr A. M. Qualtrough [*sic*] for 7.30 p.m. in connection with my insurance business I was unable to find the address and I enquired at 25 Menlove Avenue West [*sic*] and I also asked at the bottom of Green Lane, Allerton, a Constable about the address. He told me there was no such an address. I then called at Post Office near the Plaza Cinema, to look at the directory but there was none there, and I was unable to find the address. I also visited a newsagent's there where there was a directory, but I was unable to find the address. It was then 8 p.m. and I caught a tramcar to Lodge Lane and then a car to West Derby Road and Belmont Road and walked home from there.

I arrived at Wolverton Street about 8.45 p.m. and I pulled out my key and went to open the front door and found it secure and could not open it with my key. I knocked gentle but got no answer. I could not see any light in the house. I then went around the back, the door leading from the entry to the back yard was closed but not bolted. I went into the back door of the house and I was unable to get in, I do not know if the door was bolted or not, it sticks sometimes, but I think the door was bolted, but I am not sure. There was a small light in the back kitchen, but no light in the kitchen. I then went back to the front. I was suspicious because I expected my wife to be in, and the light on in the kitchen. I tried my key in the front door again and found the lock did not work properly. The key would turn in it, but seemed to unturn without unlocking the door. I rushed around to the back, and saw my neighbours, Mr and Mrs Johnstone, [*sic*] coming out of 31 Wolverton Street. I said to them 'Have you heard any suspicious noises in my house during the past hour or so.' Mrs Johnstone [*sic*] said They hadn't. I said then, I couldn't get in and asked them if they would wait a while while I tried again. I then found the back kitchen door opened quite easily. I walked in by the back kitchen door. I found kitchen light out, I lit it and found signs of disturbance in the kitchen a wooden case in which I keep photographic stuff in had been broken open and the lid was on the floor. I then went upstairs and entered the middle bedroom, but saw nothing unusual. I then entered the bathroom but this was correct. I then entered the back room and found no disturbance there. I then entered the front room, struck a match and found the bed upset. The clothes being off. I don't think my wife left it like that. I then came down and looked into the front room, after striking a match and saw my wife lying on the floor. I felt her hand and concluded she was dead. I then rushed out and told my Mr and Mrs Johnstone [*sic*] what had happened saying something but I cannot remember what I did say. After my neighbours had been in Mr Johnstone [*sic*] went for the Police and a Doctor, I asked him to go. I afterwards found that about £4 had been taken from a cash box in the kitchen but I am not sure of the amount. When I discovered my wife lying on the floor I noticed my macintosh [*sic*] lying on the floor at the back of her. I wore the macintosh [*sic*] up to noon today, but left it off owing to the fine weather. My wife has never worn the macintosh [*sic*] to my knowledge. You drew my attention to it being burnt, but it was not like that when I last saw it and I cannot explain it. I have no suspicion of anyone.

Signed William Herbert WALLACE.

There was a dog whip with a lash in the house which I have not seen for 12 months, but I have not found it up to now. It usually hung on the hall stand. The handle was wood, 12" long and 1" thick, I don't think there was any metal about it.

Appendix 2

The Wallace Diaries

The writings of William Herbert Wallace fall into three main categories: his private diary, containing entries in the years before the murder and several others made in the months that followed it; his 'life story', ghosted after the appeal by a Fleet Street journalist; and a series of five articles, again ghosted, which appeared in the *John Bull* magazine in the spring of 1932 under the title 'The Man They Did Not Hang'. Half a century later, Wallace's writing style (and that of his Boswell, a newspaper man called George Munro) seems a trifle prissy and self-important. W. F. Wyndham-Brown, the author of *The Trial of William Herbert Wallace*, has a point, however, when he attributes to Wallace 'a power of lucid and accurate, and even, at times, picturesque expression much above that of the average man'.

Wallace's diaries have disappeared, mislaid – according to Jonathan Goodman, who tried to trace them in the late sixties – by Wyndham-Brown, who selected only a handful of entries for inclusion in his 1933 book on the case. The pre-murder entries are, presumably, contemporaneous; those dated during the investigation, trial and appeal were probably written up sometime later. All the extant entries are reproduced here without comment, other than brief notes explaining the context.

1929

13 February: On the way home with —— had a discussion on religion. I find he is like myself indifferent to the dogmas and ritual of the Churches and Chapels, and agrees that if there is a hereafter the man without any so-called religious beliefs, and a non-church attender, but who lives a decent life, and who abstains from telling lies, or cheating, or acts of meanness, and who honestly tries to do good, has as much chance of getting there as the professed Christian who attends his place of worship regularly.

29 March: Listened in to *The Master Builder* by Ibsen. This is a fine thing and shows clearly how a man may build up a fine career, and as the world has it, be a great success, and yet in his own mind feels that he has been an utter failure, and how ghastly a mistake he has made to sacrifice love, and the deeper comforts of life in order to achieve success. Curious that Julia did not appreciate this play! I feel sure she did not grasp the inner significance and real meaning of the play.

9 September: . . . At four o'clock Julia and I left for home, but getting lost we had to return to Settle, so that it was five o'clock before we really got away. The roads were crowded with cars, and at Clitheroe all cars were being held up for inspection of licences. Probably the police were trying to comb out in order to get some line on the motorist who ran down a police

constable on the previous Thursday, leaving him to die in the road. If they get him, I hope he gets ten years hard labour for his callousness.

1930

25 March: Julia reminds me today it is fifteen years ago yesterday since we were married. Well, I don't think either of us regrets the step. We seem to have pulled well together and I think we both get as much pleasure and contentment out of life as most people. Our only trouble is that of millions more, shortage of £ s d.

26 October: No one has ever had any knowledge of a previous existence. If I previously existed as a thinking organism I probably argued much as I do now, and now that I am here, I recognised clearly that immortality means absolutely nothing to me. Any individuality I possessed formerly has gone. So, too, when I pass out of this existence, individual immortality is meaningless, unless I am able to retain something of my present, and the fact that my previous existence has also no meaning for me. So why worry about a life hereafter which for me has no meaning?

1930

6 November: The tournaments [chess] are now up, and I see I am in class three. This about represents my strength of play. I suppose I could play better, but I feel it is too much like hard work to go in for chess wholeheartedly, hence my lack of

practice keeps me in a state of mediocrity. Good enough for a nice game, but no good for really first-class play.

15 December: On arriving home found that Julia had not returned. I waited until nearly 1 a.m., then thinking something surely must have happened went off to Anfield Road police station to see if there was any report of any accident to hand. None. So went back home and found that she [Scholefield Allen at the committal quoted 'her ladyship'] had just turned up. It seems a laundry van had been smashed up on the railway line, the train derailed, and the line blocked. Julia waited at Southport Station until after ten o'clock and as she had apparently no hope of getting a train she decided to take a bus. She arrived in Liverpool at 12.30 and reached home at 1. It was a relief to know she was safe and sound, for I was getting apprehensive, feeling she might have been run over by a motor car or something.

1931

7 January: A night of keen frost and heavy fog caused a wonderful appearance on all the plants and trees. Every twig and leaf was most beautifully bordered and outlined with a white rim of frost. Holly leaves, owing to their wavy edges, presented a most charming appearance, and I cannot recollect an occasion on which the hoar had produced such wonderfully beautiful effects. After dinner I persuaded Julia to go into Stanley Park. She was equally charmed. A gradual thaw seems to be setting in now.

[The next three entries, covering the murder period, trial and appeal, were evidently written up retrospectively.]

19 January: The fateful day on which I received the telephone message.

20 January: Returned home from the Menlove Gardens East journey to find Julia brutally murdered in the front room. How can I ever write in these pages the agony of mind, that sense of loneliness and darkness which followed? Even now, as I am making this entry on June 15th – nearly five months after – my desolation and depression are as great as ever. To forget is impossible, and I can only hope time may soothe and calm the anguish and poignancy of our separation.

2 February: Arrested and charged with the 'wilful murder of my wife'. And yet I would not willingly have hurt a single hair on her dear head. Julia, if you can now know what is happening, you know this is very truth, and if it should be that you and I meet in the great beyond, we can meet each other knowing no wrong has been done between us. More and more do I now realise how much you loved me, and that I, too, loved you. Too often are our secret thoughts overridden by the cares and worries of the daily life, and yet I feel that you did know you were dearly loved, and found your happiness and contentment in loving and being loved. All I have left is the memory of your loving affection for me, and of the joy and happiness we shared together.

16 May: Left Walton for Pentonville guarded by officers. Had to submit to handcuffs which were not taken off until I was

safely in Pentonville. A taxi took me right up the Lime Street platform, and I had only a few yards to cross to the reserved carriage with drawn blinds. Even so, it had obviously leaked out, as there were a number of railway officials and some of the public present. Strange how this morbid curiosity draws people, who, if they would only reflect, must know it is a torture to the person under observation. Going down in the train I was very greatly impressed by the green and wonderful beauty of the country. I had seen little but high walls and iron-barred windows for about sixteen weeks, and it was something to cheer me, and take my mind off the grim horrors of the position. The officers did their best to make me comfortable.

Entering Pentonville was a melancholy ordeal. The prison is grim and forbidding, and I felt despondent and depressed beyond measure. Here again was that never-ending jingling of keys – symbols of despair had they become. I was searched, and then re-clothed and marched off to the condemned cell. I was a prey to the deepest dejection. I had little hope that my appeal would succeed. I knew if my appeal was dismissed my chance of a reprieve was slight.

18 May: Day of my appeal. Off to Court at 10.30. Handcuffed but in my own clothes. At 11 a.m. I was called to appear, and once again I faced the Court. This time my position was undeniably grave. After five hours the Court adjourned and I was taken back to Pentonville.

19 May: After the close of counsel's speeches the Lord Chief Justice said their Lordships would retire for a short while to consider their decision. I was taken out of Court into the

corridor behind, and there for about an hour I paced to and fro, alternately hopeful and depressed. It was a terrible strain. Freedom or death awaited me, and I had become insensible to all other considerations. Minute after minute passed by and I now began to think that the long wait was in my favour, in contrast to the long wait at the Assizes when I felt the delay was against me.

At last their Lordships returned and I was again taken into the dock. The Court was hushed to an almost uncanny silence. No one moved. Not a paper rustled. The very breathing of all there seemed suspended. After what seemed an eternity of time the Lord Chief Justice began to deliver judgment. I could not follow all he said. My mind lost all receptiveness, and all I remember is that my obsession to betray no emotion was as strong as ever. Tensely I waited, oblivious to all but that slow, dreadfully slow utterance of the Lord Chief Justice. I could not grasp all he said, my brain refused to function. It was as if I was suspended in space and detached from everything. Slowly, slowly went on the voice, miles away as it were, and then I heard the Lord Chief Justice end by saying: 'The Court allows the appeal and the conviction of the Court below is quashed.'

Was it true or were my ears mocking me? Immediately there began a buzz, and the beginning of a cheer, instantly suppressed. Then I realised I had won, and that I was free.

6 June: My dear Julia is seldom out of my thoughts, and now I am on my own I realise the fight I am going to have in this battle against loneliness and desolation. Julia, Julia, how can I do without you! The anguish in my soul rises up and distils itself in tears which not all my resolution can hold back. Little

did I ever think that grief and sorrow would so utterly unman me, and, yet, I must fight it down. Nothing can bring her back, nothing can undo the past. Even if he who did that foul deed is caught it cannot bring consolation to me. The only consolation I can find is in the thought of our happy life, and the realisation that she at any rate did find a large measure of happiness and content in her life.

7 June: After tea had an enjoyable ramble through the park to the woodland. I could not keep my mind off Julia, thinking how she would have enjoyed it. I am afraid these lovely walks will depress me for some time. My heart is in tears as I go along, and all the real pleasure of the walk vanished. If I could only believe in existence after death, then I could be more content. If, as the spiritualists assert, this is true, then my dear Julia will know that she is seldom out of my thoughts.

15 June: I think I must definitely abandon the idea of returning to a Liverpool agency as the ill-feeling against me is evidently stronger than I expected.

16 June: Find all the neighbours up against me. They are the rottenest crowd I ever struck. Mean and paltry brained. I feel it a wicked insult to Julia. How she would have scorned the whole thing!

[In mid-June 1931 Wallace prepared to move from Liverpool to a bungalow at Bromborough, a dormitory town on the Wirral peninsula.]

25 June: My dear Julia would have absolutely revelled in this house and garden, and it hurts me to realise that this is her long wanted house, and now she is not here to enjoy its peace and beauty. A thousand times more than ever do I wish she could share it with me. What joy she would have had in that lovely garden! What wonderful happiness and content would have been hers! And now all is gone, and if I take this house as I feel I must, my happiness and peace in it will ever be tinged with sadness and regret at her absence.

28 June: Met old —— The pompous old ass evidently did not want to speak to me, and after passing the time of day drew in to gaze in a shop window. Shallow but common artifice ... I suppose this feeling against me will probably persist for some time and I may never really live it down. Well, after all, so long as I know I am innocent why should I worry?

25 August: Quite a fine experience this morning. As I was going to catch my train I passed a man, and to my great surprise he said – 'Good morning Mr Wallace,' and introduced himself as a Mr ——. He had heard of my coming to live in Bromborough, and, believing me to be an innocent man, desired to be friends. It was a kind action for which I am immensely grateful. To know that I am not an object of scorn and suspicion to everyone is something. And to go about feeling that one is shunned by nearly everyone is a terrible ordeal, and though I try to fight it down and ignore it, the whole business depresses me beyond words. Perhaps, after a while I may get immersed in some new hobbies to take my mind off the terrible tragedy. What I fear is the long nights. But, perhaps,

the wireless will help me to overcome the desperate loneliness I feel.

8 September: The last few days I have been depressed thinking of my dear Julia. I'm afraid this will be a very lonely winter for me. I seem to miss her more and more, and cannot drive the thought of her cruel end out of my mind.

14 September: Just as I was going to dinner Parry stopped me, and said he wanted to talk to me for a few minutes. It was a desperately awkward position. Eventually I decided not to hear what he had to say. I told him I would talk to him someday and give him something to think about. He must realise that I suspect him of the terrible crime. I fear I let him see clearly what I thought, and it may unfortunately put him on his guard. I wonder if it is any good putting a private detective on to his track in the hope of something coming to light. I am more than half persuaded to try it.

6 October: I cannot disguise from myself that I am dreadfully nervous about entering the house after dark. I suppose it is because my nerves are all so shattered after the ordeal, and this, together with the recurring fits of grief and anguish over my dear Julia's end make me horribly depressed and apprehensive . . . Left to myself I am for ever trying to visualise what really did happen. Although I am convinced Parry killed her, yet it is difficult to get proof. It would be a great relief if he could only be caught, and the foul murder brought home to him.

25 November: Julia is never far out of my thoughts. The sadness and sorrow at her absence is still very real with me, but I suppose I am now accepting the inevitable. Nothing can ever bring her back, and however much I want her, or however much I miss her loving smiles and aimless chatter, I realise that life is insistent and demands first attention . . . I seem unable to concentrate on the violin. I think it is because it carries too many poignant memories of those happy hours we spent together. Every time I handle the pieces of music she loved and played so delightfully, memories crowd in upon me until I am compelled to put the fiddle down. Music has its delights, but it also brings great oceans of sadness, which sometimes, overwhelms, and brings up torrents of tears for utterly hopeless longings. So I must carry on to the end in sadness and sorrow.

1932

20 March: There are now several daffodils in bloom, and lots of tulips coming along. How delighted dear Julia would have been, and I can only too sadly picture how lovingly she would have tended the garden. Today I have been very much depressed, full of grief and tears. Julia, Julia, my dear, why were you taken from me? Why, why should this have been so? It is a question to which I can get no answer, and I must fight this dread feeling of utter loneliness as best I can. Black despair! When shall I be able to find peace!

31 March: Got —— book on ——. I see I am included in the list of great criminals. The thing is too hideous to think about. I, who could not have hurt any living thing, I am supposed to

have most brutally murdered Julia – Julia who was the whole world to me, my only companion with whom I could have trusted my life. If there is a God in Heaven, why, oh, why! Has she solved the great mystery of the beyond, or is it utter extinction? Does she know how I grieve for her, or is it the end? I am tortured by doubts.

[According to W. F. Wyndham-Brown, the last entry in Wallace's diary was made on 12 April 1932 and referred to the garden.]

Appendix 3

Comments by Raymond Chandler

*Letter to Carl Brandt**

14 December 1951

. . . The *American Weekly* suggestion strikes me as quite down my alley *in principle*, as the negotiators say . . .

The choice of the case is very difficult since the really good ones have been written up so much and all the best cases that I'm really familiar with are English. Three of the best of all time, and certainly my three favorites, because of their huge elements of doubt, their strange characters and the richness of their background, are: the Wallace case, which I would call The Impossible Murder; the Maybrick case,† or Why Doesn't an Arsenic Eater Know When He's Eating Arsenic; and the Adelaide Bartlett case,‡

* Chandler's literary agent in New York.
† Another Liverpool case, that of Florence Maybrick, convicted in 1889 of the murder of her husband James, a wealthy cotton broker. Her sentence was eventually commuted to penal servitude for life, and she was released after fifteen years.
‡ That of the wife of a London merchant, acquitted in 1885 of her husband's murder. The unfortunate Edwin Bartlett died from drinking liquid chloroform.

or The Man Who Didn't Get Up Half an Hour Early for Breakfast. The Wallace case is the nonpareil of all murder mysteries, but it has been done to a turn by Dorothy Sayers,* and whole books have been written about it. It is still not completely analysed, but the sort of analysis which remains to be done would probably not appeal to the *American Weekly*. The Maybrick case is just too damn difficult. Even the facts are in dispute. In the Wallace case an important fact is in dispute, a question of time. It is vital to the extent that if it had been decided one way Wallace would not have been convicted, and yet if it had been decided the other way the circumstances are all in favor of Wallace's innocence. I call it the impossible murder because Wallace couldn't have done it, and neither could anyone else . . .

Letter to James Sandoe[†]

21 November 1949

. . . Sending *The Wallace Case*[‡] back today. Rowland makes it as dull as Wallace himself must have been.

Three or four little points struck me:

(1) Why had Wallace, a man who travelled Liverpool widely on his rounds, no map of the city? It's the first place I would look for a strange address.

(2) Why would he not want to know something about this Qualtrough merely for selling purposes? An insurance man would have certain sources of information.

* In *The Anatomy of Murder*.
† Mystery-novel critic of the *New York Herald Tribune*.
‡ By John Rowland.

(3) When, in the course of his vain search for Menlove Gardens East he went to a newsvendor's shop and asked her where the street was and then to look up her accounts to see if she delivered papers to that address, why did he not mention the *name* to the newsvendor? Qualtrough was apparently an uncommon name in those parts.

(4) The prosecution attempted to make something of the fact that the gas jet Wallace lit in the living room, where his wife's body was lying, was not the nearest to the door, and why did he not light the most accessible jet? The defense pooh-poohed this on the ground that when you live in a house with gaslight you habitually light the same burner on entering a room. My point here is, who says the one he lit was the habitual burner, who besides Wallace himself?

To some slight extent all these points are against Wallace, but they are too slight to mean anything. It's a very unsatisfactory case, because you feel that if the police and medical work had been any good there wouldn't have been any chance of Wallace getting away with it, if he was guilty, or of being arrested and tried if he was innocent. The doctor sits around for hours timing the rigor mortis, but never records the temperature of the room or the loss of heat by the body. He never examines the stomach contents to see how far digestion has proceeded.* There is no search for strange fingerprints . . . and no scrapings from Wallace's fingernails. There is a lot of

* Not so (see p. 290).

magoozlum about blood splashes, but we end up with a very vague idea about how much and how far.

It also seems to be assumed even by the prosecution that Wallace could not have had more than twenty minutes in which to batter his wife to death, put out the fire, go upstairs and get cleaned up if he had his clothes on and get dressed if he had not, get his blood-pressure back to normal and appear perfectly calm and composed on a tram several blocks away. The number of blows struck shows a frenzy of either fear or hate, since the first blow was fatal, but the judge was the only one to point out that a man may plan a murder very coolly and yet lose his head in the execution of it. But this man got his head back again awfully damn quick . . .

From Chandler's Working Notes

. . . But if you assume Qualtrough to be the murderer, let's see where that puts us. The motive must be robbery, because nothing else makes any sense . . . But if it is robbery, the only thing to steal is Wallace's collections. So Qualtrough has to know when they will be worth stealing, although he is unlucky this particular night. He has to know how and when to make that phone call and just what to say to interest Wallace; just what address to give, Menlove Gardens East, assuming rightly that Wallace knows . . . there are Menlove Gardens* and will take it for granted that Menlove Gardens East will be near Menlove

* In fact, Wallace said he did not know of the existence of Menlove Gardens, but took them to be in the vicinity of Menlove Avenue, a major thoroughfare.

Gardens West ... Is it possible to believe that Qualtrough knew so much about Wallace, and Wallace knew so little about Qualtrough? He has to know the Wallaces and their affairs pretty damn well. But it doesn't seem that *anybody* knew the Wallaces that well.

Dorothy Sayers seems to feel that what was written in Wallace's diary after his trial and conviction and the reversal of the conviction has considerable significance in proving his innocence. I'm not convinced. I feel that with a man of Wallace's type a diary is the only outlet. And as a very occasional diarist I also feel that the moment a man sets his thoughts down on paper, however secretly, he is in a sense writing for publication ... There is nothing quoted from Wallace's diary after the trial which ... I could not imagine a guilty man writing in the circumstances. There is such a thing as remorse; there is such a thing as the wish to believe that the irrevocable had never happened ...

Wallace has posed to himself as a stoic; in his behavior after the murder there is something more than pose. In his diary he clings to the last shred of pride he has – his pride in this stoical behavior, the last stability of a ruined life.

The Wallace case is unbeatable; it will always be unbeatable.

Acknowledgements

I would like to thank a great many people who have helped in the preparation of this book. I am grateful for the forbearance of numerous colleagues at Radio City who suffered with me during its preparation, to Deborah Levey for her encouragement, to Kieran Devaney, Michael Green and Nicky Slater for their help in the research, and to City's Managing Director, Terry Smith, for the use of material contained in the programmes *Who Killed Julia?* and *Conspiracy of Silence*.

Dozens of people gave freely of their time to share with me their knowledge of the case, or to provide facilities. I owe a special debt of gratitude to Jonathan Goodman and Richard Whittington-Egan in this regard, sadly both now deceased. Others include the late Hector Munro, his son Donald Munro, J. R. Pearson (clerk to the Liverpool justices), Professor Keith Simpson, Lord Devlin, the late Mr Christmas Humphries, Alderman Sir Joseph Cleary, Leslie Williamson, Les Hill, Ted Holmes, Russell Johnston, Emily Hoer, Robert Keel, Douglas Metcalf, Lilian Olsen (née Kelly), Dr Charles St Hill, Allison Wildman, Harold Jones, H. A. L. Brown, Ray Holmes, Bill Rogers, Leslie Walsh, Dan Nicholas, Michael Unger (formerly

Editor, *Liverpool Daily Post*), Neville Willasey (Picture Editor, *Liverpool Daily Post and Echo*), Colin Hunt (Librarian, *Liverpool Daily Post and Echo*), John Harrison (Secretary, Swift Register), Jimmy Tattersall, staff at Liverpool Central Libraries, staff at Liverpool Register Office, Mrs Elizabeth Roberts, Mrs Judith Philip, R. H. Montgomery, Ray Jackson, Philip Chadwick, staff (past and present) of Merseyside Police, John Tanner (Editor) and staff of the *North Wales Weekly News*, staff at Liverpool City Engineers' Department, staff at Birkenhead Library, John Kelly, Joe Curry, Josephine Young, Stephen Roberts, Geoffrey Deyes, Albert Johns, Gordon Atkinson, Dolly Atkinson, John Parkes senior, John Parkes junior, Norman Hayward, George Hill, Robert Parry MP, Keith Johnson, Harry V. Bailey, Derek Johnston, Michael Kennedy (Northern Editor, *Daily Telegraph*), David Bamber, Peter Simpson, Dr Eric Midwinter, J. M. Maycock, George Holt, Bill Morrison, Lesley Clive, staff at the Police Staff College Library, Bramshill, Ralph Clarke, John Elphick, Graham and Philip Roberts.

The book would never have happened but for the interest and encouragement of Jean Frere, Maureen Rissik and Euan Cameron of The Bodley Head, and of my agent, Shelley Power.

The comments by Raymond Chandler in Appendix 3 are taken from *Raymond Chandler Speaking*, published by Hamish Hamilton in 1962 and reprinted by Allison & Busby in 1984, and are reproduced here by kind permission of the copyright holders, Mrs Helga Greene and College Trustees Ltd.

I apologise for any inadvertent omissions in these acknowledgements, and stress that while I am indebted to all these people for their help, any errors in the text are mine alone.

Bibliography

Non-fiction

The Trial of William Herbert Wallace by W. F. Wyndham-Brown (Gollancz, 1933).

Six Trials by Winifred Duke (Gollancz, 1934).

'The Murder of Julia Wallace' by Dorothy L. Sayers in *The Anatomy of Murder* (The Bodley Head, 1936).

The Wallace Case by John Rowland (Carroll and Nicholson, 1949).

'Corpse in the Parlour' in *Liverpool Colonnade* by Richard Whittington-Egan (Philip, Son & Nephew, 1955).

Two Studies in Crime by Yseult Bridges (Hutchinson, 1959).

The Killing of Julia Wallace by Jonathan Goodman (Harrap, 1969).

Murderer: Scot-Free by Robert F. Hussey (David & Charles, 1972).

According to the Evidence by Gerald Abrahams (Cassell, 1958).

Murder Most Mysterious by Hargrave Lee Adam (Sampson Low & Co., 1932).

Why Did They Do It? by Benjamin Bennett (Howard B. Timmins, 1953).

The Meaning of Murder by J. Brophy (Whiting & Wheaton, 1966).

Raymond Chandler Speaking by Raymond Chandler (Hamish Hamilton, 1962).

Trials – and Errors by Belton Cobb (W. H. Allen, 1962).

Rogue's March by George Dilnot (Bles, 1934).

Crime Man by Stanley Firmin (Hutchinson, 1950).

Great Murder Mysteries by Guy H. B. Logan (Stanley Paul & Co., 1931).

Ego 6 by James Agate (Harrap, 1944).

The Murder and the Trial by Edgar Lustgarten (Odhams, 1960).

Verdict in Dispute by Edgar Lustgarten (Wingate, 1949).

Five Famous Trials by M. Moiseiwitsch (Heinemann, 1964).

Background to Murder by Nigel Morland (Werner Laurie, 1955).

Tales of the Criminous by William Roughead (Cassell, 1956).

Murder by Persons Unknown by John Rowland (Mellifont Press, 1941).

More Criminal Files by John Rowland (Arco Publications, 1958).

A Second Companion to Murder by E. Spencer Shew (Cassell, 1962).

William Herbert Wallace by F. J. P. Veale (Merrymeade, 1950).

Tales of Liverpool Murder, Mayhem and Mystery by Richard Whittington-Egan (Gallery Press, 1967).

Encyclopaedia of Murder by Colin Wilson and Patricia Pitman (Barker, 1961).

The Murderers' Who's Who by J. H. H. Gaute and Robin Odell (Harrap, 1979).

Murder 'Whatdunnit' by J. H. H. Gaute and Robin Odell (Harrap, 1982).

'The Murder of Julia Wallace', *Famous Northern Crimes, Trials and Criminals* by Jane Sterling (G. W. & A. Hesketh, 1983).

Fiction

The Jury Disagree by George Goodchild and Bechofer Roberts (Jarrolds, 1934).

Skin for Skin by Winifred Duke (Gollancz, 1935).

The Telephone Call by John Rhode (Bles, 1948).

The Last Sentence by Jonathan Goodman (Hutchinson, 1978).

29, Herriott Street by John Hutton (The Bodley Head, 1979).

One Foot in the Grave by Marten Cumberland (Hurst and Blackett, 1952).

Call the Witness by Edna Sherry (Dodd, Mead and Co., 1961).

The Borrowed Alibi by Leslie Egan (Harper, 1962).

Qualtrough by Angus Hall (Herbert Jenkins, 1968).

Other Sources

Portrait of Liverpool by Howard Channon (Hale, 1970).

Liverpool and the Mersey by Francis E. Hyde (David & Charles, 1971).

Britain Between the Wars by Charles Loch Mowat (University Press, 1968).

Spike Island by James McClure (Macmillan, 1980).

Merseyside Transport (Merseyside Tramway Preservation Society, 1976).

The Mersey Tunnel (The Mersey Tunnel Joint Committee, 1951).

The Queen's Courts by Peter Archer (Penguin, 1956).

English Journey by J. B. Priestley (Heinemann, 1934).

Kelly's Directories.

Liverpool Daily Post.

Liverpool Echo.

Liverpool Evening Express.

The Times.

Daily Telegraph.

North Wales Weekly News.

Abergele Visitor.

John Bull.

Liverpool Red Books.

Liverpool and District Telephone Directory.

Liverpool A–Z.

Index